Interpreting Remote Sensing Imagery

Human Factors

Interpreting Remote Sensing Imagery
Human Factors

Edited by

Robert R. Hoffman, Ph.D.
Arthur B. Markman, Ph.D.

CRC Press
Taylor & Francis Group
Boca Raton London New York

CRC Press is an imprint of the
Taylor & Francis Group, an **informa** business

First published 2001 by Lewis Publishers

Published 2018 by CRC Press
Taylor & Francis Group
6000 Broken Sound Parkway NW, Suite 300
Boca Raton, FL 33487-2742

First issued in paperback 2019

No claim to original U.S. Government works

ISBN 13: 978-0-367-45534-7 (pbk)
ISBN 13: 978-1-56670-413-7 (hbk)

Visit the Taylor & Francis Web site at
http://www.taylorandfrancis.com

and the CRC Press Web site at
http://www.crcpress.com

Library of Congress Cataloging-in-Publication Data

Interpreting remote sensing imagery : human factors / edited by Robert R. Hoffman,
Arthur B. Markman,
     p. cm.
  Includes bibliographical references and index.
  ISBN 1-56670-413-8 (alk. paper)
  1. Remote sensing. 2. Geographical perception. I. Hoffman, Robert R.
II. Markman, Arthur B.
G70.4.I58 2000
621.36'78—dc21   00-050680
                                                CIP

Library of Congress Card Number 00-050680

Preface

Creation of this book has been a labor of love, but a labor indeed. The first and highest hurdle stemmed from the simple fact that the main topic of this volume, human factors in the interpretation of remote sensing imagery, is truly interdisciplinary. Dealing as this volume does, with psychological aspects of remote sensing—perception, conceptualization, expertise—it would seem that some sort of venue in experimental psychology would be most appropriate. But the volume's focus on the domain of remote sensing makes it seem distant from the topics that are close to the heart of mainstream psychology. Conversely, dealing with psychological aspects of remote sensing makes this volume seem distant from the traditional concerns of mainstream remote sensing. In remote sensing, whenever the term "interpretation" is used, it is taken as a reference to automated methods for image analysis. We are very pleased to have found a receptive ear at Lewis Publishers/CRC Press.

The psychological factors in remote sensing are abundantly clear. I became aware of them some 20 years ago when physicist friend Dr. Walter Carnahan of Indiana State University demonstrated his project on thermography. "How were the colors assigned to the temperatures?," "How can you tell that that green blob is a house that needs better insulation?" Clearly, the then-new field of remote sensing was ripe for the analytical eye of the experimental psychologist. The first step was to pursue training, acquired with the support of the U.S. Army Corps of Engineers—which just happened to need an experimental psychologist to help determine how to elicit expert knowledge for the creation of expert systems for aerial photointerpretation. Psychological factors including knowledge, experience, and perception quickly manifested themselves as important considerations. There was no research base of studies on how experts interpret images, how the color codings for nonliteral imagery are devised, etc.

The editors of this volume came together at the suggestion of a colleague, mentor, and friend, Dr. Dedre Gentner of Northwestern University, a world-renowned pioneer in the study of concept formation and analogical reasoning. I approached her with a discussion of the topic of remote sensing, to make a point about the state of the art in psychological research on concept formation. True to its tradition in the academic laboratory, psychological research on concept formation has tended to rely upon highly controlled, some would say artificial, experimental materials and tasks. My view was that the field of remote sensing offered a prime opportunity to study the processes of concept formation using a "real world" domain of abundant imagery and diverse image types that could be useful in studies of concept formation. Dr. Gentner arranged for me to meet her former student, Art Markman, then at Columbia University, not far from Adelphi University on Long Island where I then taught. That led to our collaboration on this volume.

Over the years of our attempts to conduct research, on such issues as expert/novice differences in the interpretation of thermograms and weather satellite images, other non-mainstream scientists started to come "out of the woodwork," including those individuals whose work we are pleased to present in this volume.

We see great hope in the continuing collaboration of remote sensing scientists and experimental psychologists in the area of remote imagery interpretation. How can research guide the design of image displays and workstations? How can we preserve the knowledge and skills of senior experts? How can we better train people? Lifetimes of research lie open and waiting. Indeed, despite advances in the computational analysis of images, the human factors will not disappear, but instead will become more salient and more important.

This book is an attempt to map this new territory and to provide guidance to future research.

Acknowledgment

The senior editor would like to thank Professor Walter Carnahan (Department of Physics, Indiana State University) for introducing him to remote sensing, stimulating his exploration of the human factor in remote sensing, and training him in the interpretation of aerial thermograms. If it were not for the fact that trees are hot in winter infrared photography, this volume would not exist. Special thanks go in memoriam to Olin Mintzer of the U.S. Army Corps of Engineers, who devoted valuable time so that the senior editor could attempt to learn terrain analysis. Thanks also to Mike Mogil for his generosity, including his willingness to share both his knowledge and his repository of remote sensing images. Finally, the senior editor would like to acknowledge the nurturing support provided by the Institute for Human and Machine Cognition and the Department of Psychology of the University of West Florida.

The editors would like to thank William Howell for assisting in the preparation of the indices.

The editors' work on this volume was supported in part by grants from the National Science Foundation and the Air Force Office of Scientific Research.

About the Editors

Robert R. Hoffman earned his B.A., M.A., and Ph.D. in experimental psychology at the University of Cincinnati, where he was awarded McMicken Scholar, Psi Chi, and Delta Tau Kappa Honors. After a postdoctoral associateship at the Center for Research on Human Learning at the University of Minnesota, Hoffman joined the faculty of Adelphi University. There, he received awards for outstanding research and service, and also served as Chair of the Institutional Review Board and the University Grants Officer. He joined the  Institute for Human and Machine Cognition of the University of West Florida in 1999, as a Research Associate.

Dr. Hoffman's first book, *Cognition and Figurative Language*, coedited by his mentor Richard Honeck of the University of Cincinnati, is now regarded as a classic. Hoffman has published widely, in journals including *Human Factors, Memory and Cognition, Organizational Behavior and Human Decision Processes, The Bulletin of the Psychonomic Society, The Journal of Psycholinguistic Research, Ecological Psychology, Applied Cognitive Psychology, Metaphor and Symbol, The AI Magazine, Weather and Forecasting,* and *The Journal of Experimental and Theoretical Artificial Intelligence.* He is a member of the board of editors for the journals *Human Factors* and *Cognitive Technology,* and is series editor for the book series, *Expertise: Research and Applications.*

Hoffman's research has focused on psychological aspects of remote sensing and meteorology, including expert reasoning, knowledge elicitation for expert systems, workstation and display design, and the development of training and performance aids. His current effort is aimed at specifying the principles of "human-centered computing" and establishing the methodologies for cognitive work analysis and cognitive field research.

Dr. Hoffman is a member of the Human Factors and Ergonomics Society, the American Association for Artificial Intelligence, the Psychonomic Society, the International Society for Ecological Psychology, the American

Meteorological Society, and the American Society for Photogrammetric Engineering and Remote Sensing. In 1994 Hoffman received a Fullbright Scholar Award and was appointed an Honorary Fellow of The British Library Eccles Center for American Studies. In 1990 he was elected Fellow of the American Psychological Society.

Arthur B. Markman completed his B.S. in cognitive science at Brown University where he was awarded the William Gaston Fund Prize for Excellence in Cognitive Science. He earned his M.A. and Ph.D. in psychology from the University of Illinois where he was awarded a fellowship in cognitive science and artificial intelligence and Sigma Xi and Phi Kappa Phi honors.

Dr. Markman was a Faculty Fellow at the Institute for Learning Sciences at Northwestern University and subsequently an Assistant Professor at Columbia University before joining the University of Texas at Austin, where he is an Associate Professor in the Psychology Department.

Dr. Markman's research has explored similarity, analogy, categorization, and knowledge representation. In 1998 he received a National Science Foundation Career Award, and in 1999 he received an honorable mention in the APA Division 3 Young Investigator Award Competition.

Dr. Markman has written over 40 scholarly papers and chapters and has written or edited three books including *Knowledge Representation* (1999), *Cognitive Dynamics* (2000), and *Cognitive Psychology, 3rd Ed.* (2001). He is a member of the editorial boards of the *Journal of Experimental Psychology: Learning, Memory, and Cognition, Memory and Cognition*, and *Cognitive Science*, and serves on the Panel on Human Cognition and Perception for the National Science Foundation.

Contributors

Demetre P. Argialas, Ph.D.
Remote Sensing Laboratory
Department of Rural and Surveying
   Engineering
National Technical University of
   Athens
Zographos, Greece

Walter H. Carnahan, Ph.D.
Department of Physics
Indiana State University
Terre Haute, Indiana

J. Kevin DeFord, Ph.D.
Department of Psychological Brain
   Sciences
University of Louisville
Louisville, Kentucky

Anthony D. Del Genio, Ph.D.
NASA Goddard Institute for Space
   Studies
New York, New York

Edward A. Essock, Ph.D.
Department of Psychological Brain
   Sciences
University of Louisville
Louisville, Kentucky

Randall W. Gibb, M.A.
USAF Academy
Colorado Springs, Colorado

Robert R. Hoffman, Ph.D.
Institute for Human and Machine
   Cognition
University of West Florida
Pensacola, Florida

Richard K. Lowe, Ph.D.
Curtin University of Technology
Perth, Western Australia
Australia

Arthur B. Markman, Ph.D.
Department of Psychology
University of Texas
Austin, Texas

Jason S. McCarley, Ph.D.
Department of Psychological Brain
   Sciences
University of Louisville
Louisville, Kentucky

G. Ch. Miliaresis, Ph.D.
National Technical University of
   Athens
Athens, Greece

H. Michael Mogil, M.S.
Certified Consulting Meteorologist
Rockville, Maryland

Richard J. Pike, Ph.D.
U. S. Geological Survey
Menlo Park, California

Michael S. Sinai, Ph.D.
Department of Psychological Brain
    Sciences
University of Louisville
Louisville, Kentucky

William R. Uttal, Ph.D.
Arizona State University
Tempe, Arizona

Contents

Section Four: Seeing the dynamics

section one

Introduction

chapter one

Overview

Robert R. Hoffman and
Arthur B. Markman

Contents

Keywords: *visualization, display design, expertise, mental models, training, topography, terrain analysis, expert systems, physiography, geomorphometry, light amplification ("night vision"), meteorology, weather charts, planetary science*

Despite advances in information processing technology, there remains a necessary and critical role for the "human in the loop" in the interpretation of remotely sensed nonliteral imagery, in domains including planetary science, earth science, meteorology, and cartography.[5] On the side of information technology, workstation and display systems play a critical role in supporting scientific visualization, and in recent years it has become widely recognized that the visualization of complex data is critical in science,[9,11,12,14,15,23] including the domain of cartography, a field with a long-standing interest in issues of communication effectiveness.[3,4,8,10,17,20,21,22] That concern has been

1-56670-413-8/01/$0.00+$.50
©2001 by CRC Press LLC

bolstered by psychological research showing that the features of display symbols, elements, and patterns can have clear effects on processes of perception and visual search.[6,7]

What are the implications of this for the field of remote sensing?

1.1   The challenge to contributors

Contributors were invited to present their newest research. Some of them are psychologists, whose research interests converge on issues in the area of remote sensing. Some of the contributors are remote sensing scientists, environmental scientists, or computer scientists. They were asked to look at their work from a psychological or human factors perspective. For most of them, this request was a challenge and a relief—they would finally have a forum for expressing their concerns about important human factors issues that the field seems to have de-emphasized. A host of questions are raised at this nexus of psychology and remote sensing, questions that formed a list of possibilities presented to the contributors:

1.1.1   Information and perception

- What is the nature of the information that is contained in remote sensing and cartographic displays?
- How is that information perceived?
- What sorts of things do experts see?
- How can individual, static displays permit the comprehension of underlying dynamics (e.g., weather, geobiological dynamics, etc.)?

1.1.2   Reasoning and perception

- How do experts reason?
- What "mental models" do experts have of the causal principles that govern the phenomena they study and that structure the information that is contained in the remotely sensed images?
- How does the expert "see through" the display to arrive at an understanding of a depicted world, its meaning, and significance?

1.1.3   Human-computer interaction

- How do experts work with their displays?
- How do the displays and workstation systems actually constrain their reasoning?
- What happens when experts "fiddle" with their displays?
- How does display interpretation integrate with the other things the experts do when performing their usual tasks?
- What are the implications of new expert systems and the role of the "human in the loop"?

1.1.4 Learning and training

- What are the phenomena of perceptual learning and concept formation that are important in display interpretation?
- What are the milestones in the developmental sequence of trainee-to-expert in image interpretation?
- What does it take to be an expert trainer?
- Can the expert trainer anticipate trainee errors, given a knowledge of the trainee's mental model?
- Given that it takes such a long time to achieve expertise at image interpretation, how can training be made more efficient?
- How can alternative approaches to training be evaluated?

As these questions show, discussions in this volume span issues ranging from the aesthetics of scientific visualization, to the mathematical analysis of perceptible objects, to the applied problems of training and interface design.

1.2 The organization of the volume

Following this Overview, the second chapter in the Introductory Section reviews some literature that attests to the role of human factors in remote sensing, and some research that helps to specify cognitive processes in a way that is pertinent to remote sensing.

Section Two focuses on topographics. Terrain analysis is the systematic study of image patterns relating to the origin, morphologic history, and composition of distinct topographic units called landforms, and their engineering significance for soil and rock identification. A great deal of experience is required to achieve expertise at terrain analysis, and senior experts possess consummate perceptual and comprehension skill.[13] In their chapter, Argialas and Miliaresis approach expertise at terrain analysis, with a focus on the creation of expert systems (see Chapter 3). Previous expert-system methods and tools that have been used to address terrain knowledge representation have modeled the landform "pattern element" approach, and have resulted in prototype expert-systems for inferring the landform of a site from user observations of pattern elements.[1,2] The first step is the formulation of a conceptual framework for knowledge, much of which can be found in books and technical manuals (interpretation "keys"). In such first-generation efforts in knowledge-based terrain-interpretation systems, knowledge related to the physiographic region of a site and to the spatial pattern of related landforms was not explicitly represented and used.

In more recent work (see Chapter 3), Argialas and colleagues have identified, named, described, and organized "book knowledge" pertaining to physiographic regions (provinces and sections), physiographic features, topographic forms, and associated landforms in terms of geomorphologic, topographic, and physiographic indicators. They have captured a number of "intermediate-level concepts" that are perhaps the most important tools available for organizing knowledge bases, both conceptually and computationally. Next, they developed an object-oriented model for the factual and structural representation of these terrain features, and a rule-base for representing the strategic knowledge needed for inferring these features from their own indicators. The conceptual scheme was formalized and implemented in a knowledge-base resulting in the Terrain Analysis eXpert (TAX-4) system, which assists the user in physiographic reasoning. In Chapter 3, Argialas et al. point out that a considerable amount of research is needed to specify the perceptual knowledge of experts.

A major thrust of research on digital information processing involves the goal of obviating the human factor through automated analysis and classification. In his chapter on geomorphometry (see Chapter 4), Richard J. Pike makes the point that mathematical analyses of terrain ultimately hinge on questions of meaning and perception. Measures of the shape and form seen in topography are needed in order for the analyst to understand natural processes and represent the Earth's surface as locus of human activity. The information content of images (e.g., synthetic aperture radar) is often extracted by traditional visual interpretation, but more effort is being undertaken to extract information by parametric computations. The key issue is how to link visual perception of terrain form with computational metrics.[16] Verbal expressions of perceived land form (e.g., "rolling hills") are ambiguous and under-specific. Also, such attributes as terrain "roughness" and spatial asymmetry must be captured in numerical terms if they are to be incorporated into models of geomorphic process, ecological interaction, and hazard identification. Because statistical descriptions, too, can be ambiguous, direct linkages are needed between perceived terrain form and its parametric expression. For example, can differences in standard deviation and kurtosis of slope curvature be detected visually in real terrain? Pike's chapter reviews morphometric representation of the ground surface and then describes selected results of an experiment designed to explore some of the important issues (see Chapter 4). An analysis of 90 small digital elevation models (sampled from 1:24,000-scale U.S. contour maps) involved fifty measures that were reduced to a provisional "geometric signature" of uncorrelated attributes. This study suggests it might be possible to "calibrate" a sample's visual appearance against its statistical characterization.

The chapters in Section Three address a basic phenomenon of expertise—experts can see things that novices cannot. Pattern recognition begins with observing something. It could be things that occur naturally, or things one sees in pictures, maps, or charts. The human mind is able to perceive the information, remember it for later use and conceptually link it to related observations. Once several similar data sets have been analyzed, a pattern can be determined.

Experimental psychologist William R. Uttal and colleagues (see Chapter 5) recently conducted some research on the ability of people to discriminate objects depicted by light amplification. Scenes viewed through light-amplifying (or "night vision") goggles produce an image that is considerably different from the view obtained with literal vision, even literal vision under conditions of dim illumination. Under certain conditions, light amplifiers provide an enormous enhancement of the observed scene. However, the displayed enhancement of luminance comes with a perceptual cost. The displayed images are degraded in terms of color, contrast, shadows, resolution, and depth cues, among other parameters. Effective use of light amplification technology requires an understanding of how humans see under these, and related conditions of degraded nonliteral viewing. Uttal and Gibb review some recent empirical findings concerning the perception of light amplified images, and go on to consider how contemporary developments in the psychology of perception may contribute, in general, to our understanding of how such important new sensing, imaging, and display devices can best be used in remote sensing and nonliteral imaging applications (see Chapter 5). The goal of the research and the theoretical considerations is, ultimately, to suggest how one might improve the observer's ability to process nonliteral informational displays, especially so as to avoid perceptual error.

In addition to seeing features and patterns that the novice cannot, the expert can also perceive dynamics. The terrain analyst sees not just terrain or even landforms, but perceives the dynamics that led to the formation of the terrain. In a meteorological satellite image, the meteorologist not only sees high and low pressure systems, fronts, and other phenomena, but also perceives the dynamics and forces that are at work. The climate and general atmospheric circulation patterns are the statistics of a large number of individual events in a rapidly changing three-dimensional fluid. A remote sensing observation, however, is a snapshot. The chapters in Section Four focus on the experts' perception of dynamics, and the displays and information processing systems that support the perception of dynamics.

In his chapter, Richard K. Lowe investigates how novices and experts perceive meteorological dynamics that are implicit in weather charts composed from remotely sensed data (see Chapter 7). This abstract type of display gives a highly selective and decontextualized presentation of a meteorological situation and depicts information that is beyond the realm of direct, everyday experience. Meteorologically, the importance of the visuo-spatial properties of chart markings lies in the way they capture particular aspects of the atmosphere that reflect its nature as a dynamic gaseous fluid. Appropriate patterning of these individual graphic elements into higher levels of meteorological organization is not apparent to the novice. Rather, the novice focuses on superficial and domain-general visuo-spatial characteristics. In Lowe's research, college student participants carried out various tasks that required them to physically manipulate or generate meteorological markings from a given weather map. These tasks included: copying then recalling markings, sorting markings into groups, drawing extensions of given (incomplete) markings, and generating predictions of future patterns. Expert meteorologists' performance during these weather map processing tasks indicates that their knowledge covering relational aspects, such as the spatial and temporal contents of a given weather map, allows them to develop a meteorologically coherent mental model of the depicted situation. In contrast, novices appear to construct limited mental models that are insufficiently constrained, lack hierarchical structure, and provide an ineffective basis for interpretation.

Although the communities of researchers studying the Earth's climate and those studying the atmospheres of the other planets barely overlap, the questions posed and the challenges to understanding in the two fields have much in common. In his chapter, Anthony Del Genio discusses the expert's perception of dynamics in the "weather" on other planets (see Chapter 8). Converting remotely sensed data into maps of physical parameters for scientific interpretation requires the application of computer algorithms based partly on physics but also partly on untested assumptions, which can introduce errors of unknown magnitude into the resulting product. Furthermore, conceptual models for the Earth's atmosphere are more advanced than those for other planets. Applying terrestrial understanding to planetary visual displays can sometimes aid interpretation but at other times might bias it. A major challenge for the planetary scientist is to use displays to deal effectively with the time domain. In many cases the important changes with time are small, and displays of *differences*, rather than data values or value averages, can be the most physically revealing. In other situations, changes with time are large, necessitating either animation or a sequence of static displays.

Ultimately, though, it is not feasible for the human to view and assimilate every image produced by every instrument on an orbiting spacecraft. To deal with the large data volumes, scientists use displays of limited segments of the data set to conceive and design computer programs that collect statistics on the phenomenon in question over the full duration of the data set. This is generally an iterative process; displays of the resulting statistics may simply confirm physical expectations, but often they reveal unanticipated behavior. The scientist must then decide whether the "objective" definition on which the algorithm is based is correct (i.e., the result is a discovery of new information) or whether the definition itself is biased and needs revision. Throughout these processes of data analysis, and despite the foundations of planetary remote sensing in physical science, psychological factors of comprehension, perception, and expertise play a critical role.

In his chapter, H. Mike Mogil takes us back to planet Earth in a discussion of the interpretation of meteorological satellite images (see Chapter 9). Since the beginning of modern meteorology about 200 years ago, meteorologists have relied upon their pattern recognition skill to gain an understanding of weather processes and to develop forecasting techniques. Currently, information gained from human-based pattern recognition efforts is being routinely used to develop automated techniques. For example, dozens of algorithms have been incorporated into the National Weather Service's new Doppler Radar system, and multispectral satellite imagery is being used in automated icing analysis programs. In asking the question, "What patterns are there in satellite imagery?" Mogil tapped into his experience at training meteorologists, and elementary school children and teachers. He had used tasks in which images and maps are sorted and classified. To his surprise, the number of patterns that novices (children and teachers) found was far greater than he had expected. A similar experiment using cloud photographs showing basic cloud types, yielded patterns involving geography, geology, colors, and other patterns. These investigations point out the myriad ways that information can be perceived and organized.

1.3 Prospectus

Chapters by experimental psychologists (Essock, et al. [see Chapter 6], Hoffman and Markman [see Chapter 2], Lowe [see Chapter 7], and Uttal, et al. [see Chapter 5]) illustrate a range of psychological research methods that can be brought to bear on issues on remote sensing, including judgment and interpretation tasks, memory tasks, and psychophysical tests of discrimination. Chapters by remote sensing scientists (Argialas and Miliaresis [see Chapter 3], Pike [see Chapter 4], DelGenio [see Chapter 8], and Mogil [see Chapter 9]) discuss the ways that human factors, including expertise and perceptual skill, play a role in their domain. A defining goal of the volume is to address issues of both basic and applied science that fall at the nexus of remote sensing and applied cognitive psychology. We hope that this volume serves as a springboard for more discussion of the issues, and more cross-disciplinary research to address the issues.

References

1. Argialas, D. P., Towards structured knowledge models for landform representation, *Z. f. Geomorphologie N.F. Supple.-Bd.*, 101, 85–108, 1995.
2. Argialas, D. P. and Mintzer, O., The potential of hypermedia to photointerpretation education and training, in *Proc. XVII ISPRS Congr.*, (Part B), Fritz, L. and Lucas, J., Eds., International Archives of Photogrammetry and Remote Sensing, Washington D.C., 1992, 375–381.
3. Bertin, J., *The Semiology of Graphics*, University of Wisconsin Press, Madison, 1983.
4. Buttenfield, B. P. and MacKaness, W. A., Visualization, in *Geographical Information Systems: Principles and Applications, Vol. 1*, Maguire, D. J. Goodchild, M. F. and Rhind, D. W., Eds., John Wiley, New York, 1991, 427–430.
5. Campbell, J. B., *Introduction to Remote Sensing*, Guilford, New York, 1996.
6. Christ, R. E. and Corso, G. M., The effects of extended practice on the evaluation of visual display codes, *Hum. Factors*, 25, 71–84, 1983.
7. Christner, C. A. and Ray, H. W., An evaluation of the effect of selected combinations of target and background coding on map reading performance. *Hum. Factors*, 3, 131–146, 1969.

8. Colwell, R. N., Ed., *Manual of Remote Sensing*, American Society for Photogrammetry and Remote Sensing, Falls Church, VA, 1983.

9. Davies, D., Bathurst, D., and Bathurst, R., *The Telling Image: The Changing Balance between Pictures and Words in a Technological Age*, Oxford University Press, Oxford, 1990.

10. DiBiase, D., MacEachren, A. M., Krygier, J. B., and Reeves, C., Animation and the role of map design in scientific visualization, *Cartography and Cartographic Information Syst.*, 19, 201–214; 256–266, 1992.

11. Durrett, H. J., Ed., *Color and the Computer*, Academic Press, New York, 1987.

12. Friedhoff, B. W., *Visualization: The Second Computer Revolution*, W. H. Freeman, San Francisco, 1991.

13. Hoffman, R. R., The problem of extracting the knowledge of experts from the perspective of experimental psychology, *The AI Mag.*, 8, (1987, Summer) 53–67.

14. Hoffman, R. R., Human factors psychology in the support of forecasting: the design of advanced meteorological workstations, *Weather and Forecasting*, 6, 98–110, 1991.

15. Hoffman, R. R., Detweiler, M., Conway, J. A., and Lipton, K., Some considerations in the use of color in meteorological displays, *Weather and Forecasting*, 8, 505–518, 1993.

16. Hoffman, R. R. and Pike, R. J., On the specification of the information available for the perception and description of the natural terrain, in *Local Applications of the Ecological Approach to Human-Machine Systems*, Hancock, P., Flach, J., Caird, J., and Vicente, K., Eds., Erlbaum, Mahwah, NJ, 1995, 285–323.

17. MacEachren, A. M., Buttenfield, B. P., Campbell, J. B., DiBiase, D. W., and Monmonier, M., Visualization, in *Geography's Inner Worlds: Pervasive Themes in Contemporary American Geography*, Abler, R. F., Marcus, M. G., and Olson, J. M., Eds., Rutgers University Press, New Brunswick, NJ, 1992, 99–137.

18. MacEachren, A. M. and Ganter, J. H., A pattern identification approach to cartographic visualization, *Cartographica*, 27, 64–81, 1990.

19. MacEachren, A. M. and Taylor, D. R. F., Eds., *Visualization in Modern Cartography*, Elsevier, NY, 1994.

20. Olson, J. M., Color and the computer in cartography, in *Color and the Computer*, Durrett, J. H., Ed., Academic Press, New York, 1987, 205–219.

21. Rudwick, M. J. S., The emergence of a visual language for geological science, 1760–1840, *Hist. of Science*, 14, 149–195, 1976.

22. Slocum, T. A. and Egbert, S. L., Cartographic data display, in *Geographic Information Systems: The Microcomputer and Modern Cartography*, Taylor, D. R. F., Ed., Pergamon Press, Oxford, 1991, 167–199.

23. Ware, C. and Beatty, J. C., Using color dimensions to display data dimensions, *Hum. Factors*, 30, 127–142, 1988.

chapter two

Angles of Regard: Psychology Meets Technology in the Perception and Interpretation of Nonliteral Imagery

*Robert R. Hoffman, Arthur Markman,
and Walter H. Carnahan*

Contents

1-56670-413-8/01/$0.00+$.50
©2001 by CRC Press LLC

Keywords: *expertise, thermography, perceptual learning, color, cartography, display design, visualization, diagrammatic reasoning, concept formation, instructional design, mental models, automated classification, visualization software*

2.1   Introduction

Advances in remote sensing are often focused on technological innovations in imaging equipment and in computational techniques that enable image data to be interpreted automatically.[83] In this chapter, we discuss the importance of the human interpreter in processing remote sensing data. To this end, we will draw on literature from both remote sensing and cognitive psychology. We will illustrate the nexus of these areas with a demonstration experiment examining novice/expert differences in the interpretation of aerial thermograms.

2.1.1   What is remote sensing?

The prototypical remote sensing situation involves a sensor taking an image of a target a great distance away. The image is often formed from some energy source outside the range of sensitivity of the human visual system. For example, a satellite in geostationary orbit might generate an infrared image of the northeast coast of the U.S. As another example, a radio telescope in the Arizona desert might generate radio-frequency images of distant space. Such images pose a number of interesting interpretation problems. First, the perspective of the image is different from what people typically see. Aerial images typically yield overhead views of a region, whereas people typically view the world from a terrestrial perspective. Second, the scale of the images is different from what people typically encounter. Third, there are many ways to map intensities of the sensed quantity (e.g., infrared radiation) onto a visible image. These choices will affect the (visible-light) perceptual properties of the image. Finally, through evolution, the human visual system has adapted to allow us to deal with the visible world. Comparable evolved mechanisms do not exist for interpretation of nonliteral images.

Remote sensing scientists are well aware of such problems, and as a result the field of remote sensing has become a unified discipline devoted to the development of tools to facilitate interpretation by humans and to create tools for automated interpretation of images (see [68,120,175]).

To be clear at the outset, while the typical case of remote sensing involves a situation like that described above, research on remote sensing also involves cases that differ from the prototype. For example:

- *The sensor does not have to be far from the object of study.*

A natural resource manager may be tracking the migrations of radio-tagged caribou, and in this case the object of study is in direct contact with the sensor, but the radio signals are tracked via a geostationary satellite that is 25,000 miles in space. The manager views the data overlaid on an aerial perspective map, as if looking down at the Earth.

- *The sensor does not have to be far from the observer.*

A meteorologist predicting the weather using a ground-based radar may be a mere ten meters from the sensor (the radar antenna), but the view is of the atmosphere scores of kilometers distant from the sensor. An astrophysicist studying quasars using a ground-based radio telescope may be tens of meters from the sensor, but the object viewed may be billions of light years away. An aircraft pilot using a light amplification ("night vision") system is in direct contact with the sensor (i.e., special goggles).

- *The sensor does not always look downward, and the perspective is not always aerial.*

An aircraft pilot uses an infrared imaging system to look downward in a nonterrestrial perspective. Weather radar looks outward and upward from its antenna. The main products from weather radars involve a transformation in which data are viewed from an aerial perspective, but weather radar is also used to generate graph displays showing height in the atmosphere on the y-axis, time on the x-axis, with winds indicated by traditional "wind speed barb" symbols that use lines to indicate wind direction and speed. Such graphs do not depict aerial perspective.

What makes remote sensing "remote" is that either (1) the sensor is distant from the object of study by a scale equal to or greater than kilometers, or (2) the observer is distant from the sensor by a scale equal to or greater than kilometers, or both (1) and (2). Hence, remote sensing can be distinguished from "proximal sensing" and "micro-sensing" These terms designate such things as medical imaging, scanning tunneling microscopy, the bubble chamber of particle physics—any technology used to study things on micro scales. In these cases, the distance from the observer to the sensor is usually on the scale of meters and the distance from the sensor to the object of study is also on that or some smaller scale.

Although remote sensing evolved from aerial photography (visible-light), remote, proximal, and micro-sensing all involve the mediation of perception through a technology that detects some forms of information-containing energy that the human sensorium cannot detect—"nonliteral" imaging.* The human eye cannot see an electron, or an ultraviolet quasar, or the isothermal patterns indicative of plankton concentrations.

2.2 The "human factor" in remote sensing

Interpreting a remote sensing image is an open-ended task. The interpreter often does not know exactly what pattern is going to appear in an image. A project examining patterns of rainfall and drainage in a region might look for specific high-level properties of an area such as drainage basins. However, the specific perceptual manifestation of these high-level properties will differ from situation to situation, and thus, there is not a one-to-one mapping between particular properties of an image and the high level-properties it depicts. The job of the human interpreter is to make this link between the images and the high-level properties.

Remote sensing is an increasingly important technology in environmental and planetary science.[37,68,94] It is also becoming salient in the culture at large. Launches of new satellites (by both governmental agencies and commercial enterprises) with evermore advanced imaging capabilities have become almost routine. Satellite and radar images are routinely shown on televised weather forecasts, images from planetary probes adorn the covers of popular periodicals, and infrared imaging was daily fare on television news broadcasts during the 1991 Gulf War. But the wealth of new image data has created a problem—the "data analysis bottleneck." It would not be an overstatement to say that there are already enough satellite data in archives to keep the available image analysts busy for decades. Indeed, much data will probably decay before it can be analyzed in detail.† One design for the

---

*Despite vast differences in data types, the same human factors issues and the same practical issues (e.g., display design) apply equally well to micro-sensing as to remote sensing (e.g., expertise and display design in radiology), magnetic resonance imaging, X-ray diffraction crystallography, and so on.

†A hypothetical satellite of the type that initiated the field of remote sensing of the weather would transmit one visible light and one infrared photograph every half hour to fifteen minutes. Over ten years that would amount to between about 350,000 to 700,000 images. In orbit today are scores of remote sensing platforms of a great many types that collectively generate thousands, if not tens of thousands, of image data sets in a single day. Over the decades of satellite observation of the Earth, few image data sets have been preserved in image hardcopy form and countless digital tapes of remotely sensed data have decayed. As a matter of routine, some data are never preserved. For instance, the National Oceanic and Atmospheric Administration (NOAA) Weather Forecasting Offices only archive data that pertain to

Earth Observation Satellite system would have entailed the generation of over a terabyte of new multispectral image data per day.

Given the ever-increasing volume of remotely sensed data awaiting analysis, and given the continuing improvements in sensors and information processing systems, the emphasis in the field of remote sensing has been on widening the bottleneck through the use of automated data analysis approaches such as pattern recognition and algorithmic spectral analysis (cf. [83,105]). However, pattern recognition and automatic image processing techniques remain inadequate.[67] The human **must** be "in the loop," since the human, unlike the computer, can perceive and can form (and re-form) concepts. As Campbell put it in his text, *Introduction to Remote Sensing*:

> Although [computer analysis of pixel values] offers the benefits of simplicity and economy, it is not capable of exploiting information contained in relationships between each pixel and those that neighbor it. Human interpreters, for example, could derive very little information using the point-by-point approach.[24]

Even if most image analysis is ultimately conducted by machine, humans will continue to make the important interpretations, and make decisions based on the interpretations. They will continue to be the agent that creates the new algorithms that are used to process the data in the first place, and they will continue to do so in part by "fiddling" with their displays (e.g., the color coding schemes), and by reasoning around the interpretation anomalies that can arise as display schemes are applied to actual data sets (see [2]). It can be argued that the essential unity of remote sensing is expressed by the concept of "remote perceiving."[85,86] That is, the ultimate purpose of all the technology of sensors and information processing systems is to support the human interpretation of data to derive meaning and make decisions on the basis of the interpretation.

The importance of the human perceiver in the field of remote sensing is underscored in Campbell's text, in which nearly every chapter includes some allusion to the critical importance of the interpreter's knowledge and skill:

> . . . it is important to recognize that the role of the equipment is much more important, and much more subtle, than we may first appreciate. Display and analysis hardware determine in part how we perceive the data, and therefore how we use them. The equipment is, in effect, a filter through which we visualize data. We can never see them without this filter because there are so many data, and so many details, that we can never see them directly.

---

interesting or otherwise special cases of weather events. In other words, we are so overwhelmed that we are losing data at a considerable rate even while plans are being laid for generating terrabytes of new data.

The human interpreter is good at distinguishing subtle differences in texture.... Direct recognition is the application of the interpreter's experience, skill, and judgment to associate the image patterns with informational classes. The process is essentially a qualitative, subjective analysis of the image using the elements of image interpretation as visual and logical clues ... for image analysis, direct recognition must be a disciplined process, with a careful, systematic examination of the image.

Today's interpreters of archived satellite imagery face some difficulties. Many of the original interpretations depended not only on the imagery itself but also on the skill and experience of the interpreters ... many critical interpretations depended on the experience of the interpreters with long experience in analysis of images—experience that is not readily available to today's analysts.

For manual interpretation, ancillary data have long been useful in the identification and delineation of features on aerial images. Such uses [are an] application of the interpreter's knowledge and experience....

The interpreter's task is not so much one of identifying separate objects as it is the accurate delineation of regions of relatively uniform composition and appearance. The goal should be to perform this mental generalization in a consistent, logical manner and to describe the procedures accurately.... The guiding principles should be the attainment of visual and logical clarity ... [supporting information] includes not only the formal written material that accompanies the map [that is produced from remote sensing imagery] but also the wider realm of knowledge that [is used to] examine and evaluate the map.[24]

Statements of precisely these kinds can be found in every text on remote sensing, and all of them serve to highlight the importance of the interpreter's knowledge, skill, and experience in the interpretation of all forms of imagery (e.g., visible-light amplification, multispectral imagery, thermal imagery, radar, etc.) and all forms of processed imagery (e.g., ratio images, false-color images, multispectral chromaticity spaces, photoclinometric images, and so on). The interpreter's knowledge is, and must be, brought to bear on all aspects of image interpretation—the recognition of soil and rock types through the perception of tones, the discrimination of plant types in normalized vegetation indexed images, and so on.

In addition to the critical role of the human interpreter in routine procedures, important discoveries have been made in remote sensing (e.g., planetary science, archaeological applications, geomorphology, and so on), not through automated analysis, but through the human perception-interpretation process.[89,93] Here are a few of the countless stories that are suggestive of the cognitive foundation of remote sensing.

- The signs [of auroras on Venus] were first noticed in 1982 when Larry Paxton, now with the Naval Research Lab, saw a "few puzzling patches of brightness" on the Ultraviolet Emissions Spectrometer about the Pioneer Venus Orbiter (UVS). . . . Paxton initially wondered if there might be something wrong with the image. A glance showed similar features on other images, so he next looked to see if there was perhaps a mistake in the mapping algorithm that had been used to make pictures from the spacecraft's data. There was such an error, it turned out, but correcting it just made the patches brighter (adapted from [49]).
- Though the National Oceanic and Atmospheric Administration (NOAA) satellites were designed with meteorologists in mind, the remote sensing community discovered that the sensors aboard the polar-orbiting satellites could be used to distinguish forest from non-forest. On one channel in the mid-infrared region, forests appear cooler and clearings warmer. This was very fortuitous (adapted from [10]).
- Analysts can make vegetation appear green or red, or even blue in the false-color composite image just by assigning different colors to different bandwidths of digital imagery. . . . The Landsat Thematic Mapper does give an analyst flexibility, but it also introduces a problem. . . . The analyst can be easily misled by the composite image . . . when swapping colors and bands if he does not understand the spectral characteristics of soil, rock, and vegetation. Typically, analysts create a standard false-color composite image by assigning bands 2, 3, and 4 to the blue, green, and red guns on the Cathode Ray Tube (CRT). [But] some analysts feel that the image "looks" better if they use band 7 instead of 2. As a result, they create a composite image that may cause wrong interpretation. . . . An interpreter can make any color associations he wishes, but he may have difficulty in interpreting the resulting composite image (adapted from [32]).
- Most of our current knowledge of galaxy morphology is based on the pioneering work of several dedicated observers who have classified and cataloged thousands of galaxies. . . . It is remarkable that . . . subjective classification labels for galaxies correlate well with physical properties such as color, dynamical properties (e.g., rotation curves and stellar velocity dispersions), and the mass of neutral hydrogen. Human classifiers will need all the help they can get to cope with the flood of data that is expected from efforts like the Sloan Digital Sky Survey, which by itself is expected to image more than a million galaxies. [To take] a first step toward finding an automated method of galaxy classification, we compiled a well-defined sample of galaxy images. . . . One of the galaxies got exactly the same classification by all six observers, but there was no such clear agreement on the other three galaxies. . . . Any classification depends on the color, size, and quality of the images used. . . . Our comparison indicates that although the [galaxy classification system] is convenient, the scatter

between observers is not negligible. Further work will focus on super-
vised [classification] to preserve human experience in multidimensional classification (paraphrased from [105], see also [60]).

- In a project involving the relocation of indigenous peoples in New
  Guinea, researchers presented false-color infrared Landsat images to a
  group of natives. "The most amazing thing that struck me every time
  was the ability of the local people to immediately and intuitively
  understand the geometry of Landsat images . . . at a glance they recognized their villages and other local features. They do not inquire
  where the pictures come from, nor do they have an inkling of the technology behind it all, but they understand the information and can use
  it immediately" (Wine Langeraar quoted in [53]).

- In the process of examining various bandwidths of Voyager data that
  came back from the moon Io, Linda Morabito of the Jet Propulsion
  Laboratory in Pasadena, CA was performing a contrast enhancement
  operation in order to resolve the faint background stars. Such an interpretation process is usually driven by its particular objectives, and
  only the objects of interest are studied. However, she observed an
  anomalous region of energy at the horizon of the moon. With a bit
  more manipulation of the contrast, it became clear that she had happened to catch a volcano in the act of erupting. The plumes would
  have been discovered eventually during systematic image processing
  and interpretation. However, this discovery of active volcanoes on
  another planetary body was very exciting (adapted from [77]).

- Beginning in 1982, a device called the Synthetic Aperture Radar was
  flown aboard Space Shuttle missions, with the purpose of mapping
  the surface of the earth. ". . . . scientists at the U.S. Geological Survey
  (USGS) saw some Shuttle Imaging Radar (SIR) pictures that changed
  their conception of the Sahara Desert's underlying structure. The
  Shuttle Imaging Radar System (SIR-A) sent back picture-like data
  revealing a vast network of valleys and smaller channels winding
  beneath the desert sands. In the Sahara's super-dry core region, the
  radar penetrated right through the sand to reveal gravel terraces and
  river banks surrounding an ancient drainage system." [169] Radars, generally, do not penetrate soils. But, unexpectedly, the SIR did penetrate
  the dry desert soils. Within a second or so of their very first glance at
  the pictures, the pictures spoke a thousand words to the USGS scientists. The initial discovery, and subsequent excavations (geological,
  hydrological, and archaeological) all made the headlines.

2.3   Psychological research related to remote sensing

As the previous section demonstrates, there are many ways in which the
human contributes to the analysis of remote sensing images. There is a
considerable amount of pertinent psychological research that has explored

phenomena including: concept formation, graphical perception, expert/ novice differences, and perceptual learning. We now summarize some of that research, organizing the discussion around aspects of perceptual learning, a concept that provides a unifying theme for this volume. Following this discussion, we present an experiment that illustrates perceptual learning in the context of remote sensing image interpretation.

2.3.1 Research on the interpretation of diagrammatic and pictorial displays

Because the human visual system is designed to recognize complex patterns, graphic displays can be developed to assist in the interpretation of complex data sets. Thus, psychological factors have become an important consideration in the display of multidimensional data (see [43,74,189]), including cartographic data[7,18,42,45,123,124,125,145,164,177] and meteorological data (e.g., satellite imagery, radar, etc.).[92] Topics in visualization and diagrammatic reasoning have become "hot" in the field of artificial intelligence (see [22]).

2.3.1.1 Diagrammatic reasoning

In concert with recent developments in scientific visualization, an extensive body of research has demonstrated that the solving of abstract problems (e.g., algebra, logic, combinatorics) and puzzles (e.g., the "Tower of Hanoi" problem) can be significantly facilitated if the problems are accompanied by diagrams that depict concepts, functions, and relations (e.g., [4,96,106,107,193]). Psychological research has shown that the comprehension of illustrations that accompany text depends on the type and difficulty level of the text, the level of expertise of the learner, the strategies the learner uses, and the relation between the type of material to be learned and the type of graphic (see [64,99,147,194,195]). Scientific material presented in textbooks can be more readily understood if accompanied by appropriate diagrams, e.g., showing clouds and the distribution of electric charges that cause lightning, diagrams showing the structure and operation of machines, electronic circuits, problems in mechanics involving pulleys and springs, etc. (see [4,108,126,139]), although textbooks often do not use graphics appropriately or effectively (see [112,197]).

An example is the work of educational psychologist Richard Mayer and colleagues.[130,131] They have conducted a number of experiments on how college-age students learn from illustrations in scientific texts. They have demonstrated that comprehension and recall of passages about common machines (e.g., the workings of a brake mechanism or a pump mechanism) and responses to a problem transfer task improve when the text is accompanied by labeled illustrations, especially for students who have had little household repair experience. Presenting the figure labels alone does not help, even though labels—for the most part—repeated information that was contained in the text. Students who saw the text with labeled illustrations showed better transfer performance (e.g., answers to what-if questions about the problem situation) and greater recall of explanation-related information. Furthermore, multiframe illustrations that showed the steps or sequences of events (e.g., what happens as a pump rod is pulled out) as well as those that labeled the parts of the mechanism were more instructive and beneficial to problem solving transfer than illustrations that just labeled the parts. In a study using animations,[130] those that were accompanied by verbal descriptions were more beneficial to problem solving transfer than when the verbal explanation was presented before the animation, even though recall of the verbal information was about the same in both conditions. Mayer's view is that labeled dynamical illustrations assist in the formation of useful mental models that combine principle-based understanding of causation with a dynamic, imagistic understanding.

2.3.1.2   Pictorial reasoning

Laboratory research on the effects of pictorial displays on performance in stimulus detection tasks, multicue judgment tasks, and memory tasks, has demonstrated that display formats can hinder or facilitate the perception and comprehension of information about spatial layouts, dynamic events, and causal processes, and the configural relations of systems that are defined by multiple variables or parameters (e.g.,[73,80]). Research has also shown that useful displays are often those that depict meanings pictorially, and dynamically mimic events and processes.[5,19,41,44,50,52,190]

Psychological studies of visual search in graphic displays have often utilized matrix-like arrays of symbols (e.g., letters, numbers, regular geometric shapes).[25,33,189,191] Psychological research using graphic displays has traditionally used highly impoverished artificial "maps" (e.g., a few simple contour lines).[34] In part, the artificiality of the stimuli is a consequence of the need for experimental control—to permit factorial manipulation of such variables as data density, the colors and sizes of areas or symbols, and target predictability. However, most of the results end up being of marginal applicability to real displays, such as maps, in which colors are variegated, shapes are convoluted, the data are multidimensional, etc.

Fortunately, some research has departed from the "artificial stimulus" tradition and investigated the perception and interpretation of remote sensing imagery.

2.3.2   Reasoning about remotely sensed imagery

While it has been argued that psychological processes are fundamental in the field of remote sensing,[86,89,92] psychological research is just beginning to examine the processes whereby experts and novices perceive and interpret remote sensing imagery (e.g.,[56,65,141,185]). While there is a tradition of research on "cognitive maps" and psychological factors in the interpretation and understanding of topographical maps and orienteering (cf. [20,51,59,81,165,180]), only recently has applied research shown that psychological factors of comprehension and memory are critical in the interpretation of meteorological charts[119] and aerial photos.[82]

> ... there has been little work in understanding the human perception or cognition of remotely sensed imagery. Despite this lack of research, we often design automated measures of image cues, such as texture or pattern, with an implicit assumption that we are emulating visual cues or at least matching human performance. ... But how do we know that such measures emulate visual cues of human processes without studying the human processes and performance?[82]

In his seminal studies on this, Hodgson[82,83] asked how much local information is needed for the human interpreter to classify a pixel. The automated analysis of pixel data to assign classification typically relies on small windows of 3×3 to 9×9 (for reasons having to do with computational efficiency, image resolution, etc.), but is such a window size adequate for the human interpreter? For smaller window sizes, neither trained nor untrained participants should perform well at a classification task, whereas for larger window sizes perhaps anyone could perform reasonably well.

In the experiment, black and white aerial photos covering the Denver metropolitan area were cropped to a range of window sizes (from 10×10 pixels up to 100×100 pixels), and the cropped images were presented to college students who had completed a course in aerial photointerpretation. Their task was to classify pixels into land-use categories (i.e., *"Is this area predominately residential, commercial, or transportation?"*). Since humans "synergistically use a number of image interpretation elements, such as tone, pattern, texture, shape, size and association"[82] in what cognitive psychologists refer to as "top-down" processing, it was expected that the optimum window size would be greater than that typically used in the automated analysis of imagery. For example, areas of commercial land use can involve large parking lots and buildings, requiring larger windows for correct classification. The research findings confirmed the notion that smaller window sizes "constrain adequate contextual analysis"[82] (i.e., top-down processing) upon which human perception depends:

> In normal circumstances, the photo interpreter may proceed from known to unknown parts of a photograph, thereby using information gained from one part of the scene in classifying other parts ... [this] calls into question the notion of using small windows, regardless of the classification algorithm. ... If the human cannot correctly classify small subimages, then should we expect an automated classifier to do so?[82]

Aesthetic judgments also come into play in the interpretation of remotely sensed imagery. Sociologist Michael Lynch[121,122] interviewed a number of expert astronomers about the "representation craft" of generating false-color displays based on multispectral data. The raw data from space probes and satellites can be portrayed using a variety of color palettes, some of which can be misleading. False-color multispectral satellite images that cover a range of visible and nonvisible bandwidths (e.g., infrared, radar, X-ray, etc.) can create special problems for display design and interpretation. A clear example is the photographs of the planets that NASA produced from Voyager data. Contrary to those brilliant and colorful depictions, most of the planets look rather like dirty tennis balls; they are not vivid. The "Great Red Spot" is not red; the moon Io does not look like a pizza (see [200]). For public relations purposes, astronomers orient explicitly to the aesthetic aspects of their images, and are unashamed to talk about the "pretty pictures" that adorn the hallways of their research facilities. For publications in popular outlets, experts sometimes change their figures to match the goals of their text and the figure captions, rather than writing captions to fit the figures. Even for technical publications, images are tailored to show the features that are being discussed (e.g., for an article about radio-emitting nebulae, an image may be recolorized to make the apparent emission pattern match a visible-light image).

The primary or scientific goal of image processing is to support scientists' accurate perception and comprehension. As one expert astronomer put it, "through a complex series of adjustments and modifications of an image. . . . [a display should] enable researchers to *see* the physics."[121] To make this point, Lynch attempted to show that the aesthetic judgments are not so distinct from the scientific ones. Most of the expert astronomers insisted that their actual scientific work involves working with raw, quantitative data, perhaps depicted graphically but even then, using a more "boring" gray-scale rather than fancy colors. However, Lynch probed the experts about what it was that made some of their color graphic products especially pleasing:

> E (expert): This is one that starts out red and then goes through yellow and white. Here's some radio data thats multicolor. I like these maps that have sort of one color, they start out dim, then go brighter, then go white. I think those are prettier than these that have many different colors.
>
> I (interviewer): Is it strictly a matter of liking one color?
>
> E: The reasons are artistic rather than scientific.
>
> I: Other people told me they like a more uniform thing because it is not misleading.
>
> E: Yes, there's that too. You show this picture to someone and you say "This is what it looks like." Now, you can't really see it; it doesn't really look like anything. But this does seem to be more realistic.
>
> I: Choice of color would have some relation if it were an extension of the spectrum . . .

E: Right. At one time I thought I wanted to make the
X-ray purple and the radio red because it gives you an idea that
this is a higher energy photon.[121]

The experts' "aesthetic" judgments clearly play a role, but do not do so in any
arbitrary way—they are driven by their foundational scientific knowledge
and their goals.

An awareness of the need for new approaches to visualization has led to
a number of collaborative research and development projects. For instance,
IBM's Lloyd A. Treinish (a space scientist by training) and Bernice E.
Rogowitz (a psychologist by training), have been developing new graphic
displays for the visualization of remotely sensed data (e.g., [154,155,162,182,183]).
Software systems that are currently in use offer a plethora of mapping choices
and tools, but provide little guidance in their application to specific tasks.
Depending on the architecture and interface of the system, the user must
either define the mapping(s) between data and pictures via the tools in such
systems, or operate within a fixed set of predefined mappings, which may
have little facility for customization or control. In both cases, the mappings
that are available are driven by the structure of the data, not the task or the
human's goal for the visualization. Hence, the design of visualizations can be
time-consuming and often requires the assistance of computer graphics
experts, who are not domain scientists.

Some of the IBM research was aimed at coping with large volumes of
rapidly produced numerical weather forecasts as well as remotely sensed
data as an aid in the presentation of information to the layman via broadcast
media and the World Wide Web. To help address this problem, Treinish
applied work done with Rogowitz on the creation of a rule-based advisory
tool for the specification of appropriate color maps.[184] Their rule-based system assists the user by ensuring that data content is reflected in images and
that perceptual artifacts are not erroneously interpreted as data features. The
system also provides advice on representation depending on whether the
goal of visualization is exploration or presentation.

The approach to visualization hinges on three premises:

• Traditional graphical representations of data will not suffice.
• Data structures have to be mapped onto perceptual structures.
• Rule-based systems can help users make good decisions about the
  visualization of data without requiring the user to become an expert in
  human vision (i.e., depth perception, color theory, etc.) or computer
  graphics (e.g., data structures, algorithms, etc.).

Instead of static or simple flip-book animations of two-dimensional
contour maps, novel three-dimensional visualization strategies have been
employed that preserve the fidelity of the original data as much as possible,
and yet allow the user to define coordinate systems onto which data may be

registered in space and time. Techniques support the registration of multiple data sets in geographic coordinates using cartographic warping of the data locations. Treinish et al. have found that the use of appropriately warped curvilinear grids can preserve the fidelity (e.g., missing data, original grid resolution) of the data—the transformations are both topologically and data-invariant. The selection of cartographic projections is dictated by the requirements of the user in the design of an appropriate visualization, as opposed to limitations of the system in use or the original characteristics of the data.

Examples of their innovative graphic products appear in Figures 2.1, 2.2, and 2.3. Figure 2.1 is a perspectival display illustrating the incorporation of multiple data types. Surface wind speed is overlaid on a surface chart (using a color palette of saturation shades of violet), and precipitation is indicated by a pastel (desaturated) "rainbow" palette. Also shown is a perspectival view of cloud structures based on radar data. Figure 2.2 is a perspectival display demonstrating a warping transformation. In this case, the column of ozone (the ozone "hole") is directly perceptible as a deformed surface. Figure 2.3 is another perspectival display illustrating how a single display

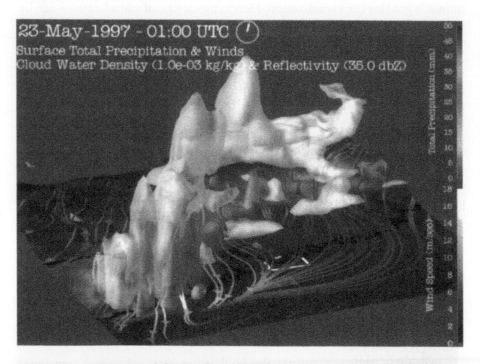

Figure 2.1 A perspectival display illustrating the incorporation of multiple data types. See color version of this figure in the color section following page 114. (From Treinish, L. A. and Rothfusz, L., *Proceedings of the Thirteenth International Conference on Interactive Information and Processing Systems for Meteorology, Oceanography and Hydrology,* American Meteorological Society, Boston, 31–34, 1997. With permission.)

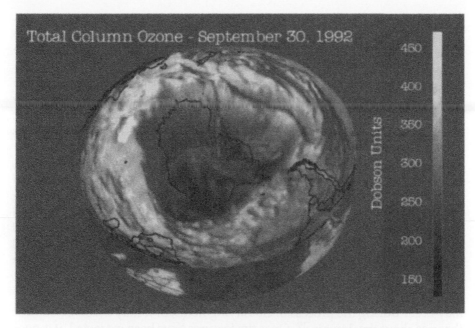

Figure 2.2   A perspectival display demonstrating a warping transformation. See color version of this figure in the color section following page 114. (From Treinish, L A. and Rothfusz, L., in *Proceedings of the Thirteenth International Conference on Interactive Information and Processing Systems for Meteorology, Oceanography and Hydrology*, American Meteorological Society, Boston, 31–34, 1997. With permission.)

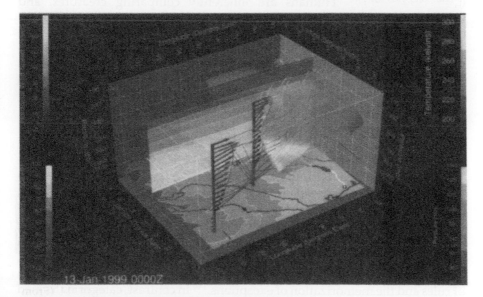

Figure 2.3   A perspectival display illustrating the incorporation of multiple data types. See color version of this figure in the color section following page 114. (Figure courtesy of L. Treinish, IBM.)

can portray multiple data types. This image portrays horizontal winds (using a color pallette of saturation shades of violet), relative humidity (using saturation shades of brown), surface temperature overlaid on the base map (using a two-tone palette of saturation shades of blue and green-blue), and air pressure (indicated in a semitransparent vertical plane using saturation shades of blue-violet and green). Also depicted are three-dimensional cloud structures. For all of these graphic products, the use of perspective, depth pseudoplanes, and animation permits the perceptual discrimination of the multiple variables (other images can be viewed at http://www.research. ibm.com/ people/l/lloydt/ and http://www.research.ibm.com/weather).

2.3.3   Research on concept formation

Recognizing that a specific pattern is an instance of a high-level feature is a perceptual classification task. Perceptual classification involves a number of important subtasks. The relevant set of perceptual features must be extracted from the items. Part of this process involves actually learning which aspects of the stimulus should be construed as features.[168] This perceptual learning may occur during the process of classifying items, or it may involve people's theories about the domain.[196] Once the features have been extracted, it is necessary to determine the combinations of properties that distinguish one category from another.[144]

An important focus of current research in categorization is how the way people interact with a set of items influences what is learned about it.[128,158,159,160,161,196] "Humans are inherently comparing creatures, and whether instructed or not we simply jump in and compare when interacting with a novel set of materials."[23] Research has confirmed the intuition that categories can be learned incidentally through exposure as well as through an intentional process of analyzing features and relations (e.g., correlated attributes), even though patterns of attention differ for incidental vs. deliberate learning (for reviews, see [17,188]). However, traditional psychological research has focused on a directed classification task in which people see a series of examples (of simple, and often artificial stimuli composed of schematic faces, geometric patterns, etc.) and they are asked to classify them (e.g., [16,58,156]).

Tasks such as interpreting remote sensing images do not typically involve this kind of trial and error learning. Instead, the high-level categories of interest in an image interpretation setting are learned in the context of identifying items in the images, using the images to solve other problems, and communicating the results to others. The categories are learned as a byproduct of this other kind of reasoning. This distinction is important, because categories learned in laboratory tasks tend to involve the formation of rules and the memorization of exceptions.[144] In contrast, categories formed incidentally to performing a primary task are less rule-governed, and tend to emphasize those features that were important for solving the primary task.[127,158,159,160,161,198,199]

2.3.4 Research on expert/novice differences

On the basis of recent psychological research on expertise,[31,55,87,111] including expert/novice differences in map interpretation and the use of cartographic visualization tools,[133] one would expect major differences between the perceptual skills of the expert and the initiate image analyst. Such differences, once specified, could have implications for instructional design, image or display design, workstation design, and the development of decision aids or expert systems. Training issues are critical since it takes many years to become an expert image analyst.

Kibbe and Stiff conducted a study of novice/trainee interpretation of aerial photographs.[100] Participants were shown aerial photographs overlaid by line drawings that outlined some of the salient features in the pictures (e.g., hill contours, roadways, etc.). Some of the line drawings were sparse, some were more detailed. Some were properly aligned with the photo that they superimposed and some were misaligned, and the participants' task was speeded recognition of (mis)alignment. Line drawings that indicated the longer features were responded to more rapidly (by about 1 s, with 10% greater accuracy) than line drawings with short lines, but only when the line drawings were properly aligned. In one condition, the participants were initially exposed to the stimuli in a task in which they themselves attempted to produce outline drawings for each of the photographs. This active engagement in the interpretation task had a positive effect in their subsequent recognition reaction time performance for the properly aligned drawings, even though the line drawings used in the task were not their own.

Moray and Richards attempted to demonstrate the expert/novice difference in a study of memory for radar-like displays.[135] A group of college-age students, a group of Royal Air Force (RAF) fighter controllers (with some experience with radar), and a group of RAF aerospace systems engineers (with more radar experience) were presented with a series of simple radar-like displays, basically showing a circle with one or more "targets" indicated by a small letter "X" somewhere within the circle. After seeing each stimulus for about 10 s (about equal to 1 radar sweep), they had to try and reproduce the targets by redrawing the stimulus, either immediately or following a delay (of up to 30 s). Both accuracy and confidence tended to decline as the delay period was increased. However, there appeared no statistically significant differences between the two expert groups in overall recall accuracy, although there was a trend for the more highly experienced of the experts to do slightly better at the task. The effect of expertise was more manifest for the more highly experienced participants in one respect—for displays involving three (as opposed to one or two) targets, the participants reported that they were able to remember the pattern, leading to better performance and increased confidence. In general, ratings of confidence were not a very good indicator of recall accuracy, a finding common in the literature on memory and expertise.[140]

As the Kibbe and Stiff[100] and Moray and Richards[135] studies suggest, quite a lot of the modern research on expertise has involved domains in which the interpretation of nonliteral imagery is a primary task. Hence, this work pertains to the topic of perceptual learning.

2.3.5   Research on perceptual learning

By tradition in psychology, the processes of perception and learning are for the most part treated separately (e.g., separate chapters in the standard textbooks). But learning is not just the accumulation or storage of propositional facts and static knowledge structures. Across development, there is a change in the way information is acquired. At first, attention is passively "captured" by salient or easily isolated stimulus features. With experience and practice, new distinctive features are discovered, permitting the active strategic search for critical information.[15,75,76,98,137] One gains an ability to rapidly detect and discriminate, and not just isolated features or cues. Rather, one learns to attend to the invariant patterns or cue configurations that specify distinctive properties, patterns which were not previously noticed or were discerned only with difficulty.[30,54,57,70,143]

Perceptual learning, operationally defined, is the increase in the ability to discriminate and extract information as a result of practice and experience, as assessed in terms of an increased specificity of the responses to stimuli.[54,70] Over the course of development, perceptual skills change, permitting the rapid search, discrimination, recognition, and comprehension of complex informational patterns, provided that the responses are mapped consistently to specific elements or patterns in the visual scene (or display).[26,36,62,78,142,148,150,172]

As one acquires a perceptual skill involving the classification of complex patterns, performance can come to reflect the underlying rules, yet the human may be unable to articulate the relevant dimensions of difference, that is, the knowledge becomes "tacit."[1,13,14,72,103,111,113–115,143,149–152,172,187,188] The explanations people give for what they are doing may be justifications rather than descriptions of the rules they are following. Furthermore, performance at the classification of complex patterns can improve without the learner developing a deep conceptual understanding of the significances in the patterns.[48,63,146,167] Rich discriminations can be made without conscious analysis, verbal labeling, or even awareness of isolated features. Indeed, at high levels of skill, complex stimuli can be perceived at a rate that precludes verbal labeling, perhaps illustrated best in the research on the learning of Morse code.[70]*

A great deal of psychological research on perceptual learning has focused on child development (e.g., depth perception, locomotion, and object perception). However, in her classic book on perceptual learning and development, Eleanor Gibson pointed to the role of perceptual learning in such expert skills as sonar interpretation, X-ray interpretation, identifying aircraft by their silhouettes, and infrared aerial photointerpretation.[70] Skill automatization has been observed in a number of studies of expertise.[27,38,39,40,11,69,170] As one expert personnel manager observed, "When I was younger I used to carefully consider all the aspects, get lots of opinions, and agonize over decisions. But now, I can generally just recognize what to do."[171] Indeed, the automatization of skill is believed to characterize the shift from novice to expert.[46,71,101,102,110]

For instance, Myles-Worsley et al. had expert radiologists and medical students observe and then attempt to recognize a series of chest X-rays.[137] Reaction time data showed that experts allocated their attention more efficiently, focusing on abnormal features that distinguished the images. Similarly, Norman et al. demonstrated the effect of perceptual learning in a study of student, intern, and resident dermatologists, in which the participants were shown 100 slides for diagnosis.[143] The researchers measured reaction time and error rates in a subsequent recognition task. The reaction time data showed that experts engaged in a rapid perceptual process that does not rely on independent analyses of separate cues. In other words, reaction times and errors were not predictable on the basis of the simple presence or absence of isolated features that are typical of each diagnostic category.

Research has shown that experts in domains as diverse as architecture, nursing, and electronic circuit design can indeed "see" and evaluate things

---

*Lewicki, Hill, and Bizot[115] conducted an experiment in which participants were run in thousands of trials, each trial consisting of a matrix of four numbers. One of the numbers was the "target," and its position would differ in the matrices across blocks of 7 trials. The task was speeded reaction-time—the participants pressed a key to indicate the position of the target on each trial. A complex rule was used to determine the sequence of target movements (e.g., if the target appeared in quadrants 3, 2, 4, and 1 in trials 1, 3, 4, and 6, then it would appear in quadrant 1 on trial 7). Over several thousand trials, participants' reaction times and error rates for trial seven decreased significantly. Yet, participants were not able to verbalize the underlying rule or even give it a coherent characterization. Interestingly, when taken out of the speeded reaction time task and asked to predict the position of the target on trial 7, they performed no better than chance. Such results obtained even when participants were offered a considerable award ($100) if they could figure out the rule, and even when participants were college faculty who knew that the experiment involved studying the nonconscious processes of perceptual learning.

that novices cannot.[98,111] When novice livestock judges confront the judgment task they can miss seeing important features of livestock that experts readily detect[171]; the eye movements of radiologists while they scan X-ray films are quite different from those of novices—the experts can selectively search for abnormalities; expert cardiologists directly comprehend cardiovascular bio-mechanical events as perceived through a stethoscope.[98] In many domains of expert decision making, such as fire fighting, power plant operation, jurisprudence, and design engineering, experts often make decisions through rapid recognition of causal factors and goals, rather than through any explicit process of generating and evaluating solutions.[101]

In an example from remote sensing, experts at the identification of rocks and landforms seem to directly recognize different types, even though they were originally taught the diagnostic features explicitly. Hoffman studied terrain analysts with the U.S. Army Corps of Engineers, experts at interpreting aerial photographs for engineering purposes.[84] The experts had behind them decades of experience at analyzing aerial photographs to assess soils, bedrock, vegetation patterns, drainage patterns, and the like. In one experiment, experts were asked to think aloud about their perceptions as they viewed aerial photographs:

> Based on what I see in this photo, this is a semiarid climate. Over here you see there's a gently rolling, irregular plain. The gullies down here are V- and U-shaped. Lots of lowlands ... rounded contours. But over here are some escarpments. The gradients are fairly uniform, so it's homogeneous rock. About midway down the slopes is a relatively thick tonal band, so there's a thick bed there, pretty thick, and at the base it's flared and a bit scalloped. This terrain is flat shale, with loess topsoil.[93]

Exactly how did the expert know that the climate is semiarid? Exactly how did the expert know that the shale is flat? Which of the expert's statements were premises about perceived features, and which were conclusions? What does it mean to say that a plain is "irregular"? Many things were being perceived, but these were stated in terms of the higher-level concepts of terrain analysis (e.g., "escarpment"), not in terms of specific perceptible cues. The informational cues were certainly there in the photos, but they could only be seen by the novice when they were pointed out and explained.

In another experiment, experts were presented a photograph for inspection, but were only allowed two minutes of viewing time—ordinarily the full systematic terrain analysis process can take hours. After the viewing period, the experts were allowed two minutes in which to report everything that could be remembered about the photo. In one particular trial, an expert began his retrospection by asserting that any personnel sent to the depicted area would need to be prepared for certain types of bacterial infection. The experimenter's response was, "You can see bacteria in a pond taken from 40,000 feet?" Here was the reasoning sequence that the expert recounted:

> The photo covered an area of tropical climate. The vegetation was mature and uniform, so the contours to the top of the tree canopy could be taken as a reflection of the contour of the underlying soil, and since the soil layer would be relatively thin, the contour to the tree canopy reflected the underlying bedrock, which appeared to be tilted interbedded limestone. The bedrock also determined the pattern to the streams and ponds, and there appeared one pond that did not have a major distributary running away from it. Given the climate, the vegetation (tropical legumes) and the stagnant water, the presence of bacteria was a sure bet.[93]

This appears to be a long chain of inferences, dependent on a great deal of conceptual knowledge. Yet, in the actual experimental trial, the expert's judgment was very rapid, the sort of judgment that one might be inclined to call "direct" or "immediate"—more of a perceptual thing than a linear, conscious, and deliberative process.

2.4   A demonstration experiment: expert/novice differences in the interpretation of aerial thermograms*

To illustrate the human factor in remote sensing, consider the false-color aerial thermogram shown in Figure 2.4. This image covers an area of about four city blocks in a small town in the midwest U.S. The depiction is of mid- and far-infrared radiometric data, displayed in terms of a "rainbow code" that is standard in this application (cf. [138]), i.e., the assessment of patterns of energy conservation.[2] The colors depict temperatures falling in the range of −5 to 7°C, a range that includes most of the wintertime variation in temperatures of surfaces (glass, brick, siding, heat vents, etc.), and other sources such as trees, small bodies of water, forested areas, etc. The high extreme temperature is coded as white (which did not fit into the 8 × 10-in. photo frame); temperatures at and below the low extreme are coded as black. Temperatures between are assigned to colors (about 0.7°C per color) based on common

---

*Walter Carnahan (Indiana State University) provided the aerial thermograms used in this study. The authors would like to thank Scott Lissner (Longwood College), Robin Akerstrom, Andrea Bubka, Stan Grabon, Garry Zaslow (Adelphi University) for helping in the collection and analysis of the data. Finally, thanks to Mark Detweiler (Pennsylvania State University) for his comments on a draft version of this material.

Figure 2.4   An aerial thermogram of a suburban area. See color version of this figure in the color section following page 114. (Indiana State University Thermography Project. With permission.)

associations: "Cold" (blue hues), "Cool" (green hues), "Warm" (red and orange hues), and "Warmer" (yellow hues).

While perhaps reasonable *a priori*, remote sensing scientists have learned that such color codes can generate interpretation anomalies when applied to actual data sets.[2,176] In the case of thermograms, flat water surfaces and metal roofs can act as infrared mirrors, reflecting the sky temperature and appearing anomalously cold (right-hand corner of Figure 2.4). As a second example, a salient color boundary (green-blue adjacent to the red) straddles a critical temperature—buildings with poor insulation get coded as red to yellow, houses with good insulation get coded as green. By design, this makes it easy for the expert to discriminate buildings in need of better insulation. Experience with students, however, suggested that the naive viewer is inclined to interpret the "green blobs" as trees. Coincidentally, trees are relatively warm in winter thermography and appear as "yellow blobs," which initiates seem inclined to interpret as houses with poor insulation.

The motivation for the studies we describe stems from the pedagogical strategy taken in most textbooks on remote sensing. The introductions of texts and manuals (e.g., [35,117,173,174,192]) invariably focus on technical information about electromagnetism and sensors. Some include one or a few examples of multispectral imagery (e.g.,[37,175]), but the reader's attention is directed only at the feature that is the focus of the application (land use, hydrology, geology, etc.). Rarely is an explanation given of how a classification was determined, or of how a false-color scheme was established. There is no guidance to interpretation; there is no encouragement to reason. We designed this study to include conditions that would emulate these aspects of the textbook pedagogical strategy.

It is known that the format and focus of instructions can shape the learner's strategies in concept formation[179] and in the learning of both simple puzzle tasks and more complex tasks such as mathematical problem solving and computer programming.[109,118,153] However, explicit introductory teaching alone does not necessarily promote skill acquisition, whether in applied contexts such as electronics troubleshooting[163] or in academic contexts such as mathematics puzzle solving.[132] In a study in which novices (college students) were taught about the process of plastic extrusion,[104] one group was first taught about the general domain concepts (mixing, injecting, etc.) and the multiple relations between the concepts, and was subsequently taught about the lower-level details (e.g., the operation of the machine screw as a function of injection pressure). Another group was taught in the opposite order (lower-level details followed by general concepts). A test of what the students had learned involved asking them to say whether domain concepts presented pairwise were or were not related. The results showed that the group that was first taught about the general level domain concepts performed better than the group that was first taught at the detailed level. For the acquisition of knowledge structures in complex domains, attention needs to be given to instruction on both the hierarchical relations (general to particular) among domain concepts, and the multiple relations between domain concepts.

Furthermore, there are important training issues involving the relation of instruction and hands-on practice vs. tests of knowledge acquired through the study of manuals. At an extreme called the "dissociation" effect, after practice at a complex task (e.g., the operation of an industrial process via a computer-driven graphical interface), people can sometimes provide a verbal description of the task while their performance remains poor. Conversely, in some conditions performance can be good and yet the person may be unable to give an adequate verbal explanation of what it is that he or she is doing in the task.[6,21,79,129,167]

What these findings from applied psychological research suggest for the pedagogical strategy used in remote sensing is that instruction should not proceed simply by diving into the gory details of electromagnetics. The hypothesis which we examined was that even for a skill that is highly reliant on perception and perceptual learning, initial verbal instructions can nevertheless make some positive difference. But this hypothesis must be qualified by "cognitive load" considerations (see [181]). In the learning of task procedures (e.g., physics problem solving), instructions can be detrimental if they require the learner to integrate multiple sources of information (e.g., diagrams, equations, worked examples, etc.) before the learner has developed an understanding of domain concepts, i.e., memory schemas that can be used to lessen the burden on working memory.[188] One goal of the present research was to see if a similar finding might obtain for the interpretation of remote sensing images—basic information about electromagnetism must be integrated with the task of picture perception. We hypothesized that providing elaborate *a priori* instructions that delve into details about thermograms might not promote identification performance, and might actually suppress the overall rate of responding in an identification task.

2.4.1 Experiment 1

The purposes of Experiment 1 were to assess expert performance at the interpretation task and conduct a reference analysis of the materials. One of the authors (R.R.H) served as the expert, having spent four years analyzing scores of aerial thermograms, visible light aerial photographs, and radar images, and hundreds of visible and infrared meteorological satellite images. He had received his training in image interpretation at the U.S. Army Corps of Engineers and the U.S. Air Force Geophysics Laboratory.

On each of nine trials, the expert was presented a thermogram and generated identifications for a period of five minutes. A sheet of celluloid was laid over each thermogram, and using a felt-tip pen the expert outlined the identified features and objects while providing a verbal description which was recorded on audiotape.

For four stimuli depicting rural regions, the expert identified an average of 27 things and features. Within an average of about three minutes the expert asserted that he had identified all of the interpretable features. For the five stimuli that depicted suburban regions, an average of 107 things were identified, but there were yet more things that could have been identified when three of the trials ended.

In most cases, confirmation of the expert's identifications (e.g., identifying a form as a house with poor insulation, identifying a road, a stream, etc.) was totally unnecessary. A few identifications had to be confirmed either by reference to training manuals or to ground truth. The few remaining uncertain identifications, all apparent thermal anomalies, were explained in light of on-going research (e.g., [28]).

According to the expert's identifications, over 60 qualitatively different things could be identified in the thermograms. The reference menu appears in Table 2.1.

2.4.2 Experiment 2

2.4.2.1 Design and procedure

The main purpose of Experiment 2 was to investigate performance at the exact opposite end of the skill continuum relative to the expert. The participants were 48 Adelphi University undergraduates. In a post-experimental ques-

Table 2.1 Categorization for Correct Responses in the Identification Task.

Transportation

Dirt trailpath, tractor path[5], sidewalk, dirt road, two-lane street[4], four-lane street[4], boulevard (divided), expressway, expressway ramp, expressway overpass, bridge, automobile, truck, railroad car, railroad track[4], parking lot[4]

Topography

Tree[4], shrub, forest, hedge rows[5], grass field[4,5], park, hill, hillock[5], puddle[5], pond, stream, river, sand or silt river or pond bank, tilled farm field[5], till rows[5], fallow farm field[5], irrigation gully[5,] crop row[5], drainage catch basins

Residential buildings

House[4], attached garage[4], unattached garage[4], porch[4], patio, trailer home[5], trailer park

Commercial buildings

Small industry[4], large industry, small commercial[4], large commercial, piping, water tank[4]

Roof and building structure

Partially insulated roof[4], poorly insulated roof[4], uninsulated roof[4], standing water on roofs[4], superstructure, composite materials[4], metal roof[4], eave, flue[4], vent, chimney[4], water damage

Thermal shine sources

Windows[4], doors, building height asymmetries[4], walls[4], roof pitch, reflecting surfaces[4], solar-load (from sidewalks, patios, etc.)

Heat phenomena

Heat shadows (e.g., from cars that had been parked during the day), compass heading (asymmetrically heated hill or hillock slopes)[5], wind direction, furnaces, heat plants, auto or truck engines, pipes[4], heat leaks, remnant heat (e.g., from car engines pausing at road intersections)[4]

Superscripts denote the figures (either 2.4 or 2.5) in which a feature can be seen.

tionnaire, only a few indicated a passing familiarity with satellite images, (i.e., from TV weather forecasts), and perhaps a vague memory of having seen one or two satellite images, typically in a high school or junior high school course in general earth science.

Aerial thermograms covering suburban areas (see Figure 2.4) manifest the regularities one might expect of aerial views of streets and houses. On the other hand, rural areas have asymmetrical ponds, forests, and farms, and meandering streams and paths. An example appears in Figure 2.5. As a consequence of physical variations (terrain texture and slope, plowing, soil moisture, etc.) and their effects on thermal emissivity, even rectangular farm

Figure 2.5   An aerial thermogram of a rural area. See color version of this figure in the color section following page 114. (Indiana State University Thermography Project. With permission.)

fields can present an asymmetrical panoply of colors and forms. We hypothesized that the uninformed viewer would be more likely to perceive the rural stimuli as abstract art rather than as aerial views.

The experiment also probed for an effect of instructions. There were four instructional conditions. In Instructional Condition 0, participants were told only that they "would be shown some pictures." In Condition 1, participants were informed that they would be shown aerial perspective pictures. In Condition 2, participants were told the pictures were aerial perspectives and they were also given a brief (350 word) explanation of thermography (i.e., that it is the detection of wavelengths outside the visible spectrum), with emphasis on the fact that the pictures do not depict the world as it appears to the human eye. The color coding scheme was not explained. In Condition 3, participants were given a fuller (500 word) description of thermography, including a discussion of the color coding scheme, and a discussion of the ways heat can manifest itself in thermograms (e.g., reflection vs. transmission of heat, thermal shine, heat leaking through poorly insulated roofs, heat coming from chimneys, etc.).

We also probed for an effect of providing an example during instruction. Easily understood "start-up" examples[153] can have a positive effect on simple and complex problem solving,[29,158,179,201] and on the acquisition of perceptual discrimination skill.[9] Practice effects can be most noticeable for participants who are given an example during instruction, especially if the example is prototypical of the test problems.[109] However, in much of the available research on this topic, it is possible for the example to *be* the instructions (i.e., *"Here's an example of the type of problem you will be seeing…"*), forcing participants to deduce the underlying scheme of the problem type (e.g., the names of mammals ordered by size). The materials and task which we were utilizing made it possible to provide examples but not explicitly engage the participants in an analytical interpretation of them. This would permit a test of the "start-up" hypothesis and would also simulate the pedagogical strategy in textbooks on remote sensing.

The final independent variable we investigated was the role of feedback, or more precisely, the way behavior might change during feedback. In the feedback conditions, during the first two trials the participants were told when a response was correct (e.g., *"Yes, that is a warm pond,"* or *"Yes, that is a street."*), and for each incorrect response the experimenter provided the correct identification (e.g., *"No, that's not a butterfly, it's an area of grassland,"* or *"No the green blob isn't a tree, it's a house"*). It is known that this type of corrective feedback can have a positive effect on the acquisition of problem solving skill.[118] Corrective feedback also can have a positive effect on category learning, concept formation, and multicue judgment, for both artificial stimuli (e.g., geometrical patterns) and for more realistic stimuli[3,61,95] including light amplification scenes.[141] (Conversely, false or delayed corrective feedback can disrupt the transition from chance-level exemplar discrimination to concept discovery and performance well above chance; see [116,129].)

Our expectation was that corrective feedback would lead to a performance improvement apart from any effect of instruction level. Especially for the suburban images, it should be easy after some feedback to generate dozens of correct identifications merely by indicating, for example, *"This is a house, this is another house, this is another house,"* and so on. Furthermore, we predicted that the effect of feedback would be modulated by stimulus type. That is, feedback with suburban stimuli might lead to performance improvement, but if stimulus type is then switched to rural, some of the gain from the prior feedback might be lost.

Participants were run individually in a small quiet room. They were shown a series of four images for five minutes per image. (The color photos were mounted in protective folders that masked the color palette and digital reference information.) During each trial, their task was to say everything they could about what they thought they saw. Their statements were audio recorded and the experimenter took notes about the image location of the things the participants identified.

2.4.2.2   *Data analysis method*

In addition to a response in which the participant showed an awareness of aerial perspective (e.g., *"This looks like the view from an airplane."*), the menu from the expert (see Table 2.1) was used to define what would count as a correct response.

A response could also be incorrect in a variety of ways. Based on pilot research, responses to be counted as incorrect could be unambiguously classified as: (1) mere repetition (correctly or incorrectly) of information that had been given in the instructions (e.g., *"The purple areas are colder."*), (2) default responses (e.g., *"All I see is a bunch of colors."*), (3) form responses (e.g., *"This white shape looks like a rabbit's head," "This area looks like a blob of green algae."*), (4) menu-coincident form responses (e.g., *"This white area has the shape of a tree."*), (5) incorrect identifications (*"This green blob looks like a tree."*), (6) incorrect thermal interpretations (e.g., *"The yellow area is where there is no shade."*), and (7) incorrect extra-menu responses. This last category was for features or objects that could appear in aerial thermograms, but which happened to not be present in the thermogram (e.g., *"This could be an airport—there's a row of lights,"* or *"This area is probably rocks."*).

We expected our participants would spend a considerable amount of time just inspecting the stimuli, and produce perhaps 20 responses at most. For Instructional Condition 0 and the rural stimuli, we expected more errors, more form responses, and even a failure on the part of some participants to realize that the stimuli were in aerial perspective. For Instructional Condition 3, we expected more correct and incorrect thermal interpretations than at the other instructional levels.

The sums for each participant on each trial of the number of correct and incorrect responses were determined. Analyses of variance were computed on total number of responses, number of correct responses, number of error responses, and proportion of correct responses. To determine the proportions, the number of correct responses was divided by the total number of responses for each participant on each trial.*

2.4.2.3 Results

For Instruction Level 0 there were proportionately more error (form and default) responses, and a trend for the number of errors to increase over trials. Participants in Instructional Condition 0 made many more errors (frequency range of 7–12) than participants in any of the other conditions, especially for the rural stimuli. Form and default responses predominated (frequencies on the order of 7–12 per participant) for all but one participant for whom (correct) menu responses (frequency = 14) and (incorrect) extra-menu responses (13) predominated. Participants in both Instructional Conditions 0 and 1 shown the rural stimuli made no thermal identifications—either correct or incorrect.

Given the newness of the task and materials to the participants, we expected that the pattern for the total number of responses would largely

---

*Further details on the experiments and the statistical analyses can be provided upon request. Although in this discussion we highlight a number of the trends in the results, we draw conclusions concerning only those trends that achieved statistical significance.

reflect the total number of errors, which it did. Thus, we focused on the proportion correct score. Only in Instructional Conditions 1, 2 and 3 did performance for some participants reach or surpass a proportion correct of 0.50, and even then most often for the suburban stimuli and in conditions in which feedback was provided. In Instructional Condition 1, there appeared fewer form responses than in Condition 0 (frequency range of 0–8 per participant), more menu responses (range of 3–20), and more extra-menu responses (range of 3–12). This trend continued across Instructional Conditions 2 and 3, where a few participants yielded no form responses. Finally, in Instructional Condition 3 there appeared a number of correct thermal identifications (typically just a few per participant but the obtained range was 0–20), and only a few incorrect thermal identifications.

We speculated that presentation of a "raw" example during instruction would have little overall effect on subsequent performance. This is a weak hypothesis, but it can be turned on its head. It is known from research on instructional design that the effectiveness of a start-up example can depend on whether there is a match or mismatch of the example and the first test problem.[29,118] We reasoned that if there could be any effect of an example it should be revealed by a comparison of two particular conditions, one in which the example type corresponded with the type of the test stimuli, and one in which it did not. Furthermore, if the suburban stimuli are more interpretable, the presentation of a suburban example during the presentation of the instructions should facilitate performance on the subsequent test trials. Conversely, the participants shown a rural example might be placed at a disadvantage.

Comparing two conditions—suburban example vs. rural example presented during the instructions, with *all* of the test stimuli being suburban— there was a general increase in proportion correct across instructional levels but only for the participants shown the suburban example, with performance uniformly surpassing proportion correct of 0.5 at Instruction Level 3. This is illustrated in Figure 2.6. Although an example might invite an interpretive process, it can also perplex it or leave it unaffected, depending on the example type and the instruction level. This is interesting because it is usually assumed that a text or manual should provide representative examples early on.

Figure 2.6 also illustrates the finding that across the instructional conditions, the proportion of correct responses tended to increase (and the number of errors tended to decrease). The greatest contrast in proportion correct, as well as in totals and errors, often resided in the comparison between Instructional Conditions 0 and 1 vs. Conditions 2 and 3. The conclusion from this seems clear—being informed that the pictures were in aerial perspective seemed to both constrain performance (fewer errors and lower total number of responses) and guide it (more menu and extra-menu identification responses). The present results show that at the earliest stages of learning a skill that is perceptually laden, basic instruction involving

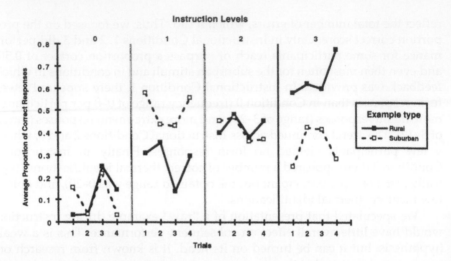

Figure 2.6 Results showing average proportion of correct responses as a function of example type, instruction level, and trials.

even a single critical concept can have a considerable and positive effect on performance.

On the other hand, the results for Instructional Conditions 1, 2, and 3 also suggest that initial instructional information can actually inhibit overall responding. Higher levels of instruction combined with the less interpretable stimuli (i.e., the rural images) seem to have inhibited overall performance, whereas at lower instruction levels the less interpretable stimuli generated the most errors. Although in Instructional Condition 3 there appeared more thermal identifications, there was a clear decrease in total number of responses and the numbers of (correct) menu identifications and (incorrect) extra-menu identifications.

We had hypothesized that the more elaborate instructions could induce a cognitive load, that is, overwhelm participants with "front-end" verbal information. While this could explain the findings, the effect we obtained could also be due to simple inhibition. That is, participants might have been less inclined to speak up having been given elaborate instructions. This interpretation is supported by the finding that across instructional conditions there was a steady increase in the number of default responses—in which the participants expressed frustration or said, "*I don't see anything.*" In Instructional Condition 3, every participant made at least one such response.

Further research could attempt to isolate the cognitive load factor from response inhibition. This would be important because it is never desirable for initial instructional information to inhibit responding—that is precisely the time when the instructor needs to know that the learner is thinking.

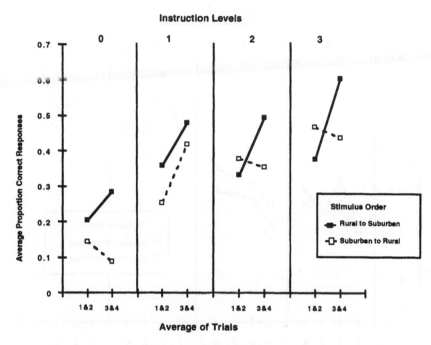

Figure 2.7   Results showing average proportion of correct responses averaging trials 1 and 2 and trials 3 and 4, as a function of stimulus order and instruction level.

The type of test stimulus did affect performance, with the stimulus difference defined here as one involving perceptual salience and interpretive significance (suburban vs. rural). For some of the conditions we ran, the first two test stimuli were rural and the second two were suburban, or vice versa. While performance generally improved across instructional conditions, the switching of stimulus type could be disruptive. Specifically, switching from suburban to rural did not significantly change performance, but switching from rural to suburban resulted in a consistent albeit modest improvement in performance. Overlaid upon this is the performance improvement across instruction levels. These results are shown in Figure 2.7.

Looking across the conditions we ran, knowing that the stimuli are in aerial perspective (Instructional Conditions 1, 2, and 3) seems to have helped, but for the rural stimuli—hypothetically less interpretable—performance showed little or no improvement across instruction levels (when no feedback was provided). Although some participants in Instructional Conditions 2 and 3 made some correct thermal identifications, participants at Instructional Levels 0 and 1 shown the rural stimuli made no thermal identifications— either correct or incorrect. In Instructional Conditions 1, 2, and 3, all of which mentioned that the pictures were in aerial perspective, the preponderance of erroneous form responses seen at Instructional Level 0 gave way to a preponderance of menu responses (both correct menu responses and incorrect

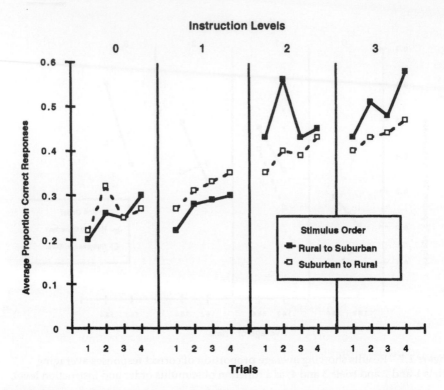

Figure 2.8   Results showing average proportion correct as a function of stimulus order, instruction level, and trials, for the conditions in which participants received feedback.

extra-menu responses). Knowing that the stimuli depict aerial perspective helped, but even with that knowledge, performance in terms of proportion correct did not consistently improve across instruction levels. In other words, when participants were confronted with the actual interpretation task, some stimuli were easier to interpret incorrectly.

Our expectation was that corrective feedback would lead to a performance improvement apart from the effect of instruction level, and also result in a clear effect of trials. Statistical testing confirmed these expectations (see footnote on page 31). Results for the feedback conditions are presented in Figure 2.8. Apparent in Figure 2.8 is the improvement in performance comparing instruction levels, and also the general improvement across trials within each of the instructional conditions.* While feedback had the effect of

---

*Notice also the "breakpoints" in Instructional Conditions 0, 2 and 3 between trials 2 and 3 in the rural-to-suburban stimulus order conditions, reflecting the effect of switching from rural-to-suburban stimuli. The effect of the switching of stimulus type seems to have been occasional and modest compared to the effects of trials and instruction level in the conditions in which feedback was provided.

increasing the total number of responses (means of 14.32 vs. 7.31), it also increased the number of errors (participant means of 9.41 vs. 4.98). In the conditions in which no feedback was provided, the number of errors decreased only slightly from Instruction Levels 0 to 1, whereas in the feedback conditions, number of errors more clearly decreased across instruction levels.

2.4.3 Implications for education in remote sensing

The study reported here was designed to merely demonstrate the viability of psychological research into the human factors of remote sensing image interpretation. The findings are entirely preliminary, and are based on only a sampling of the important variables. In addition, our small sample size in terms of the number of participants in our experimental conditions allowed individual differences to percolate through and cloud the interpretation of some of the statistical interactions we obtained. Nevertheless, the results dovetail with other research on the effects of examples, instructions, and feedback (e.g., [29,118]).

For example, the results suggest that illustrative introductory examples should be used in texts in a particular way:

- Introductory exercises should be engaged *before* the student is burdened with the details of electromagnetism, sensor systems, optics, thermodynamics, etc. The examples should follow only a very brief explanation of the electromagnetic spectrum.
- The introductory examples should be in sufficient number to illustrate the diversity and variety of remote sensing imagery. Some research on learning has shown that variability as well as prototypicality of practice items can enhance transfer (e.g., [11,12]). The presentation of a range of examples—covering the critical attributes, salient feature contrasts, degrees of difficulty, etc.—is especially conducive of initial concept learning.[8,9,116,179]
- Every example should be accompanied by specific, step-wise guidance allowing the student to conduct an interpretation and engage his or her perceptual and reasoning processes.
- That interpretation task should *not* be the mere "pointing out" of some particular salient feature (e.g., *"In this aerial photograph you can see the fracture line indicating faulted bedrock."*). Rather, the task should be more engaging (e.g., *"Can you explain the hot swath across the playing field?"*).
- Some introductory exercises should be conducted with an instructor who would provide immediate, explanatory, elaborative feedback. Those exercises should be conducted so as to encourage and facilitate the initiate's verbalization of his or her reasoning, without fear of error or criticism.

A number of modern theories of perceptual learning and categorization emphasize the importance of concept coherence and the perception of family resemblances or prototypes (e.g., [136,157]). An important question that stems from such theories is: what is the nature of the information presented by remote sensing images?[82,93] In the suburban thermograms there seems to be sufficient information to support the perception of aerial perspective and the identification of certain features (e.g., streets, houses, trees, etc.). Not all of the responses in Instructional Condition 0 were form responses—some responses showed that the participants were able to discover the aerial perspective on their own. But expert performance shows that there is also information sufficient to indicate such things as compass orientation, effects of solar heating, the internal structure of roofs, underground steam pipes, and so on. The instructions for Level 3 involved elaborating the notion of thermography, and so we expected that at Level 3 we would obtain more thermal identification responses than we did. The paucity of *incorrect* thermal identifications suggests that once the color coding is explained, some of the meaning in the thermograms become discernable—the color coding scheme is somewhat effective in informing about thermal properties.

2.5   Conclusions and prospects

We submit that there are two important take-home messages from this exploration of the psychological "angle of regard" on remote sensing.

1. A number of psychological processes are, and will remain, critical to the enterprise of remote sensing. Foremost among these are:
   - the acquisition of a rich and highly organized knowledge base that supports the formation of mental models, and
   - the acquisition of perceptual skills.

The achievement of expertise relies on fundamental cognitive processes such as concept formation, but it also relies upon judgmental processes, hypothetical reasoning, aesthetic analysis, feedback, and so on. The last two decades have witnessed a significant migration of psychological research away from the traditional artificial laboratory into applied domains (see [90,91]) including the study of expertise (see [31,55,88]), and we look forward to much more research on the psychological foundations of remote sensing.

2. Psychological research in collaboration with remote sensing scientists can lead to new advances and approaches.
   These would include new approaches to instructional design and training, in order to accelerate the progression from trainee to expert, and new methods of visualization and display design—new "cognitive technologies"— to support and amplify the performance of the remote sensing scientist. For all forms of nonliteral imagery, we are

hopeful that further specification of the information that is available, through psychological research, would permit the design of displays and instructional and feedback conditions that would facilitate the perceptual learning and interpretation processes and also contribute to efforts at automation.

References

1. Anderson, J. R., Skill acquisition: compilation of weak-method problem solutions, *Psychol. Rev.*, 94, 192–210, 1987.
2. Artis, D. A. and Carnahan, W. H., Survey of emissivity variability in thermography of urban areas, *Remote Sensing Environ.*, 12, 313–329, 1982.
3. Balzer, W. K., Doherty, M. E., and O'Connor, R., Effects of cognitive feedback on performance, *Psychol. Bull.*, 106, 410–433, 1989.
4. Bauer, M. I. and Johnson-Laird, P. N., How diagrams can improve reasoning, *Psychol. Sci.*, 4, 372–378, 1993.
5. Bennett, K. B. and Flach, J. M., Graphical displays: implications for divided attention, focused attention, and problem solving, *Hum. Factors*, 34, 513–533, 1992.
6. Berry, D. C. and Broadbent, D. E., On the relationship between task performance and associated verbalizable knowledge, *Q. J. Exp. Psychol.*, 36A, 209–231, 1984.
7. Bertin, J., *The Semiology of Graphics*, University of Wisconsin Press, Madison, 1983.
8. Biederman, I., Human image understanding: recent research and a theory, *Comput. Vision, Graphics, Image Proc.*, 32, 29–73, 1987.
9. Biederman, I. and Shiffrar, M. M., Sexing day-old chicks: a case study and expert systems analysis of a difficult perceptual-learning task, *J. Exp. Psychol. Learning, Mem. Cognit.*, 13, 640–645, 1987.
10. Booth, W., Monitoring the fate of forests from space, *Science*, 243, 1428–1429, 1989.
11. Bransford, J. D., Franks, J. J., Morris, C. D., and Stein, B. S., Some general constraints on learning and memory research, in *Levels of Processing in Human Memory*, Cermak, L. S., and Craik, F. I. M., Eds., Wiley, New York, 1979, 331–354.
12. Bransford, J. D., Franks, J. J., Vye, N. J., and Sherwood, R. D., New approaches to instruction: because wisdom can't be told, in *Similarity and Analogical Reasoning*, Vosniadou, S., and Ortony, A., Eds., Cambridge, Cambridge University Press, 1989, 470–497.
13. Broadbent, D. E. and Aston, B., Human control of a simulated economic system, *Ergonomics*, 21, 1043–1053, 1978.
14. Brooks, L., Nonanalytic concept formation and memory for instances, in *Cognition and Categorization*, Rosch, R., and Lloyd, B., Eds., Erlbaum, Hillsdale, NJ, 1978, 169–211.
15. Bruner, J. S., *Going Beyond the Information Given*, Harvard University Press, Cambridge, MA, 1957.
16. Bruner, J. S., Goodnow, J. J., and Austin, A. A., *A Study of Thinking*, Wiley, New York, 1956.
17. Burns, B. C., Ed., *Percepts, Concepts and Categories*, Elsevier Science Publishers, Amsterdam, 1992.
18. Buttenfield, B. P. and MacKaness, W. A., Visualization, in *Geographical Information Systems: Principles and Applications, Vol. 1*, Maguire, D. J., Goodchild, M. F., and Rhind, D. W., Eds., John Wiley, New York, 1991, 427–4430.

19. Buttigieg, M. A. and Sanderson, P. M., Emergent features in visual displays for two types of failure detection tasks, *Hum. Factors*, 33, 631–651, 1991.
20. Byrne, R. W., Memory for urban geography, *Q. J. Exp. Psychol.*, 31, 147–154, 1979.
21. Camerer, C. F. and Johnson, E. J., The process-performance paradox in expert judgment: how can experts know so much and predict so badly? in *Toward a General Theory of Expertise: Prospects and Limits*, Ericsson, K. A. and Smith, J., Eds., Cambridge University Press, New York, 1991, 195–217.
22. Chandrasekaran, B., Narayanan, N. H., and Iwasaki, Y., Reasoning with diagrammatic representations: a report on the Spring symposium, *The AI Magazine* (1993, Summer) 49–56.
23. Callaghan, T. C., Commentary, in *Percepts, Concepts and Categories*, Burns, B. C., Ed., Elsevier Science Publishers, Amsterdam, 1992, 492–493.
24. Campbell, J. B., *Introduction to Remote Sensing*, Guilford, New York, 1996.
25. Card, S. K., Visual search of computer command menus, paper presented at the Tenth Int. Symp. on Attention and Performance, Venlo, Netherlands, July 1982.
26. Carlson, R. S., Sullivan, M. A., and Schneider, W., Practice and working memory effects in building procedural skill, *J. Exp. Psychol. Learning, Mem., Cognit.*, 15, 517–526, 1989.
27. Carmody, D. P., Kundel, H. L., and Toto, L. C., Comparison scans while reading chest images: taught but not practiced, *Investigative Radiol.*, 19, 462–466, 1989.
28. Carnahan, W. H. and Larson, R. C., An analysis of an urban heat sink, *Remote Sensing Environ.*, 33, 65–71, 1990.
29. Catrambone, R. and Wachman, R. M., The interaction of principles and examples in instruction, in *Proc. 14th Annu. Meet. Cognit. Sci. Soc.*, Erlbaum, Mahwah, NJ, 1992, 749–754.
30. Chase, W. G. and Simon, H. A., Perception in chess, *Cognit. Psychol.*, 5, 55–81, 1973.
31. Chi, M. T. H., Glaser, R., and Farr, M. J., Eds., *The Nature of Expertise*, Erlbaum, Mahwah, NJ, 1988.
32. Childs, C. M., Interpreting composite imagery requires training, *Tech-Tran*, Newsletter of the Engineer Topographic Laboratories, U.S. Army Corps of Engineers, 13, Fort Belvoir, VA, 3, 1988.
33. Christ, R. E. and Corso, G. M., The effects of extended practice on the evaluation of visual display codes, *Hum. Factors*, 25, 71–84, 1983.
34. Christner, C. A. and Ray, H. W., An evaluation of the effect of selected combinations of target and background coding on map reading performance, *Hum. Factors*, 3, 131–146, 1961.
35. Clark, J. D., Ed., The GOES User's Guide, National Environmental Satellite Data and Information Service, National Oceanic and Atmospheric Administration, Washington, D.C., 1983.
36. Cleermans, A. and McClelland, J. L., Learning the structure of event sequences, *J. Exp. Psychol. Gen.*, 120, 235–253, 1991.
37. Colwell, R. N., Ed., *Manual of Remote Sensing*, American Society for Photogrammetry and Remote Sensing, Falls Church, VA, 1983.
38. Crandall, B. W., A comparative study of think out loud and criticial decision knowledge elicitation methods, in Special Issue on Knowledge Acquisition, *SIGART Newsletter*, 108, Special Interest Group on Artificial Intelligence, Association for Computing Machinery, New York, 1989, April, 144–146.

39. Crandall, B. and Calderwood, R., Clinical assessment skills of experienced neonatal intensive care nurses, Report, Klein Associates, Yellow Springs OH, 1989.
40. Crandall, B. and Getchell-Reiter, K., Critical Decision Method: a technique for eliciting concrete assessment indicators from the intuition of NICU nurses, *Adv. Nursing Sci.*, 16, 42–51, 1993.
41. Crossman, E. R. F. W., Cooke, J. E., and Beishon, R. J., Visual attention and the sampling of displayed information in process control, in *The Human Operator in Process Control,* Edwards, E. and Lees, F. P., Eds., Taylor & Francis, London, 1974.
42. Curran, P. J., Remote sensing methodologies and geography, *Int. J. Remote Sensing*, 8, 1255–1275, 1987.
43. Davies, D., Bathurst, D., and Bathurst, R., *The Telling Image: The Changing Balance between Pictures and Words in a Technological Age*, Oxford University Press, Oxford, 1990.
44. De Keyser, V., How can computer-based visual displays aid operators? *Int. J. Man-Machine Sys.*, 27, 471–478, 1987.
45. DiBiase, D., MacEachren, A. M., Krygier, J. B., and Reeves, C., Animation and the role of map design in scientific visualization, *Cartography and Cartographic Inf. Sys.*, 19, 201–214; 256–266, 1992.
46. Dreyfus, H. L. and Dreyfus, S. E., *Mind over Machine: The Power of Human Intuition and Expertise in the Era of the Computer*, Free Press, New York, 1986.
47. Durrett, H. J., Ed., *Color and the Computer*, Academic Press, New York, 1987.
48. Durso, F. T., Cooke, N. M., Breen, T. J., and Schvaneveldt, R. W., Is consistent mapping necessary for high speed search? *J. Exp. Psychol. Learning, Mem. Cognit.*, 13, 232–229, 1987.
49. Eberhart, J., The night skies of Venus: another kind of aurora? *Sci. News*, 130, 364–365, 1988.
50. Edlund, C. and Lewis, M., Comparing ecologically constrained and conventional displays in control of a simple steam plant, in *Proc. Hum. Factors and Ergonomics Soc. 38th Annu. Meet.*, The Human Factors and Ergonomics Society, 1994, 486–490.
51. Eley, M. G., Determining the shapes of land surfaces from topographical maps, *Ergonomics*, 31, 355–376, 1988.
52. Endsley, M. R., Toward a theory of situation awareness in dynamic systems, *Hum. Factors*, 37, 32–64, 1995.
53. EOSAT, Mapping New Guinea using LANDSAT and dugout canoes, *LANDSAT Data Users Notes*, 5, 3–4, 1990.
54. Epstein, W., *Varieties of Perceptual Learning*, McGraw Hill, New York, 1967.
55. Ericsson, K. A. and Smith, J., Eds., *Toward a General Theory of Expertise: Prospects and Limits*, Cambridge University Press, New York, 1991.
56. Essock, E. A., Sinai, M. J., McCarley, J. S., Krebs, W. K., and DeFord, J. K., Perceptual ability with real-world nighttime scenes: image-intensified, infrared, and fused color imagery, *Hum. Factors*, 41, 438–452, 1999.
57. Estes, W. K., Of models and men, *Am. Psychol.*, 12, 609–617, 1957.
58. Estes, W. K., *Classification and Cognition*, Oxford University Press, Oxford, 1994.
59. Evans, G. W. and Pezdek, K., Cognitive mapping: knowledge of real-world distance and location information. *J. Exp. Psychol. Hum. Learning Mem.*, 6, 13–24, 1980.

60. Fayyad, U. M., Djorgovski, S. G., and Weir, N., From digitized images to online catalogs: data mining a sky survey, *AI Mag.* (1996, Summer) 51–66.

61. Fischhoff, B. and Slovic, P., A little learning. . . Confidence in multicue judgment tasks, in *Attention and Performance VIII*, Nickerson, R. S., Ed., Erlbaum, Mahwah, NJ, 1980, 770–801.

62. Fisk, A. D., High performance cognitive skill acquisition: perceptual/rule learning, in *Proc. 31st Annu. Meet. Hum. Factors Soc.*, Human Factors Society, Santa Monica, CA, 1987, 652–656.

63. Flach, J. M. and Grunzke, P. M., Automatic processing through the back door, in *Proc. 31st Annu. Meet. Hum. Factors Soc.*, Human Factors Society, Santa Monica, CA, 1987, 1054–1056.

64. Fleming, M. L., Designing pictorial/verbal instruction: some speculative extensions from research to practice, in *The Psychology of Illustration, Vol. 2: Instructional Issues*, Houghton, H. A. and Willows, D. M., Eds., Springer Verlag, New York, 1987, 136–157.

65. Foyle, D. C. and Kaiser, M. K., Pilot distance estimation with unaided vision, night-vision goggles and infrared imagery, *Digest of Technical Papers of the International Meeting of the Society for Information Display*, Society for Information Display, Playa del Rey, CA, 1991, 314–317.

66. Friedhoff, B. W., *Visualization: The Second Computer Revolution*, W. H. Freeman, San Francisco, 1991.

67. Friedl, M. A., Estes, J. E., and Star, J. L., Advanced information extraction tools in remote sensing for earth science applications: AI and GIS, *AI Appl. Nat. Resour. Manage.*, 2, 17–30, 1988.

68. Fussell, J., Rundquist, D., and Harrington, J. A., On defining remote sensing, *Photogrammetric Eng. Remote Sensing*, 52, 1057–1511, 1986.

69. Getty, D. J., Pickett, R. M., D'Orsi, C. J., and Swets, J. A., Enhanced interpretation of diagnostic images, *Invest. Radiol.*, 23, 240–252, 1988.

70. Gibson, E. J., *Principles of Perceptual Learning and Development*, Prentice-Hall, Englewood Cliffs, NJ, 1969.

71. Glaser, R., Thoughts on expertise, in *Cognitive Functioning and Social Structure over the Life Course*, Schooler, C. and Schaie, W., Eds., Ablex, Norwood, NJ, 1987, 81–94.

72. Graeser, A. C. and Clark, L. F., *Structures and Procedures for Implicit Knowledge*, Ablex, Norwood, NJ, 1985.

73. Greeno, J. G., Situations, mental models, and generative knowledge, in *Complex Information Processing: The Impact of Herbert A. Simon*, Klahr, D. and Kotovsky, K., Eds., Erlbaum, Hillsdale, NJ, 1989, 285–318.

74. Hall, S., *Mapping the Next Millennium*, Random House, New York, 1991.

75. Hammond, K. R., Clinical inference in nursing, II: a psychologist's viewpoint, *Nursing Res.*, 15, 27–38, 1966.

76. Hammond, K. R., Naturalistic decision making from a Brunswikian viewpoint: its past, present, and future, in *Decision Making in Action: Models and Methods*, Klein, G., Orasanu, J., Calderwood, R. and C. E. Zsambok, C. E., Eds. Ablex, Norwood, NJ, 1993, 205–227.

77. Hansen, C., Personal communication, Jet Propulsion Laboratory, Pasadena, CA, 1987, May.

78. Hartman, M., Knopman, D. S., and Nissen, M. J., Implicit learning of new verbal associations, *J. Exp. Psychol. Learning, Mem. Cognit.*, 15, 1070–1082, 1989.

79. Hayes, N. A. and Broadbent, D. E., Two modes of learning for interactive tasks, *Cognition,* 28, 249–276, 1988.
80. Hess, S. M., Detweiler, M. C., and Ellis, R. D., The effects of display layout on monitoring and updating system states, in *Proc. 38th Annu. Meet. Hum. Factors and Ergonomics Soc.,* Human Factors and Ergonomics Society, Santa Monica, CA, 1994, 1336–1340.
81. Hintzman, D. L., O'Dell, C. S., and Arndt, D. R., Orientation in cognitive maps, *Cognit. Psychol.* 11, 375–394, 1981.
82. Hodgson, M. E., What size window for image classification? A cognitive perspective, *Photogrammetric Engin. Remote Sensing,* 64, 797–807, 1998.
83. Hodgson, M. E. and Lloyd, R. E., Cognitive and statistical approaches to texture, *ASPRS Annu. Convention Tech. Papers,* 4, 407–416, 1986.
84. Hoffman, R. R., The problem of extracting the knowledge of experts from the perspective of experimental psychology, *AI Mag.* (1987, Summer) 53–67.
85. Hoffman, R. R., Remote perceiving: a step toward a unified science of remote sensing, *Geocarto Int. Multidisciplinary J. Remote Sensing,* 5, 3–13, 1990.
86. Hoffman, R. R., Human factors psychology in the support of forecasting: the design of advanced meteorological workstations, *Weather Forecasting,* 6, 98–110, 1991.
87. Hoffman, R. R., Doing psychology in an AI context, in *The Psychology of Expertise: Cognitive Research and Empirical AI,* Hoffman, R. R., Ed., Erlbaum, Mahwah, NJ, 1992, 3–11.
88. Hoffman, R. R. Ed., *The Psychology of Expertise: Cognitive Research and Empirical AI,* Erlbaum, Mahwah, NJ, 1992.
89. Hoffman, R. R. and Conway, J. A., Psychological factors in remote sensing: a review of some recent research, *GEOCARTO Int.,* 4, 3–21, 1989.
90. Hoffman, R. R. and Deffenbacher, K. A., An analysis of the relations of basic and applied science, *Ecological Psychol.,* 5, 315–352, 1993.
91. Hoffman, R. R. and Deffenbacher, K., A brief history of applied cognitive psychology, *Appl. Cognit. Psychol.,* 6, 1–48, 1992.
92. Hoffman, R. R., Detweiler, M., Conway, J. A., and Lipton, K., Some considerations in the use of color in meteorological displays, *Weather Forecasting,* 8, 505–518, 1993.
93. Hoffman, R. R. and Pike, R. J., On the specification of the information available for the perception and description of the natural terrain, in *Local Applications of the Ecological Approach to Human-Machine Systems,* Hancock, P., Flach, J., Caird, J., and Vicente, K., Eds., Erlbaum, Mahwah, NJ, 1995, 285–323.
94. Holz, R. K., Ed., *The Surveillant Science: Remote Sensing of the Environment,* 2nd. ed., Wiley, New York, 1985.
95. Homa, D. and Cultice, J., Role of feedback, category size, and stimulus distortion on the acquisition and utilization of ill-defined categories, *J. Exp. Psychol. Learning, Mem., Cognit.,* 10, 83–94, 1984.
96. Houghton, H. A. and Willows, D. M., Eds., *The Psychology of Illustration, Vol. 2: Instructional Issues,* Springer Verlag, New York, 1987.
97. Jacoby, L. L. and Dallas, M., On the relation between autobiographical memory and perceptual learning, *J. Exp. Psychol. Gen.,* 110, 306–346, 1981.
98. Jenkins, J. J., Acoustic information for objects, places and events, in *Persistence and Change: Proceedings of the First International Conference on Event Perception,* Warren, W. H. and Shaw, R. E., Eds., Erlbaum, Hillsdale, NJ, 1985, 115–138.

99. Kalyuga, S., Chandler, P., and Sweller, J., Levels of expertise and instructional design, *Hum. Factors*, 40, 1–17, 1998.
100. Kibbe, M. P. and Stiff, J., Operator performance in pattern matching as a function of reference material structure, in *Proc. 38th Annu. Meet. Hum. Factors and Ergonomics Soc.*, The Human Factors and Ergonomics Society, Santa Monica, CA, 1994, 1280–1284.
101. Klein, G. A. and Hoffman R. R., Perceptual-cognitive aspects of expertise, in *Cognitive Science Foundations of Instruction*, Rabinowitz, M., Ed., Erlbaum, Hillsdale, NJ, 1993, 203–226.
102. Klein, G. and MacGregor, D., Knowledge elicitation of recognition-primed decision making, Report MAD903-86-C-0170, U.S. Army Research Institute, Alexandria, VA, 1987.
103. Kolers, P. A., Reading a year later, *J. Exp. Psychol. Hum. Learning Mem.*, 2, 554–565, 1976.
104. Koubek, R. J., Clarkston, T. P., and Calvez, V., The training of knowledge structures for manufacturing tasks: an empirical study, *Hum. Factors*, 37, 765–780, 1994.
105. Lahav, O., Naim, A., Buta, R. J., Corwin, H. G., de Vaucouleurs, G., Dressler, A., Huchra, J. P., van den Bergh, S., Raychaudhury, S., Sodré, L., and Storrie-Lompardi, M. C., Galaxies, human eyes, and artificial neural networks, *Science*, 267, 959–962, 1995.
106. Larkin, J. H., The role of problem representation in physics, in *Mental Models*, Gentner, D. and Stevens, A., Eds., Erlbaum, Hillsdale, NJ, 1983, 75–98.
107. Larkin, J. H., Display-based problem solving, in *Complex Information Processing: The Impact of Herbert A. Simon*, Klahr, D. and Kotovsky, K., Eds., Erlbaum, Hillsdale, NJ, 1993, 319–341.
108. Larkin, J. H. and Simon, H. A., Why a diagram is (sometimes) worth ten thousand words, in *Models of Thought, Vol. 2*, Simon, H. A., Ed., Yale University Press, New Haven, CT, 1989, 413–437.
109. LeFevre, J. A. and Dixon, P., Do written instructions need examples? *Cognit. Instruction*, 3, 1–30, 1986.
110. Lesgold, A. M., Acquiring expertise, in *Tutorials in Learning and Memory: Essays in Honor of Gordon Bower*, Anderson, J. R. and Kosslyn, S. M., Eds., W. H. Freeman, San Francisco, 1984, 31–60.
111. Lesgold, A. M., Rubinson, H., Feltovich, P., Glaser, R., Klopfer, D., and Wang, Y., Expertise in a complex skill: diagnosing X-ray pictures, in *The Nature of Expertise*, Chi, M. T. H., Glaser, R., and Farr, M. J., Eds., Erlbaum, Mahwah, NJ, 1988, 311–342.
112. Levin, J. R. and Mayer, R. E., Understanding illustrations in text, in *Learning from Textbooks: Theory and Practice*, Britton, B. K., Woodward, A., and Binkley, M., Eds., Erlbaum, Hillsdale, NJ, 1993, 95–113.
113. Lewicki, P., Processing information about covariance that cannot be articulated, *J. Exp. Psychol. Learning, Mem. Cognit.*, 12, 135–146, 1986.
114. Lewicki, P., Czyzewska, M., and Hoffman, H., Unconscious acquisition of complex procedural knowledge, *J. Exp. Psychol. Learning, Mem. Cognit.*, 13, 523–530, 1987.
115. Lewicki, P., Hill, T., and Bizot, E., Acquisition of procedural knowledge about a pattern of stimuli that cannot be articulated, *Cognit. Psychol.*, 20, 24–37, 1988.

116. Lewis, M. W. and Anderson, J. R., Discovery of operator schemata in problem solving: learning from examples, *Cognit. Psychol.*, 17, 26–65, 1985.
117. Lillesand, T. M. and Kiefer, R. W., *Remote Sensing and Image Interpretation*, Wiley, New York, 1979.
118. Lovett, M. C., Learning by problem solving versus by examples: the benefits of generating and receiving information, in *Proc. 14th Annu. Meet. Cognit. Sci. Soc.*, Erlbaum, Mahwah, NJ, 1992, 956–961.
119. Lowe, R., Constructing a mental representation from an abstract technical diagram, *Learning Instruction*, 3, 157–179, 1993.
120. Luney, P. L. and Dill, H. W., *Remote Sensing with Special Reference to Agriculture and Forestry*, National Academy of Sciences, Washington, D.C., 1970.
121. Lynch, M., Laboratory space and the technological complex: an investigation of topical contextures, *Sci. Context*, 4, 51–78, 1991.
122. Lynch, M. and Edgerton, S. Y., Aesthetics and digital image processing: representational craft in contemporary astronomy, in *Picturing Power: Visual Depictions and Social Relations*, Fyfe, G. and Law, J., Eds., Routledge, London, 1988, 184–220.
123. MacEachren, A. M., Buttenfield, B. P., Campbell, J. B., DiBiase, D. W., and Monmonier, M., Visualization, in *Geography's Inner Worlds: Pervasive Themes in Contemporary American Geography*, Abler, R. F., Marcus, M. G., and Olson, J. M., Eds., Rutgers University Press, New Brunswick, NJ, 1992, 99–137.
124. MacEachren, A. M. and Ganter, J. H., A pattern identification approach to cartographic visualization, *Cartographica*, 27, 64–81, 1990.
125. MacEachren, A. M. and Taylor, D. R. F. Eds., *Visualization in Modern Cartography*, Elsevier, Tarrytown, NY, 1994.
126. Mandl, H. and Levin, J. R., Eds., *Knowledge Acquisition from Text and Pictures*, North-Holland, Amsterdam, 1989.
127. Markman, A. B. and Makin, V. S., Referential communication and category acquisition, *J. Exp. Psychol. Gen.*, 127(4), 331–354, 1998.
128. Markman, A. B., Yamauchi, T., and Makin, V. S., The creation of new concepts: a multifaceted approach to category learning, in *Creative Thought: An Investigation of Conceptual Structures and Processes*, Ward, T. B., Smith, S. M., and Vaid, J., Eds., American Psychological Association, Washington, D.C., 1997, 179–208.
129. Mathews, R. C., Buss, R. R., Chinn, R., and Stanley, W. B., The role of explicit and implicit learning processes in concept discovery, *Q. J. Exp. Psychol.*, 40A, 135–165, 1988.
130. Mayer, R. E. and Anderson, R. B., Animations need narrations: an experimental test of the dual-coding hypothesis, *J. Educ. Psychol.*, 83, 484–490, 1991.
131. Mayer, R. E. and Gallini, J. K., When is an illustration worth ten thousand words? *J. Educ. Psychol.*, 82, 715–726, 1990.
132. Mayer, R. E. and Greeno, J. G., Structural differences between learning outcomes produced by different instructional methods, *J. Edu. Psychol.*, 63, 165–173, 1972.
133. McGuinness, C., Expert/novice use of visualization tools, in *Visualization in Modern Cartography*, MacEachren, A. M. and Taylor, D. R. F., Eds., Elsevier, Tarrytown, NY, 1994, 185–199.
134. Medin, D. L. and Smith, E. E., Strategies and classification learning, *J. Exp. Psychol. Hum. Learning Mem.*, 7, 29–37, 1981.

135. Moray, N. and Richards, M., Memory for radar-like patterns, Report EPRL-90-03, Engineering Psychology Research Laboratory, Department of Mechanical and Industrial Engineering, University of Illinois, Urbana-Champaign, 1990.

136. Murphy, G. L. and Medin, D. L., The role of theories in conceptual coherence, *Psychol. Rev.*, 92, 289–316, 1985.

137. Myles-Worsley, M., Johnston, W. A., and Simons, M. A., The influence of expertise on X-ray image processing, *J. Exp. Psychol. Learning, Mem. Cognit.*, 14, 553–557, 1988.

138. NASA, NASA color thermographs show how much heat homeowners are losing, Flyer produced by the National Aeronautics and Space Administration, Washington, D.C., 1977.

139. Nelson, I. and Lee, J., Conversations with graphics: implications for the design of natural language/graphics interfaces, *Int. J. Hum.-Comput. Stud.*, 40, 509–541, 1994.

140. Neisser, U. and Hirsch, N., Phantom flashbulbs: false recollections of hearing the news about Challenger, in *Affect and Accuracy in Recall: Studies of "Flashbulb Memories,"* Winograd, E. and Neisser, U., Eds., Cambridge University Press, New York, 1992, 9–31.

141. Niall, K. K., Reising, J. D., and Martin, E. L., Distance estimation with night vision goggles: a little feedback goes a long way, *Hum. Factors*, 41, 495–506, 1999.

142. Nissen, M. J. and Bullemer, P., Attentional requirements of learning: evidence from performance measures, *Cognit. Psychol.*, 19, 1–32, 1987.

143. Norman, G. R., Rosenthal, D., Brooks, L. R., Allen, S. W., and Muzzin, L. J., The development of expertise in dermatology, *Arch. Dermatol.*, 125, 1063–1068, 1989.

144. Nosofsky, R. M., Palmeri, T. J., and McKinley, S. C., Rule-plus-exception model of classification learning, *Psychol. Rev.*, 101, 53–97, 1994.

145. Olson, J. M., Color and the computer in cartography, in *Color and the Computer*, Durrett, J. H., Ed., Academic Press, New York, 1987, 205–219.

146. Oransky, N. A., Skedsvold, P. R., and Fisk, A. D., The interaction of bottom-up and top-down consistency in the development of skills, in *Proc. 31st Annu. Meet. Hum. Factors Soc.*, The Human Factors Society, Santa Monica, CA, 1987, 1044–1048.

147. Peeck, J., The role of illustrations in processing and remembering text, in *The Psychology of Illustration, Vol. 1: Basic Research*, Willows, D. M. and Houghton, H. A., Eds., Springer Verlag, New York, 1987, 115–151.

148. Perruchet, P., Galego, J., and Savy, L., A critical reappraisal of the evidence for unconscious abstraction of deterministic rules in complex experimental situations, *Cognit. Psychol.*, 22, 493–516, 1990.

149. Reber, A. S., Implicit learning of synthetic languages: the role of instructional set, *J. Exp. Psychol. Hum. Learning Mem.*, 2, 88–94, 1976.

150. Reber, A. S., Implicit learning and tacit knowledge, *J. Exp. Psychol. Gen.*, 118, 219–235, 1989.

151. Reber, A. S., Cassin, S. M., Lewis, S., and Cantor, G., On the relation between implicit and explicit modes of deriving a complex rule structure, *J. Exp. Psychol. Hum. Learning Mem.*, 6, 492–502, 1980.

152. Reber, A. S. and Milward, R. B., Probability learning and memory for event sequences, *Psychonomic Sci.*, 3, 431–432, 1968.

153. Rissland, E. L., Examples and learning systems, in *Adaptive Control of Ill-Defined Systems*, Selfridge, O. G., Rissland, E. L. and Arbib, M. A., Eds., Plenum, New York, 1981, 149–163.

154. Rogowitz, B. E. and Treinish, L. A., An architecture for perceptual rule-based visualization, *Proc. IEEE Comput. Soc. Visualization '93*, IEEE, New York, 1993, 236–243.

155. Rogowitz, B. E. and Treinish, L. A., How not to lie with visualization, *Comput. Phys.*, 10, 268–274, 1996.

156. Rosch, E. and Lloyd, B. B., Eds., *Cognition and Categorization*, Erlbaum, Hillsdale, NJ, 1978.

157. Rosch, E. and Mervis, C. B., Family resemblances: studies in the internal structure of categories, *Cognit. Psychol.*, 7, 573–605, 1975.

158. Ross, B. H., Discrimination of superficial similarities: different effects on the access and use of earlier problems, *J. Exp. Psychol. Learning, Mem. Cognit.*, 15, 456–468, 1989.

159. Ross, B. H., The use of categories affects classification, *J. Mem. Language*, 37, 240–267, 1997.

160. Ross, B. H., Post-classification category use: the effects of learning to use categories after learning to classify, *J. Exp. Psychol. Learning, Mem. Cognit.*, 25(3), 743–757, 1999.

161. Ross, B. H., The effects of category use on learned categories, *Mem. Cognit.*, 28(1), 51–63, 2000.

162. Rothfusz, L. P., McLaughlin, M. R., and Rinard, S. K., An Overview of NWS Weather Support for the XXVI Olympiad, *Bull. Am. Meteorological Soc.*, 79, 845–860, 1998.

163. Rouse, W. B. and Morris, N. M., On looking into the black box: prospects and limits in the search for mental models, *Psychol. Bull.*, 100, 349–363, 1986.

164. Rudwick, M. J. S., The emergence of a visual language for geological science, 1760–1840, *Hist. Sci.*, 14, 149–195, 1976.

165. Sadalla, E. K., Burroughs, W. J., and Staplin, L. J., Reference points in spatial cognition, *J. Exp. Psychol. Hum. Learning Mem.*, 6, 516–528, 1980.

166. Sanderson, P. M., Verbalizable knowledge and skilled task performance: association, dissociation, and mental models, *J. Exp. Psychol. Learning, Mem. Cognit.*, 15, 729–747, 1989.

167. Schneider, W., Training high-performance skills: fallacies and guidelines, *Hum. Factors*, 30, 539–566, 1985.

168. Schyns, P. G., Goldstone, R. L., and Thibaut, J. P., The development of features in object concepts, *Behav. Brain Sci.*, 21(1), 1–54, 1998.

169. *Science News*, April 21, 1984; Vol. 125, No. 16, 244.

170. Scribner, S., Thinking in action: Some characteristics of practical thought, in *Practical Intelligence: Nature and Origins of Competence in the Everyday World*, Sternberg, R. J. and Wagner, R. K., Eds., Cambridge University Press, Cambridge, 1986, 14–30.

171. Shanteau, J., Some unasked questions about the psychology of expert decision makers, in *Proc. 1984 IEEE Conf. Syst., Man, Cybernetics*, El Hawary, M. E., Ed., IEEE, NY, 1984, 23–45.

172. Shiffrin, R. M., and Dumais, S. T., The development of automatization, in
     Cognitive Skills and Their Acquisition, Anderson, J. R., Ed., Erlbaum, Hillsdale,
     NJ, 1981, 111–140.
173. Short, N. M., *The LANDSAT Tutorial Workbook: Basics of Satellite Remote
     Sensing,* National Aeronautics and Space Administration, Washington,
     D.C., 1982.
174. Short, N. M., Lowman, P. D., Freden, S. C., and Finch, W. A., *Mission to Earth:
     LANDSAT Views the World,* National Aeronautics and Space Administration,
     Washington, D.C., 1976.
175. Siegal, B. S. and Gillespie, A. R., *Remote Sensing in Geology,* Wiley, New York,
     1980.
176. Silverman, J., Mooney, J. M., and Shepherd, F. D., Infrared video cameras, *Sci.
     Am.* March, 1992, 78–83.
177. Slocum,T. A. and Egbert, S. L., Cartographic data display, in *Geographic
     Information Systems: The Microcomputer and Modern Cartography,* Taylor, D. R. F.,
     Ed., Pergamon Press, Oxford, 1991, 167–199.
178. Tarmizi, R. and Sweller, J., Guidance during mathematical problem solving,
     J. Edu. Psychol., 80, 424–436, 1988.
179. Tennson, R. D. and Park, O.-C., The teaching of concepts: a review of
     instructional design research literature, *Rev. Edu. Res.,* 50, 55–70, 1980.
180. Thorndyke, P. W. and Hayes-Roth, B., Differences in spatial knowledge
     acquired from maps and navigation, *Cognit. Psychol.,* 14, 560–589, 1982.
181. Tindall-Ford, S., Chandler, P., and Sweller, J., Cognitive load theory and
     instructional design, *Cognit. Tech.,* 2, 49–59, 1997.
182. Treinish, L. A., Unifying principles of data management for scientific
     visualization, in *Animation and Scientific Visualization Tools and Applications,*
     Earnshaw, R. and Watson, D., Eds., Academic Press, New York, 1993, 141–169.
183. Treinish, L. A., Visualization of disparate data in the earth sciences, *Comput.
     Phys.,* 8, 664–671, 1994.
184. Treinish, L. A. and Rothfusz, L., Three-Dimensional visualization for support
     of operational forecasting at the 1996 Centennial Olympic Games, in *Proc. 13th
     Inter. Conf. Interactive Information Proc. Syst. Meteorology, Oceanography and
     Hydrology,* American Meteorological Society, Boston, 1997, 31–34.
185. Uttal, W. R., Baruch, T., and Allen, L., Psychological foundations of a model of
     amplified night vision in target detection tasks, *Hum. Factors,* 36, 488–502, 1994.
186. Ward, M. and Sweller, J., Structuring effective worked examples, *Cognit.
     Instruction,* 7, 1–39, 1990.
187. Wagner, R. K. and Sternberg, R. J., Tacit knowledge and intelligence in the
     everyday world, in *Practical Intelligence: Nature and Origins of Competence in the
     Everyday World,* Sternberg, R. J. and Wagner, R. K., Eds., Cambridge University
     Press, Cambridge, 1986, 51–83.
188. Ward, T. B. and Becker, A. H., Learning categories with and without trying:
     does it make a difference? in *Percepts, Concepts, and Categories,* Burns, B., Ed.,
     Elsevier Science Publishers, Amsterdam, 1992, 451–493.
189. Ware, C. and Beatty, J. C., Using color dimensions to display data dimensions,
     Hum. Factors, 30, 127–142, 1988.
190. Wickens, C. D., Ed., Attention and Situation Awareness: a NATO AGARD
     Workshop, Aviation Research Laboratory, University of Illinois,
     Urbana-Champaign, 1996.

191. Williams, L. G., The effect of target specification on objects fixated during visual search, *Percept. Psychophysics*, 1, 315–318, 1966.
192. Williams, R. S. and Carter, E. D., Eds., *ERTS-1: A New Window on Our Planet*, U.S. Geological Survey, Department of the Interior, Washington, D.C., 1976.
193. Willows, D. M. and Houghton, H. A., Eds., *The Psychology of Illustration, Vol. 1: Basic Research*, Springer Verlag, New York, 1987.
194. Winn, W., Charts, graphs, and diagrams in educational materials, in *The Psychology of Illustration, Vol. 1. Basic Research*, Willows, D. M. and Houghton, H. A., Eds., Springer Verlag, New York, 1987, 152–198.
195. Winn, W., The design and use of instructional graphics, in *Knowledge Acquisition from Text and Pictures*, Mandl, H. and Levin, J. R., Eds., North-Holland, Amsterdam, 1989, 125–144.
196. Wisniewski, E. J. and Medin, D. L., On the interaction of theory and data in concept learning, *Cognit. Sci.*, 18, 221–282, 1994.
197. Woodward, A., Do illustrations serve an instructional purpose in U.S. textbooks? in *Learning from Textbooks: Theory and Practice*, Britton, B. K., Woodward, A., and Binkley, M., Eds., Erlbaum, Hillsdale, NJ, 1993, 115–134.
198. Yamauchi, T. and Markman, A. B., Category learning by inference and classification, *J. Mem. Language*, 39, 124–148, 1998.
199. Yamauchi, T. and Markman, A. B., Learning categories composed of varying instances: the effect of classification, inference, and structural alignment, *Mem. Cognit.*, 28, 64–78, 2000.
200. Young, A. T., What color is the solar system? *Sky and Telescope*, May, 1985, 399.
201. Zhu, X. and Simon, H. A., Learning mathematics from example and by doing, *Cognit. Instruction*, 4, 137–166, 1987.

section two

The Communication of Topographic Perspectives and Forms

chapter three

Human Factors in the Interpretation of Physiography by Symbolic and Numerical Representations within an Expert System

Demetre P. Argialas and
George Ch. Miliaresis

Contents

Keywords: *digital elevation model, expert system, factual knowledge, formalization, fuzzy set, geomorphometry, heuristic knowledge, human factors, image interpretation, knowledge acquisition, knowledge quantification, knowledge representation, knowledge base, landform interpretation, lexical uncertainty, linguistic variable, membership value, NEXPERT OBJECT, object oriented programming, pattern elements, physiographic analysis, region growing segmentation, remote sensing, SMART ELEMENTS, symbolic representation, terrain analysis, terrain knowledge conceptualization, terrain feature extraction*

" *. . . nothing is great or little otherwise than by Comparison* "

In Gulliver's Travels[29]

3.1   Introduction

This chapter examines the role of human factors in both symbolic and numerical terrain representations for the interpretation of physiography from remotely sensed images. In illustrating the human factors involved, it draws heavily on the work of the authors on expert terrain interpretation systems and physiographic feature quantification through image processing, geomorphometric and fuzzy set techniques.

   This chapter is organized as follows: the introduction presents the photo-interpretation tasks and problems for physiography and landforms, earlier efforts in knowledge-based terrain representation, and the detailed objectives of the chapter. Then, the chapter follows the knowledge-based physiographic representation including the description of the study area and the implementation of the symbolic and numerical representations. Human factors and subjectivity in terrain representation and quantification are addressed throughout the chapter.

   During the early part of this century, the study of regional scale geomorphology was termed "physiography."[9] Physiographic analysis was based on the partition of terrain to physiographic units by taking into account the form and spatial distribution of their component features through fieldwork and visual interpretation of topographic maps and aerial photographs.[11] Today, physiography is being stimulated by the need to explain enigmatic landscapes, newly explored on the surfaces of other planets through remotely sensed data.[9]

   While physiographic analysis is concerned with regional scale geomorphology, terrain analysis is concerned with local (medium scale) geomorphology and involves the systematic study of image patterns relating to the origin, morphologic history, and composition of distinct terrain units, called landforms.[2,15,20] Landforms are natural terrain units, which when developed from the same soil and bedrock or deposited by a similar process (under similar conditions of climate, weathering, and erosion), exhibit a distinct and predictable range of visual and physical characteristics on aerial images, called "pattern elements."[33] Typical pattern elements examined include topographic form, drainage texture and pattern, gully characteristics, soil tone variation and texture, land use, vegetation, and special features.[33]

The shaded relief map of Figure 3.1[27] shows a part of the basin and range physiographic province and the landform alluvial fan commonly found in this province with its typical pattern elements: fan-shaped form, semiconical 3-D shape, dichotomic drainage pattern, medium soil tones, and barren landcover.

Problem solving for landform and physiographic region interpretation is an art.[7] The procedural framework for terrain interpretation problem solving is missing: books do not elaborate on the strategies needed to guide a novice to the terrain interpretation process through a step-by-step question-and-answer scenario. Landforms, pattern elements, physiographic features, and relevant indicators are vital and poorly described components of the landscape. Interpretation of pattern elements of a site relies on the education and experience of the interpreter, his perceptual skills, his ability for trial-and-error experimentation, his use of interpretation heuristics, his personal judgement, and his intuition. The use of prior knowledge on a specific geographic region and the use of available maps (physiographic, landcover, geologic, etc.) and bibliographic information can greatly assist terrain interpretation.

There is, therefore, a need to methodically study the physiographic and terrain-analysis reasoning process and, to better understand and formalize these processes and guide novice interpreters in terrain problem solving, develop computer-assisted interpretation procedures.

Knowledge-based expert systems (KBES) is a field of artificial intelligence that addresses complex, domain specific, problem solving that requires unique expertise.[12,14] Knowledge-based expert systems offer methods and tools for representing problem solving procedures within interactive computer programs and thus can assist in the discovery and formalization of terrain interpretation procedures. Expert system success is largely determined by the effective computer representation of domain knowledge. Knowledge representation takes place by employing facts, objects, frames, rules, and inexact reasoning procedures.

For the past twenty-five years, scientists working toward knowledge-based landform interpretation have implemented expert system prototypes for terrain analysis using different methods of knowledge representation such as rules, frames, Bayesian reasoning under uncertainty, and fuzzy descriptors.[2,6,7,21] These earlier developed prototype terrain expert systems

Figure 3.1 Study area. The state of Nevada as it appears in the color landform atlas of U.S. The Death Valley Intermontane Basin is pointed out and an enlarged view of the basin in a Landsat Thematic Mapper (TM) image is provided. A block diagram is included showing an alluvial fan (A). See color version of this figure in the color section following page 114. (From Sterner, R., 1999, http://fermi.jhvapl.edu/states/maps1/nv.gif. With permission.)

assisted the interpreter to infer the landform of a site through a step-by-step question-and-answer scenario. The user was queried for all pattern element values of a site and the degree of certainty ascribed to each value. Based on the user's responses, the system inferred the landform of the site, indicating also a certainty value for each decision (e.g., the inferred landform is sandstone with certainty, 0.95).

While the earlier developed landform interpretation procedures are still used, in this research effort knowledge related to the physiographic region of a site and to the spatial pattern of related landforms is also represented, formalized, and programmed.

Building this new physiographic expert system involved identifying, naming, describing, and organizing knowledge pertaining to physiographic regions (provinces and sections), and their component features in terms of their distinguishing indicators. The conception of the various indicators encompassed a study of physiographic books and reports and it was achieved through trial-and-error experimentation.[3] The compiled factual and structural descriptions were represented within an expert system tool by using appropriate definitions of classes, subclasses, hierarchies, spatial relations, and rule structures.[3,4,5]

The expert system representation has the drawback in that it employs mostly qualitative terrain indicators which occasionally can be vague and ambiguous to novice and inexperienced interpreters. There are three different approaches to partially assist in the representation of ambiguity of these terrain terms.

- The first is the use of a terrain visual vocabulary composed of definitions, diagrams, and aerial images describing each terrain term that can be used concurrently with the consultation of the expert system to enhance the perceptual and mental models of the novice. Such a terrain visual vocabulary was implemented through a hypermedia system.[6]
- The second approach, discussed in the following, is the computer-assisted segmentation of digital elevation models into discrete landforms through image processing operators and geomorphometric techniques and the subsequent quantification (parametric representation) of the discrete landforms and physiographic regions based on geomorphologic attributes.[16,17,24]
- The third approach, discussed also in the following, is using fuzzy sets[34] to handle the ambiguity or lexical uncertainty of terrain indicators. In particular, fuzzy sets are used as a calculus for the representation of a natural geomorphic language in the Great Basin geomorphologic context.[17,18]

Despite the common misconception that computer representation—symbolic or numerical—makes terrain interpretation "objective," it entails much human intervention and subjectivity. The resulting subjectivity affects (1) the symbolic representation of physiography within an expert system, (2) the surface parameterization into spatially discrete landforms, and (3) the fuzzy set representation of the physiographic indicators in the Great Basin context. Human factors and subjectivity are addressed throughout the chapter.

3.2 Knowledge-based physiographic interpretation

3.2.1 Study area

The methodology was implemented for the Basin and Range Province of the Southwest U.S. The province, centered principally in the state of Nevada (see Figure 3.1), is a large area, approximately one tenth of the U.S., occupied mostly by wide desert plains, generally almost level, interrupted by great, largely dissected, north trending, roughly parallel mountain ranges (see Table 3.1). The Province of Basin and Range is further subdivided to five sections, each at a different erosion stage, such as the Great Basin (mainly in the youthful erosion stage) and the Sonoran Desert (maturity erosion stage).[11] The Great Basin is known as such because its drainage waters do not reach the sea but evaporate in saline lakes on the plains between the mountain ranges. The space taken by the mountains is about half of the total. The Sonoran Desert has mountain ranges that are smaller and perhaps older, occupying one fifth of the space. Moreover, large areas are without concave basins of internal drainage and the section belongs to the maturity erosion cycle.

Each physiographic section was partitioned into its component physiographic features, and each physiographic feature into its component topographic forms, and each topographic form into its component landforms.[23] The physiographic features observed within the Basin and Range Province are (1) the mountain ranges, (2) the major desert valleys, and (3) the intermontane basins. Close intermontane basins are also called bolsons while open basins are also called semibolsons. The topographic forms observed within an intermontane basin are (1) the Piedmont slope, a gross topographic form, forming a gently sloping surface parallel to mountain front and surrounding the mountain belts, and (2) the basin floor. Figure 3.2 shows typical mountain ranges, intermontane basins, Piedmont slopes and basin floors. The common landforms expected within the Piedmont slope are the alluvial fan, pediment, and bahada, while the common landforms within the basin floor are the valley fill, the playa, and the saline lake. Death Valley is a typical (closed) intermontane basin of the Basin and Range Province. Figure 3.2(a) shows the landforms (LFs) and topographic forms (TFs) interpreted from a Landsat Thematic Mapper (TM) image,[30] and Figure 3.2(b) shows the relief and spatial relationships between these landforms and topographic forms.

Table 3.1 Physical and perceptible characteristics of the physiographic features in the Great Basin section. (From Fenneman, N., *Physiography of Western United States*, McGraw-Hill, N.Y., 1931. With permission.)

Mountain Range						Basin	Spatial arrangement
1. Size	2. Shape	3. Elevation	4. Relief	5. Roughness	6. Process		
Lengths of 80–110 km and widths of 10–24 km are common. The mountain ranges are of all sizes from mere hills or buttes up to ranges and *there are more small than larger ones.*	Ranges are elongated and oriented mainly in N-S direction.	Ranges' most frequent altitudes are 2000 to 3000 m above sea level.	The local relief of ranges is between 910–1500 m.	Within its length there is no great variation in height.	The mountains in the Great Basin are either in the first erosion cycle (youthful) or in the second erosion (maturity) cycle.	The average gradient of a basin is about 3%. Each basin has its own base level.	Roughly parallel mountain ranges separated by desert basins. The total area of the section is about evenly divided between mountains and basins. Piedmont slopes occupy narrow belts some miles in width surrounding the mountain ranges.

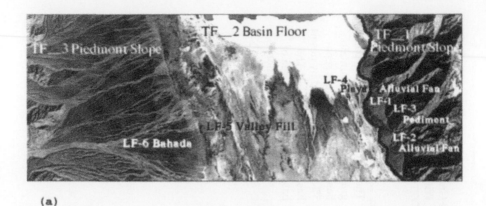

(a)

(b)

Figure 3.2   The Death Valley Intermontane Basin. **(a)** Landforms (LF) and topo-graphic forms (TF) of Death Valley interpreted from a Landsat Thematic Mapper (TM) image. (From U.S. Geological Survey, *Landsat-Thematic Mapper Image of Death Valley,* Order: 0119612270019, 1884. With permission.) **(b)** Block-diagram simulating the 3-D representation of Figure 3.2(a).

A conceptual framework for the representation of factual, structural, inferential, and strategic knowledge is now presented.

3.2.2   Factual and structural knowledge representation

For the factual and structural representation of physiographic knowledge, an object-oriented representation structure was developed that uses frames as classes, subclasses, objects, subobjects, and slots as properties.

First, we named and described by their properties (see Table 3.1), and organized into class-subclass hierarchies the following terrain classes (see Figure 3.3):

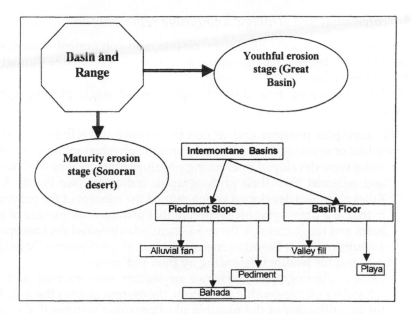

Figure 3.3 Organization and spatial relationships of physiographic provinces and features, topographic forms, and landforms for Basin and Range.

- Class of physiographic provinces and sections; subclass of basin and range; sub-subclasses: basin and range youthful stage, basin and range maturity erosion stage
- Class of physiographic features; subclass of intermontane basins; sub-subclasses of bolson and semibolson
- Class of topographic forms; subclasses of Piedmont slope, basin floor
- Class of landforms with subclasses alluvial fan, playa, etc.

Through the class-subclass hierarchy, properties are inherited down each hierarchy so as to be shared by all the members of each class.

Then, we defined an object-subobject or whole-part hierarchy thus defining the "whole-part terrain organization" (see Figure 3.3). For example, each topographic form is composed of a set of landforms and conversely each landform is part of a topographic form.

Finally, we defined class members or *instances* of each class or subclass so that the expert system to use them for symbols inferred features of each class during our consultation. These instances are dynamic objects generated during the consultation of the expert system. Thus when a topographic form is inferred, the system creates an instance TF1 belonging to the proper topographic form class and when a landform is inferred, the system creates an instance LF1 belonging to the proper landform class.

3.2.3   Inferential and strategic knowledge representation

Having defined the classes, subclasses, objects, and component objects, we use them now to describe the inferential and strategic knowledge through a rule-based formalism.

We have conceived four distinct aspects of strategic physiographic reasoning:

1. Physiographic province and section inferencing and refining to either youthful or maturity erosion stage by specific physiographic indicators,
   - Rules were developed inferencing physiographic regions (provinces and sections) from their physiographic indicators (see Figure 3.4). Rules were also developed which refined the concept of the province to that of a physiographic section of that province. In the case of the basin and range concept, the refinement rules inferred the concept of a youthful (Great Basin) or mature erosion stage (Sonoran Desert).
2. Physiographic feature inferencing by their indicators,
   - Once a physiographic province or section was inferred and/or refined by physiographic indicators, the system queries the user for the identification of the possible physiographic features that could be evident in the study area.
3. Topographic form inferencing by spatial association,
   - Once a physiographic feature (e.g., an intermontane basin) was inferred based on the user's input of the relevant indicators, the

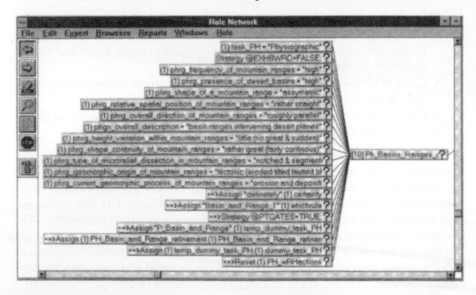

Figure 3.4 Physiographic rule inferring the Basin and Range Province. Indicators like "frequency of mountain ranges," "shape of mountain ranges," etc., as used by Fenneman in his physiographic descriptions (see Table 3.1) could be inferred from the shaded relief map of Figure 3.1 or from Landsat Thematic Mapper images such as the one shown in Figure 3.2.

possible types of topographic forms that could be evident within that physiographic feature would be posed for examination to the user.

4. Landform inferencing by pattern elements, geomorphologic indicators, and spatial association to interpreted landforms,
   - Once a topographic form was inferred, then the user was guided for the identification of the expected landforms within that topographic form according to user-specified pattern elements and spatial constraints.

3.2.4   Formalization of physiographic knowledge with NEXPERT OBJECT

The earlier developed object oriented representation structure and the associated inference rules were programmed in the expert system tool NEXPERT OBJECT (recently renamed SMART ELEMENTS).[22]

NEXPERT OBJECT provides a graphical representation of the object and rule structure as it exists before the program execution or as it unfolds during the dynamic consultation of the expert system. These graphical networks are more declarative than the alternative textual representations and therefore they are used in the figures to demonstrate the system operation. Classes and subclasses are shown in circles while the class-subclass relationships are shown with links (lines) connecting a class (circle) with another class. Class properties are indicated with the little squares, while inherited properties are shown replicated in the subclasses as they appear in the parent class. Dynamic class instances (objects) are shown as little triangles and they are created during consultation. They are assigned (linked) to the proper class they belong to based on the inference process.

The inferential knowledge for determining the physiographic context of the Basin and Range Province was expressed in rules. Figure 3.4 shows a graphical representation of a typical rule for establishing the Basin and Range Province. Any rule like this in NEXPERT OBJECT is composed of three parts: the hypothesis to be established or rejected (PH_Basin_and_Range) in the right, the physiographic conditions (indicators) in the left to be asked to the user in order to prove/disprove the hypothesis (e.g., frequency of mountain ranges, presence of desert basins), and the "then" actions of the rule, shown to the left with the prefix "+=>", executed if and only if the rule fires. Once the hypothesis of the basin and range is verified, a rule is triggered by the hypothesis PH_Basin_and_Range_Refinement that refines the basin and range context to either maturity (Great Basin) or youthful (Sonoran Desert) stage.

The outcome of a hypothesis that was proved true is the creation of a dynamic object (e.g., an instance of the relevant class established during execution). For example, in Figure 3.5A we observe the dynamic object PH_1 derived by the rule in Figure 3.4 that was assigned to the class Basin and Range. In Figure 3.5B we see that the dynamic objects are linked with part-of

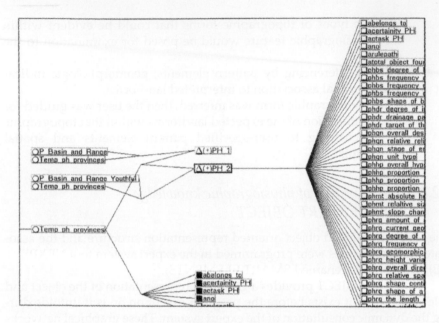

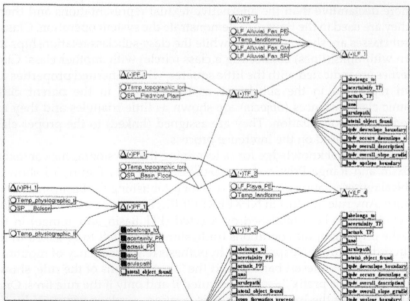

Figure 3.5 Dynamically created objects. Top: Inferred objects PH_1 and PH_2 are members of the basin and range physiographic class. Object PH_2 was further refined and assigned to the youthful erosion stage class. Bottom: The landform object LF_1 is an alluvial fan inferred from pattern elements (PEs), geomorphologic criteria (GMs) and spatial associations (SPs) while LF_4 is a playa inferred only from pattern elements. LF_1 is a part-of a Piedmont plain object (TF_1) while LF_4 is a part-of a basin floor object (TF_2). Both objects TF_2 and TF_1 are parts of the physiographic feature PF_1 that is a kind-of closed intermontane basin (bolson).

relationships to each other based on their spatial association. So the dynamic object LF_1 is a kind-of alluvial fan established from pattern elements (LF_Alluvial_Fan_PE), geomorphologic criteria (LF_Alluvial_Fan_GM), and spatial association criteria (LF_Alluvial_Fan_SR). At the same time LF_1 is part-of the topographic form TF_1 which is a kind-of Piedmont plain. TF_1 and TF_2 (basin floor) are part-of of the physiographic feature PF_1 that is a kind-of intermontane basin of bolson type.

3.2.5 Testing and evaluation

The lack of a detailed published procedure used by experts conducting physiographic analysis precludes the comparison of our own research prototype to such a source. We have tested the developed system for a number of interpretation scenarios mostly in the Basin and Range Province. For the cases tested, the system's reasoning was satisfactory and conformed to our interpretations. Further testing with other users needs to be conducted to evaluate the features of the system.

3.2.6 Human factors in building the physiographic expert system

The developed landform and physiographic interpretation expert systems are characterized as *research prototypes* in the sense that they are exploratory tools of the potential of the expert system paradigm in the typology, structuring, and formalization of photointerpretation knowledge. The formalized knowledge of the physiographic expert system was compiled from examples and case studies found in engineering, physiographic, and geomorphologic books[3,4,5] and mainly from Fenneman,[11] and Peterson.[23] Our own education, experience, expertise, trial-and-error experimentation, heuristics, and intuition have also greatly contributed to the developed representations. We did not generate any new knowledge; instead, we have turned the "implicit knowledge" available in books and in our mental models into "explicit knowledge" formalized through terrain classes and hierarchies, and inferential and strategic rules. These formal representations were implemented in an expert system tool and the resulting prototype expert system guides the novice interpreters in a step-by-step question and answer procedure to investigate various strategic interpretation scenarios and inferential paths for physiographic reasoning. We have captured within the rule system what we conceived as reasonable stages in terrain interpretation and have made available this interactive consultation guidance to novice users through the physiographic expert system. Despite this subjectivity, the physiographic expert system prototype contains a partial formal backbone object and rule structure for experimentation, evaluation, revision, improvement, and extension. What is important is that this backbone structure contains explicit and declarative terrain knowledge in the form of classes, objects, and rules and as such it is easier to be inspected, criticized, expanded, transferred, and understood than if it was available in textual form.

Terrain representation with an expert system paradigm entails much human intervention and subjectivity. At the level of terrain, problem identification is subjective in the selection of the geographic scale of the problem studied, the terrain features to be reasoned with, the tasks, subtasks, and hypotheses that the system considers, the choices given to the user, and the assumptions made within the problem solving space. At the level of conceptualization, identification is subjective in the selection of the hypotheses and reasoning paths to be investigated, the class-subclass and whole-part relations adopted, and the approach for handling uncertainty and inexactness. At the level of knowledge formalization, it is subjective in the selection of a specific tool chosen for programming the developed representations.

The developed physiographic expert system representation has a drawback in that it employs mostly qualitative terrain indicators, such as those appearing in Table 3.1, which occasionally can be vague and ambiguous[26,32] to novice and inexperienced interpreters. The next section presents surface parameterization into spatially discrete mountain ranges, and a fuzzy set representation for the natural geomorphic language used in the expert system. The application was made for the Great Basin section of the Basin and Range Province.

3.3 *Physiographic feature quantification*

According to Hoffman and Pike[13] the task of automating all parts of the terrain analysis process requires (1) an analysis of the language used to describe terrain, and (2) an analysis of the optical information about terrain that is available to the perceiver. In this particular study, the language that describes the mountain ranges in the Great Basin Section was related to a set of attributes concerning their size, shape, and geomorphologic characteristics.[11] These attributes were used earlier for the representation of physiographic reasoning within an expert system.

The symbolic representations are quite vague and ambiguous although interpreters communicate successfully.[26] In addition, the imprecision that is inherent in most words ("lexical uncertainty") is context dependent.[1] For example, in the expression of Fenneman, "there are more small than larger ones (mountain ranges)" the words "small" and "large" are both perceived in a specific physiographic context, that of the Great Basin physiographic section.[11] In a different province, it is possible for the largest mountain ranges observed in the Great Basin to be comparatively small. Thus, there is the need for capturing a geomorphometric terrain description (perceived optical information) and relate it to the symbolic representation (language). That is achieved by the use of fuzzy sets that relate the symbolic representations to the numeric representations and thus producing "digital words" that can be used for reasoning in a computer system.[32]

In order to quantify the natural geomorphologic language in the Great Basin context, the mountain features will be interpreted from digital elevation models[17] and will be numerically represented by a set of attribute values.[16] These values will specify the fuzzy set representation of the Fenneman's attributes in the Great Basin's physiographic context.[18,19]

3.3.1 Mountain feature extraction

The basis used for the extraction of mountain features was the GTOPO30[31] Digital Elevation Model (DEM) with spacing 30 arc-s since it provides a digital global representation of the earth's relief appropriate for regional scale (1:1,000,000) comparative studies. In a mountain, two parts are often distinctive: (1) the gently sloping summit, and (2) the steep mountainsides.[10] The process for the identification of mountains is based on the assumption that the summit or ridge pixels form the initial set of mountain pixels which needs to be expanded downslope taking into account the gradient values present in their neighborhood. The employed algorithms first identify the summits and then label the pixels around the summits as mountain pixels as long as their gradients were greater than a certain threshold[17]:

- The summits were extracted and labeled by imlementing runoff simulation. In this approach, a single water unit is imported in every cell of the DEM and travels according to the upslope aspect pointing direction. The water units imported in each cell are counted and finally, the derived values represent the runoff per cell. The cells with runoff values greater than a certain threshold should belong to the ridge network. Human expertise is required in order to judge whether the resulting ridge network resembles the usual ridge network observed on maps in the current physiographic context. In this case study, it was learned that the threshold should be equal to nine.[17] The resulting ridge pixels are given in Figure 3.6(a).

- Then the gradient was computed (see Figure 3.6(b)). The gradient value depends on (1) the computation method, and (2) the accuracy specification and grid size of the DEM. Due to the accuracy specification of the GTOPO30[31] a kernel of size 9 × 9 was selected for gradient computation. The gradient values represented in Figure 3.6(b) differ to a degree from the values an interpreter observes in the field and additional expertise should be developed by landform specialists in order to deal with this kind of computer derived image. Statistical analysis of training areas indicated that the gradient of the mountainsides should be greater than 6°.[17] Note that if the gradient threshold chosen was greater than 6°, then the resulting mountains would have been smaller in size; while if it was less than 6°, then the resulting mountains would have been larger in size. This threshold is by no means applicable to other physiographic regions since their mountainsides could be less or more steep than the mountainsides observed in the Great Basin. Additionally, if a different relief representation and/or a

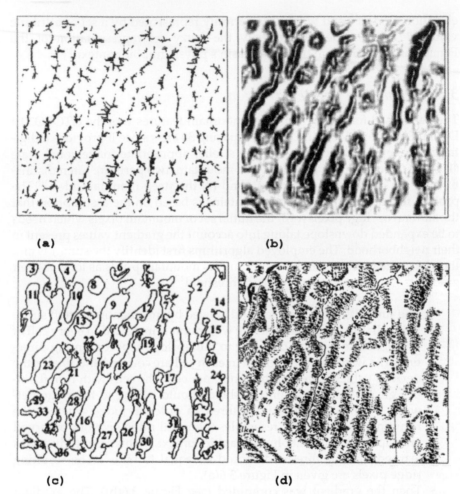

Figure 3.6 Extraction of Mountains. **(a)** Initial set of mountain seeds generated by runoff simulation in the upslope direction. **(b)** Gradient derived from the GTOPO30 DEM. Gradient values (minimum is 0 and maximum is 35°) were rescaled to the interval 255 to 0 (the lighter a pixel is the lower its gradient is). **(c)** Boundary and label identification of mountain objects in the study area. (From Miliaresis, G. Ch. and Argialas, D. P., in *Comput. Geoscience,* 25(7), 715–728, 1999. With permission from Elsevier Science.) **(d)** Shaded relief map of the study area. (From Atwood, W. W., *Map of the Landforms of California and Nevada,* Ginn and Co., Boston, 1895. With permission.)

different algorithm for gradient computation were going to be used, then a different gradient threshold would have been derived even for the Great Basin.

• Then, an iterative region growing segmentation algorithm was applied to label the mountain pixels,[17] the boundary of the mountain features was delineated, and a unique integer identifier was assigned to each mountain (see Figure 3.6(c)).

Visually comparing the extracted mountain features to the mountain ranges compiled by Atwood[8] that could also be interpreted from the shaded relief map of the study area shown in Figure 3.6(d), it is observed that there is a fairly good correspondence between them (e.g., for each of the Atwood ranges there is at least one range in the map of extracted mountain ranges). It is, however, observed that some of the mountain ranges of Atwood appear rather broken in the map of extracted mountains. This discrepancy could be explained either by the level of generalization induced by human and machine or by the intrinsic nature of the mountain ranges in Great Basin.[11] Atwood could have used human expertise and fieldwork and thus, he might have connected isolated mountains and adjacent mountain ranges applying a generalization process.[8]

The mountain feature extraction techniques are subjective to a degree. Human expertise is needed in order to deal with the discrete representation of the terrain at various scales and select the most suitable algorithms that could deal with the elevation and positioning errors of the available datasets. Usually one has to use a specific dataset that is available and thus a particular expertise should be developed in order to deal with the derived images and models. The selection of thresholds for gradient or for runoff is performed through a trial-and-error procedure and through comparison of the derived images to our mental images and models for this particular physiographic context. In the next section quantitative attributes for the mountains will be defined.

3.3.2   *Mountain feature parametric representation*

To create a parametric representation of the extracted mountain features, one first needs to select their attributes. We have selected such attributes for the Great Basin mountain ranges based on the descriptions of Fenneman[11], some of which appear briefly in Table 3.1. The selected attributes were then defined quantitatively after study of published geomorphometric parameters[9] and image processing operators:[16]

1. *Size.* The natural logarithm of the object's "diameter" was used for the quantification of size
2. *Elongation.* Eccentricity (E) was used for the quantification of elongation
3. *Orientation* (Φ)
4. *Mean elevation* (H)
5. *Roughness* (R). The standard deviation of elevation
6. *Local relief* (LR). The difference between the highest and the lowest elevation occurring in a mountain feature
7. *Hypsometric integral* (HI). Pike and Wilson[25] defined it as the ratio of Mean Altitude-Lowest Altitude to Local Relief. HI reflects the stage of landscape development. Areas with HI values above 0.6 are in the youthful erosion phase, values below 0.35 correspond to the monadnock phase while HI values in the range 0.6 to 0.35 correspond to equilibrium[28]
8. *Mean gradient* (G)

Table 3.2. Parametric representation of some of the mountain features (see Figure 3.6(c)) in the Great Basin. (From Miliaresis, G. Ch. and Argialas, D. P., *Proc. Inter. Conf. Assoc. Math. Geol.*, International Association for Mathematical Geology, 1998, 892–897. With permission.)

	Ln D	E	Φ	H	R	LR	HI	G
No	Km^2	0..1	Deg	M	m	m	0..1	Deg
1	3.60	0.32	58.3	1769	172	852	0.37	9.1
2	5.02	0.57	68.6	2231	355	1625	0.32	15.7
3	3.16	0.08	48.2	1601	221	954	0.33	13.2
4	3.73	0.24	54.9	1817	296	1415	0.34	13.2
5	5.16	0.60	70.2	1634	292	1445	0.43	14.0
6	3.48	0.26	34.6	1671	217	762	0.39	12.1
7	4.68	0.66	72.9	1954	185	1065	0.37	9.3
8	3.53	0.05	47.2	1797	254	1034	0.38	12.7
9	4.58	0.29	56.6	1841	248	1491	0.29	11.0
10	4.15	0.48	64.9	1778	306	1679	0.36	14.9

Table 3.2 shows the attribute values computed for a subset of the mountain features extracted. The presented parametric representation as a computed abstraction of reality simplifies their shape and morphologic complexity while at the same time it leads to their numeric representation which allows the use of (1) statistics, and (2) algorithms to further process and analyze them. Furthermore mountain feature parametric representation techniques are subjective in many respects. First, human expertise is needed in the selection of an attribute (e.g., elongation and size). The attributes selected are by no means universally applicable to other physiographic contexts. For example, elongation is a well-accepted attribute for the Great Basin physiographic context but it might be meaningless for a context with eroded, almost circular mountain remnants. In the next section, an effort will be made to use the parametric representation for the quantification of the geomorphologic words for the Great Basin.

3.3.3 *Fuzzy set representation of mountains*

Fuzzy sets have been developed as a calculus for the representation of natural language in various domains and are being used in the following for representation of the imprecision of the qualitative mountain attributes (linguistic variables) used in our knowledge base. A variable is called linguistic if it can take words in a natural language as its values.[26] The words are represented by fuzzy sets defined in the domain of the linguistic variable. More specifically, a linguistic variable is characterized by:

1. The name of the variable (e.g., Local Relief)
2. The set of linguistic labels that the variable takes (e.g., low, moderate, high)

3. The actual physical domain in which the linguistic variable takes its quantitative values (e.g., {300, 1200})
4. A semantic rule that relates each linguistic label of a variable with a fuzzy set in the actual physical domain[34]

Thus, in order to quantify the natural geomorphologic language, all four elements should be determined. The names of the linguistic variables and their labels were determined directly by physiographic descriptions (see Table 3.1). The quantitative values of the actual physical measurements were computed through the geomorphometric parameterization of each extracted mountain feature to a set of attribute values (see Table 3.2).

A fuzzy partition of the physical domain was next implemented and a sub-domain for each linguistic label was derived. This was achieved based on geomorphological knowledge and trial-and-error experimentation.

The semantic rules that relate each linguistic label with a fuzzy set in the actual physical domain were expressed through membership functions.[34] For a continuous variable (x), the "membership function" (MBF) describes the compatibility between the linguistic label and the degree of membership (DMB), that is [DMB = MBF (x)]. The DMB and its values are in the interval 0 to 1. The membership function of a linguistic label is (1) subjective, (2) context-dependent, and (3) influenced by new numerical data and knowledge.[32] There is no general method to determine an MBF.[1] Its specification is a matter of definition, rather than of objective analysis.[32]

Many different shapes of MBFs have been proposed in the literature and the most practical implementations use the so-called standard MBFs[1] that are normalized (maximum is always 1 and minimum 0). The definition of a standard MBF includes the following steps:

- Define the value of the domain that best fits to the meaning of the label and assign DMB equal to 1
- Define the rightmost and the leftmost values (DMB = 0) of each linguistic label assuming that adjacent labels have usually 60% overlap[1]

For example, the fuzzy sets that correspond to each label of the linguistic variable "Size of the mountain Ranges in the Great Basin physiographic context"[18] are given in Figure 3.7.

The fuzzy sets allowed the fuzzy partitioning of the domain of geomorphic variables in the Great Basin and the quantitative representation of the geomorphic language in that physiographic context. Their definition was based on both (1) well-accepted physiographic knowledge, and (2) the geomorphometric data acquired for the study area (physical domain).

Thus, the geomorphic language describing the mountain ranges was quantified for the Great Basin context.[18] So a user of a computer system could be assisted during the interpretation process by recalling the knowledge base of Great Basin and by using it to interpret the numeric data acquired from

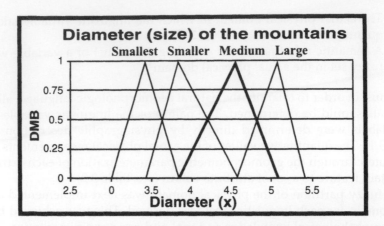

Figure 3.7 Fuzzy set representation of the linguistic variable Diameter (size) of the Mountains in the Great Basin physiographic context. (From Miliaresis, G. Ch. and Argialas, D. P., *Proc. 25th Conf. Remote Sensing Soc.*, 1999. With permission.)

aerial photographs and digital elevation models. The computer system projects the values he gave to the domain of the Great Basin digital words and would give responses like, "This mountain feature is small in size and elongated in a Great Basin physiographic context."[19]

Human factors are crucial for the fuzzy partition of the domain and for the selection of the MBF types. The last selection influences the interpretation process and is performed by a trial-and-error procedure on the basis of human expertise and the derived quantitative data (domain). Although there is degree of subjectivity, a novice interpreter could be assisted and make judgements on the basis of the relative (context-dependent) knowledge base of "digital words." In the future, when perhaps a more complete and tested knowledge base can be made available for various physiographic regions, it will lead to the creation of an absolute definition (noncontext dependent) of the geomorphic words and terms.

3.4   Conclusion

This chapter has demonstrated some of the lessons learned in attempting to conceptualize, represent, interpret, segment, and quantify terrain features from DEM and satellite imagery through expert systems and geomorphometry. All the procedures employed involved judgement calls.

The hardest part of conceptualization—and quite subjective in nature—is the identification of terrain-related objects, their organization, their relations, and their combinations in creating inference and strategic rules. Identification of this conceptual structure involves both discovery and invention of the key abstractions and mechanisms that form the vocabulary of terrain analysis problem solving, and it strongly depends on the bibliographic sources and mental models of the knowledge engineers and the terrain analysis experts. We have made an extra effort in capturing a number of "intermediate-level concepts" in physiographic reasoning which are perhaps the most important tools available for organizing knowledge bases, both conceptually and computationally.

The numerical description of mountain features involves subjectivity in (1) the discrete representation of the earth surface (DEM) including methods of preprocessing and generalizing, (2) the segmentation of the DEM into mountain ranges through selected algorithms and associated thresholds, (3) the selection of parameters of 3-D form, and (4) the computation of these parameters through selected geomorphometric and image processing operators.

The subsequent fuzzy set representation resulted in the quantification of geomorphologic words and concepts, by assigning to each numeric representation a linguistic label that interpreters easily conceive and computer systems are able to process. Subjectivity is also induced, however, since in the fuzzy partitioning of the physical domain, the linguistic labels and the membership functions are also subjective and context dependent. Their specification is a matter of *definition*, rather than of objective analysis. "Definition" indicates human expertise and evaluation by trial-and-error procedures.

Quantification involves subjectivity. Expertise is needed in order to deal with geomorphometric descriptions. The main advantage of quantification is that (1) it approaches the complexity of the real world while at the same time simplifies it to a degree, and (2) it provides numerical representations that can be used for statistical comparisons.

We thank the Editors, Professors Hoffman and Markman, for their kind and extensive reviews. They contributed greatly to the improvement of the original manuscript both in style and in the emphasis on human factors.

References

1. Altrock, C., *Fuzzy Logic and Neurofuzzy Applications Explained*, Prentice-Hall, Upper Saddle River, NJ, 1995.
2. Argialas, D. P., Towards structured knowledge models for landform representation, *Z. f. Geomorphologie N.F. Supple.-Bd.*, 101, 85–108, 1995.
3. Argialas, D. P. and Miliaresis, G. Ch., Physiographic knowledge acquisition: identification, conceptualization and representation, *Proc. Am. Soc. Photogrammetry and Remote Sensing*, American Society for Photogrammetry and Remote Sensing, Baltimore, MD, 3, 311–320, 1996.
4. Argialas, D. P. and Miliaresis, G. CH., Landform spatial knowledge acquisition: identification, conceptualization and representation, *Proc. Am. Soc. Photogrammetry and Remote Sensing*, American Society for Photogrammetry and Remote Sensing, Seattle, WA, 3, 733–740, 1997.
5. Argialas, D. P. and Miliaresis, G. CH., An object oriented representation model for the landforms of an arid climate intermontane basin: case study of Death Valley, CA, *Proc. 23rd Conf. Remote Sensing Soc.*, The Remote Sensing Society, Reading, U.K., 1997, 199–205.

6. Argialas, D. P., and Mintzer, O., The potential of hypermedia to photointerpretation education and training, in *Proc. XVII ISPRS Cong.* (Part B), Fritz, L. and Lucas, J., Eds., International Archives of Photogrammetry and Remote Sensing, Washington, D.C., 1992, 375–381.
7. Argialas, D. P., and Narasimhan, R., TAX: a prototype expert system for terrain analysis, *J. Aerosp. Eng.*, l, 151–170, 1988.
8. Atwood, W. W., *Map of the Landforms of California and Nevada*, Ginn and Co., Boston, 1895.
9. Baker, V. R., Regional landform analysis, in *Geomorphology from Space, a Global Overview of Regional Landforms*, Short, N. M. and Blair, R. W., Eds., NASA SP–486, Washington, D.C., 1986, 1–22.
10. Bates, R. L. and Jackson, J. A., Eds., *Glossary of Geology*. American Geological Institute, Alexandria, VA, 1987.
11. Fenneman, N., *Physiography of Western United States*, McGraw-Hill, New York, 1931.
12. Hayes-Roth, F., Waterman, D., and Lenat, D., *Building Expert Systems*, Addison-Wesley, Reading, MA, 1983.
13. Hoffman, R. R. and Pike, R. J., On the specification of the information available for the perception and description of the natural terrain, in *Local Applications of the Ecological Approach to Human-Machine Systems*, Hancock, P., Flach, J., Caird, J., and K. Vincente, Eds., Erlbaum, Mahwah, NJ, 1995, 285–323.
14. Jackson, P., *Introduction to Expert Systems*, Addison-Wesley, Reading, MA, 1986.
15. Lillelsand, T. and Kiefer, R., *Remote Sensing and Image Interpretation*, 2nd ed., John Wiley & Sons, New York, 1979.
16. Miliaresis, G. CH. and Argialas, D. P. (1998). Parametric representation and classification of mountain objects extracted from moderate resolution digital elevation data. *Proceedings of 4th International Conference of the Association for Mathematical Geology* (pp. 892–897). Ischia, Italy: International Association for Mathematical Geology.
17. Miliaresis, G. CH. and Argialas, D. P., Segmentation of physiographic features from the global digital elevation model/GTOPO30, *Comput. Geosciences*, 25 (7), 715–728, 1999.
18. Miliaresis, G. CH. and Argialas, D. P., Formalization of the photo-interpretation process by a fuzzy set representation of mountain objects in the geomorphic context of the Great Basin section, *Proc. 25th Conf. Remote Sensing Soc.*, The Remote Sensing Society, Cardiff, U.K., 1999, 745–750.
19. Miliaresis, G. CH. and Argialas, D. P., Fuzzy pattern recognition of compressional mountain ranges in Iran, *Proc. 5th Inter. Conf. Assoc. Math. Geo.*, International Association for Mathematical Geology, Trondheim, Norway, 1999, 227–233.
20. Mintzer, O. and Messmore, J., *Terrain Analysis Procedural Guide for Surface Configuration* (Technical Report ETL-0352), U.S. Army Corps of Engineers, Engineer Topographic Laboratory, Fort Belvoir, Virginia, 1984.
21. Narasimhan, R. and Argialas, D., Computational approaches for handling uncertainties in terrain analysis, *Proc. Annu. Conv. Am. Soc. Photogrammetry and Remote Sensing*, American Society for Photogrammetry and Remote Sensing, Baltimore, MD, 3, 302–310, 1989.
22. Neuron Data, *SMART ELEMENTS (User Guide)*, Neuron Data, Palo Alto, CA, 1993.
23. Peterson, F., *Landforms of the Basin and Range Province Defined for Soil Survey*, Technical Bulletin 28, Agricultural Experiment Station, Nevada, 1981.

24. Pike, R. J., Geomorphometry-process, practice and prospects, in *Z. f. Geomorphologie N.F. Supple. Bd.*, Pike, R. J. and Dikau, R., Eds., 101, 221–238, 1995.
25. Pike, R. J., and Wilson, S. E., Elevation-relief ratio, hypsometric integral and geomorphic area-altitude analysis, *Geol. Soc. Am. Bull.*, 82, 1079–1084, 1971.
26. Ross, T. J., *Fuzzy Logic with Engineering Applications*, McGraw-Hill, New York, 1995.
27. Sterner R., Shaded relief map of Nevada, 1999, http://fermi.jhuapl.edu/states/maps1/nv.gif
28. Strahler, A. N., Hypsometric (area-altitude) analysis of erosional topography, *Geol. Soc. Am. Bull.*, 63, 1117–1142, 1952.
29. Swift, J., *Gulliver's Travels* (A voyage to Brobdingnag, Chapter I) 1726, http://www.jaffebros.com/lee/gulliver
30. U.S. Geological Survey, *Landsat-Thematic Mapper Image of Death Valley*, Order: 0119612270019, 1984.
31. U.S. Geological Survey, *GTOPO30: 30 Arc Seconds Global Digital Elevation Model*, 1998, http://edcwww.cr.usgs.gov/landdaac/gtopo30/gtopo30.html
32. Wang, P., The interpretation of fuzziness, *IEEE Trans. Syst. Man Cybernetics*, 26(2), 321–326, 1996.
33. Way, D., *Terrain Analysis*, McGraw-Hill, New York, 1978.
34. Zadeh, L. A., The concept of a linguistic variable and its application to approximate reasoning I, II, III. *Inf. Sci.*, 8, (I) 199–251; 8, (II) 301–357; 9, (III) 43–80, 1975.

chapter four

Scenes into Numbers: Facing the Subjective in Landform Quantification

Richard J. Pike

Contents

1-56670-413-8/01/$0.00+$.50
©2001 by CRC Press LLC

Keywords: *analog modeling, classification, clustering, correlation, DEM, digital elevation model, digital terrain analysis, extraterrestrial terrain, feature abstraction, feature identification, geometric signature, geomorphology, geomorphometry, hill shading, image analysis, impact craters, index numbers, landform geometry, landform interpretation, landforms, landscapes, landslide hazards, Mars, measurement, Mercury, meteorite craters, modeling, Moon, morphometry, multi-ring basins, multivariate analysis, parameterization, pattern, perception, photointerpretation, photoclinometry, photogrammetry, planetary surfaces, principal components analysis, quantitative terrain analysis, radargrammetry, redundancy, relief, river basins, sampling, sand dunes, SAR, signatures, slope, statistical analysis, surface features, synthetic-aperture radar, terrain analysis, terrain modeling, terrain perception, topography, transformation, Venus, visualization, volcanoes*

> *However tempting it may seem to leave everything to the computer, knowledge discovery is still a collaborative process that involves human expertise in a fundamental way.*
>
> Brodley, et al.[4]

4.1 Introduction

This chapter addresses the role of human factors in quantifying terrain features from remotely acquired photographs and digital images. After introducing the practice of surface quantification, this methodological essay examines six links in the chain of inference that connects the perception of topographic form with its understanding:

- defining a measurable form
- sampling a population of landforms
- choosing descriptive parameters
- measuring or enumerating parameters
- analyzing the data
- making sense of the results

Human judgment pervades not only these stages of investigation but also the analytical procedures, ten of which are discussed here.

Most examples of this uncertainty are from the author's studies of impact craters and volcanoes during early exploration of the Solar System. The chapter closes with some lessons learned from the experience.

4.2 Surface quantification

The traditional vocabulary by which topographic information has been extracted from a scene—"rolling hills," "strong relief," "concave slopes"—no longer suffices. Verbal, qualitative, expression of surface form not only is ambiguous but fails to deliver full content of the scene. A more quantitative approach is needed. Numerical abstraction of terrain proceeds directly from the visual appraisal of a scene. Characterization of a landscape as, say, "rolling hills" presupposes a perceptual process that links the optic array containing information about the scene[12] with a mental integration of terrain form that is not arbitrary but rather grounded in observational principles. If topography can be perceived as it is and described from criteria shared by a consensus of observers, then sufficient information must be present in the optic array to specify the terrain in concrete, quantitative terms.[20]

Measurement of the relief and pattern observed in topography is essential to understanding land-shaping processes and representing Earth's surface as the locus of human activity. Its origins—older than Renaissance hydrology, Roman civil engineering, or Egyptian surveying—are lost in antiquity. The first systematic measurement of topography preceded the early quantification of Earth's surface-form by Alexander von Humboldt and later German geographers.[34] From telescopic measurements of craters on the Moon, the astronomer Johann Schröter[60] calculated volumes of the raised rim and inner depression—and found them, on the average, equivalent (see "Schröter's Rule"[39]). Figure 4.1(a) shows Humboldt, a large crater of the type Schröter measured, and Figure 4.1(b) shows the geometric quantities that translate the visual perception of these craters into computable numbers. In describing human factors in the quantitative analysis of topography from remote data, this chapter draws heavily from Schröter's legacy.

The art, science, and technology of ground-surface quantification are known by various terms, such as (geo)morphometry.[51] Practice is mainly parametric, that is, "capturing" the character of topography by slope, relief, spacing, directional orientation, and other metrics of form.[7,48] Topography also is quantified by automated techniques of visualization, such as relief shading.[50] Recently revolutionized by the mass-production of digital elevation models (DEMs) and square-grid arrays of terrain heights,[7,51] the discipline is preparing for explosive growth as synthetic-aperture radar (SAR) and other instruments image Earth's surface and return unprecedented volumes of topographic data.[4,66,69]

Despite the common assumption that its mathematics makes it "objective," terrain quantification entails much human supervision. This subjectivity affects landforms and landscapes alike.[7] Landforms—river basins, landslides, volcanoes, sand dunes, meteorite craters—are spatially discrete and readily outlined on a map or image. Landscapes are *continuous* tracts of terrain that do not comprise a mosaic of well-defined landforms. The interpretation of

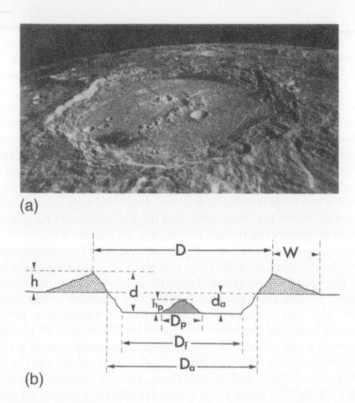

Figure 4.1   **(a)** Lunar scene at about 27° S, 81° E. The large *complex* Humboldt crater contrasts morphologically with the small *simple* craters within. Scene is 250 km across. Apollo 15 mapping-camera photo 2513. **(b)** Geometric abstraction of a lunar landform. Nine quantities that characterize the morphology of large impact craters such as Humboldt.

landforms is subjective in various respects: identifying and defining a feature, selecting and measuring its dimensions, analyzing the data, and understanding the results. Analysis of the continuous landscape introduces added uncertainties.[51] This chapter focuses on landforms, the more tractable of the two modes of surface quantification. The first step is recognition of the feature.

4.3   Landform identification

4.3.1   Landslides

The recognition of landforms remotely is sensitive to variance in human expertise.[3,8] Landslides are mapped from aerial photos in order to obtain a regional inventory of this hazard. In addition to the usual problems arising from photo quality, scale, and time of year and day, the topographic criteria for recognizing landslides are complex and subtle. Not all analysts use the same criteria or interpret them similarly.[36] Some observers are more inclusive of landslides than others; some will map both the landslide scar and the deposit, others only the deposit; some are better at recognizing landslides in certain types of bedrock, terrain, or vegetative cover. The variance in experience and "personal equation" are evident in different inventories of landslides for the same area by different analysts. Such variations may bias statistical models of vulnerability to slope failure.[35,36] Field work can resolve some discrepancies resulting from uncertainty in photointerpretation, but on-the-ground verification is too costly for large areas. In space exploration, however, ground truth is largely unavailable.

4.3.2   Large impact craters

Remoteness of Earth's Moon and the planets poses a special challenge to recognizing surface features.[4,16] Percival Lowell's misidentification of canals on the planet Mars, a classic blunder in signal recognition, remains a caveat to all who push the limits of perception. Less celebrated examples include the long delay in correctly identifying the Moon's craters as having formed by the impact of meteoroids. The last proponents of a volcanic origin for the craters pressed their case from photographic analogies with terrestrial features,[14] a qualitative argument vanquished by the analyses of crater geometry described in this chapter.

A debate over the Solar System's largest landforms, multi-ring basins, illustrates many of the uncertainties in feature identification on the planets.[30,64] Impact craters form a size-dependent morphologic continuum[13] starting at *simple* craters, the small bowl-shaped depressions with featureless interiors shown in Figure 4.1(a). It progresses through larger, *complex*, forms with interior terraces and a flat floor surrounding a central peak or cluster of peaks—exemplified in Figure 4.1(a) by the Humboldt crater. The continuum ends in multi-ring basins, broad depressions ringed by concentric scarps. Figure 4.2 shows the archetypal lunar basin Orientale and four of its concentric raised rings. Ranging from two to perhaps six per basin, the rings vary in form and commonly diminish in relief and completeness—and thus ease of recognition—with distance outward from the center.[52,67]

Multi-ring basins were first mapped on the Moon by Hartmann and Kuiper,[17] who discovered a systematic spacing of adjacent rings: an interval of about $\sqrt{2} \times$ diameter (D), or 1.4 D.[17] Figure 4.3 reveals this spatial order in a plot of each ring diameter against that of the topographically most prominent ("main") ring in its basin. Combined, the 78 rings of 17 lunar basins define 7 linear clusters, ranked I–VII in Figure 4.3. The ranked clusters shown here all are spaced about 1.4 D apart. A similar 1.4 D interval was identified in multi-ringed craters on Mars and Mercury,[52] and Earth.[25,47] This consistency in ring spacing is important because it constrains hypotheses for the origin of the basins.[64]

Reality of the spacing interval became disputed as missions to the planets and rocky satellites returned images of older, less distinct basins.[52] The subdued and fragmented appearance of many rings, absence of the 1.4 D spacing on icy satellites, and dependence of choice of the main ring on photogeologic expertise raised doubts of even the existence of more than two

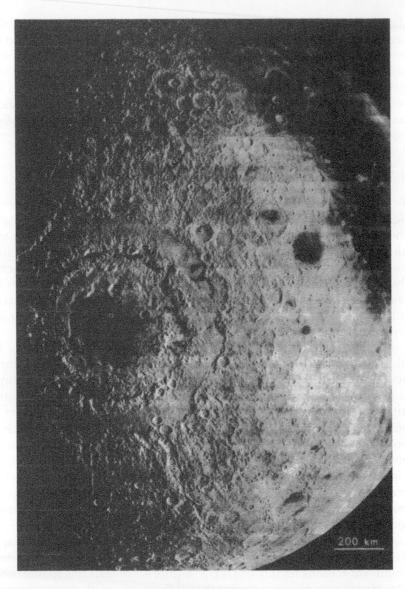

Figure 4.2   The lunar multi-ring basin Orientale. Outermost visible ring, about 930 km across, is "main" ring—equivalent to rim crest of a smaller impact crater; two faint larger rings are not evident at this scale. Lunar Orbiter IV frame 187M.

or three concentric rings per basin. Melosh[29,30] and Alexopoulos and McKinnon[1] also took issue with interpretations of basin origin that built on the constant ring spacing.[52,64] The dispute extended to Earth. Because most meteorite craters are deeply eroded, their observable features are structural—ring-shaped geologic faults and folds that formed at depth. These features are difficult to equate with their now-vanished (eroded) topographic

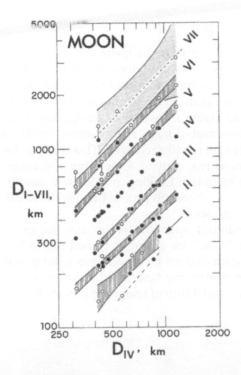

Figure 4.3 Plot exemplifying order in lunar landforms: similar spacing between 7 clusters (ranks I–VII) of ring diameters (D) for 17 basins. See text for explanation. D_{IV} is main ring. Open circles are faint rings; vertical lines join split segments of one ring. Shading shows statistical confidence for equations (at the 95% level) fit to 6 clusters; only rank VII is weak; two small rings suggest a rank below I. Orientale's 6 rings form part of second column of dots from right.

counterparts—the raised rings by which terrestrial craters are compared with planetary basins.[47] This subjectivity in linking topography to its subsurface structure weakened inferences drawn from combined Earth and planetary data.[15]

A cultural clash of authorities, recalling that of Alfred Wegener and his opponents,[38] informs the ring debate. Both disagreements arose from narrowness in expertise and the absence of a formational model. Wegener's critics could conceive of no mechanism for continental drift. Similarly, current physically based models of the impact process explain no more than two basin rings.[29,32] This prompted theoreticians—unfamiliar with the nuances of photointerpretation—to reject the more cryptic rings identified by empiricists,[30] while empiricists Pike and Spudis[52,64] rejected the theoreticians' cratering model for its failure to account for the many rings they observed. The debate ended only with recognition of 1.4 D ring spacings for basins on Venus[18,58] and for the multi-ring meteorite craters Chicxulub in Yucatán[61] and Sudbury in Ontario.[63] Rarely has agreeing on the validity of a landform and its sampling aroused such controversy.

4.4   Sampling the population

Once identified, a landform must be measured in quantities sufficient for analysis. The adequacy of a sample depends on objectives. Landslides are atypical in that the most complete inventory possible is needed for hazard mapping. A sample of about 30–50 landforms suffices for the more usual requirements, such as stable measures of correlation and other statistics. For many landforms—sand dunes, river basins, small impact craters— these modest numbers are readily achieved. This is not so for rare features— multi-ring basins, meteorite craters, some large volcanoes—for which all examples tend to be included. Lacking an adequate sample, one can either discard that landform or choose to proceed under the usual risks attending the statistics of small numbers.

A sample also should span the entire size range of the landform. Schröter's venerable "rule," for example, turned out to be wrong. Because Schröter's equipment limited his measurements to large features, he missed the small craters for which rim and bowl volumes are not equivalent.[39] Similarly, the uneven availability of images and maps limits sample size and

Figure 4.4   A Martian scene at 79° N, showing barchan dunes imaged at 3 m/pixel by Mars Global Surveyor in March 1999. Scene is 2.1 km across. Image P-50279.

variety.[36] Combining observations from different sources, at different scales, can result in a nonuniform data set and increase uncertainty in subsequent analysis. Finally, clarity of a landform and variations in freshness influence sampling. Well-formed features invite measurement; degraded or poorly exposed forms tend to be ignored.[36]

Figure 4.4 shows barchan dunes recently imaged on Mars, which illustrate some of the sampling issues. On Earth, these crescent-shaped landforms threaten desert settlements, the speed of their migration varying with sand supply, dune size, and terrain form.[3] Barchan dimensions, needed to model their movement and predict location, can be measured remotely,[3,57] but aerial photos and satellite images rarely span their entire size range. Recalling Schröter, instrumentation limited the sample of Sarnthein and Walger[57] to barchans more than 25 m across, leaving 200 smaller dunes unmeasured. Any size-dependent differences in the morphology of smaller barchans will go unrecorded by such incomplete ("truncated") samples, possibly leading to incorrect understanding of their mechanics of migration. Figure 4.4, by contrast, is so detailed that it can be processed to extract any parameters of barchan form—length, height, horn-to-horn width, and angles of windward and lee slopes. The linear sand dunes portrayed by shaded relief in Figure 4.5 are too small to sample any parameters accurately.

4.5   Parameters of surface form

Landforms selected for sampling must be "captured" from images and maps by describing their shape in ways that distinguish them from other landforms. This abstraction of shape is accomplished by measuring geometric attributes[22,24,60] and by recording the presence or absence of morphologic features.[45] The analyst's judgment guides both the choice of parameters and making the measurements. Selecting diagnostic parameters requires familiarity with past work, intimate knowledge of how landforms are portrayed on source maps and images, and experience in measurement. A parameter that cannot be measured accurately across the entire sample is an unwise choice, and individual landforms on which defensible measurements cannot be taken should be dropped from the sample—often a painful decision.[45]

Uncomplicated landforms, like the near-circular impact craters shown in Figure 4.1(a) and the volcano diagrammed in Figure 4.6, can be specified for most purposes by the few measures in Figures 4.1(b) and 4.6—diameters of the rim, flank, and floor; depth; and height of the rim above exterior datum.[2,41,60] The circularity index, area of an inscribed circle divided by that of a circumscribed circle, expresses symmetry of the rim-crest outline.[42,44] (Most volcanic craters, for example, have circularities of 0.40–0.70, most impact craters 0.75–0.85.) Distinction among crater sub-types requires added information—on such morphologic details as bowl shape, flat floor, terraced rim, and central peak.[45,49] The geometry of landslides, sand dunes, and most other landforms is irregular and thus harder to specify.[24]

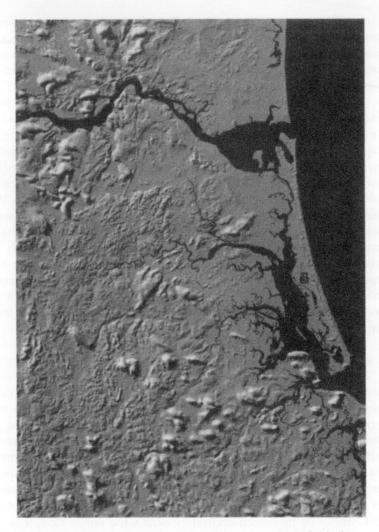

Figure 4.5 A terrestrial scene (Massachusetts). Landforms in a shaded-relief image: cluster of drumlins (lower right) and long line of small dunes (adjacent island). Computed from 30-m DEM; linears are raised roadbeds; scene is 22 km across.

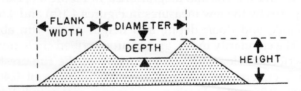

Figure 4.6 Parameters that quantify volcano shape. Profile from averaged dimensions for 12 "pseudocraters" formed by lava flowing over saturated ground. Base diameter 135 m.

Experiments with river basins have resulted in many descriptive measures, such as the hypsometric integral (elevation skewness), crenulation of the basin outline, and drainage density. Groups of river-channel segments are represented collectively, by measures that describe their topology and spatial pattern.[7,22,33,56] A good parameter, however, is of little value if it cannot be measured accurately.

4.6   Making measurements

Remote measurement of topography dates to Galileo's first estimates of relative height on the Moon from the length of cast shadows. Taken visually at the telescope, the dimensions of craters measured by Schröter and his successors varied in accuracy and precision with instrumental error, disturbances in Earth's atmosphere, location on the Moon, and the observer's idiosyncracies.[2,27] Historically, measurements of crater diameter have been consistent, but those of depth and rim height are not. Because shadow tips are indistinct, many relief estimates were low and reflect shadows that were not on the floor of a large crater, at the center of a bowl-shaped crater, or beyond the foot of the exterior rim.[44,45] Sources of vertical error did not disappear with the advent of photography.[9] Only during the post-Sputnik race to the Moon were sufficient resources committed to shadow-length photography to reduce its uncertainties to an acceptable level, by automating identification of the shadow tip.[55] Even so, the depth and rim-height data generated by the U.S. Air Force for its lunar maps were uneven in quality and required careful screening.[39,40]

Uncertainties in the remote capture of landform data remain despite advances in technology. Current methods all require human intervention. Photoclinometry ("shape from shading"), which extracts terrain slope from image brightness, is used on Mars and satellites of the outer planets where photogrammetry cannot be applied.[65] It requires careful internal calibration.[21] Photoclinometry's inverse, digital relief-shading, creates a brightness map from terrain slope. It, too, relies on experience to generate a high quality image.[50] The drumlins (low, rounded hills formed beneath glaciers[26]) shown in shaded-relief in Figure 4.5 are sufficiently clear that their length, width, and correspondence to an ellipse can be measured. Although photogrammetry yields the most accurate relief values, pre-Apollo maps contoured photogrammetrically[37] decreased in reliability with distance from the center of the lunar disk and had to be used selectively.[39,40] Experts still must judge the suitability of base/height ratios for planetary photogrammetry, as well as evaluate the performance of SAR imaging degraded by steep or forested terrain.[11,54]

The inaccuracies inherent in images, maps, and DEMs obtained by remote sensing are compounded by ambiguities in measuring the landforms on them. Even morphologically uncomplicated features, such as the radially symmetric craters in Figures 4.1(a) and 4.2, can require many operational decisions.[44,45] Photogrammetry from returned Apollo film improved the precision of lunar data but did not eliminate the need for human judgment. For measuring crater-rim height in uneven terrain, for example, one must choose several elevations on the rim crest, decide on a reasonable radial distance outward, and then choose more heights.[44] That radial distance, rim width, remains the most uncertain of all crater dimensions, an ambiguity not eliminated by laser altimetry[10] or planetary DEMs.[23] Crater diameters can be uncertain. Isolated fragments of subdued basin rings must be carefully mapped before fitting a circle to them.[52]

Similar ambiguities complicate the quantification of terrestrial landforms. Measuring the base diameter of a volcano that merges gradually into the surrounding terrain can require a geologic map to locate the extent of the form. Obtaining the rim outline of a volcano's summit crater to measure its circularity also can be difficult because many rims are fragmentary or eroded; reconstructing a rim crest requires good judgment and restraint. Analogous problems in defining landform extent from remote data arise in measuring landslides, glacial cirques (erosion hollows in mountainous terrain[8]), and the drumlins shown in Figure 4.5. The many small decisions required in measuring these landforms are an essential prelude to their analysis.

4.7 Landform analysis

Landforms are interpreted from their measurements by methods that are subjective, despite the scientific objectivity sometimes claimed for them. Ten analytical practices are discussed in this section:

1. Arraying landforms by size or morphology
2. Stratifying a sample by relative age
3. Searching for correlations
4. Assigning varying importance to descriptive data
5. Transforming a parameter's scale of measurement
6. Deriving index numbers
7. Sorting variables to reduce redundancy
8. Obtaining an optimal set of parameters
9. Classifying landforms by multiple measures
10. Modeling morphometric relations and formational process

4.7.1 Initial sorting

Subdividing a landform sample prior to numerical analysis is something of an art. Interpretation of impact craters, for example, requires recognizing qualitative differences within the size-dependent array of morphologies. Dence[5] distinguished the first of these transitions, from a simple (deep, bowl-shaped) to a complex (shallow, several interior features) shape, in Earth's meteorite craters. Figures 4.7 and 4.8 illustrate (in detail not present in

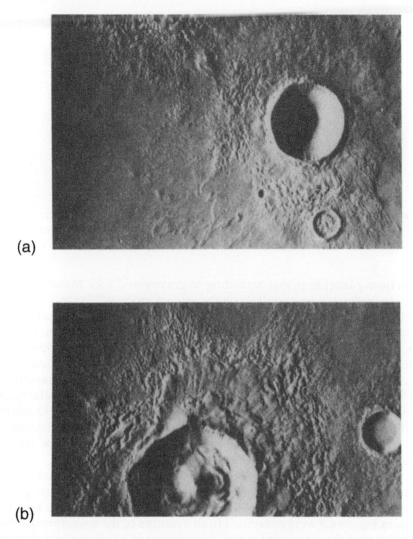

Figure 4.7 A quantifiable contrast in landform morphology: examples of fresh simple (a) and complex (b) impact craters on Mars. See text for explanation. Craters are 8 and 14 km across. Viking Orbiter frames 645A09 and 645A01.

Figures 4.1(a) and 4.2), this transition for craters on Mars. The simple crater in Figure 4.7(a) differs qualitatively from the larger complex crater in Figure 4.7(b)—with its central peak, flat floor covered with slumped material, and scalloped and terraced rim. The data for seven of these morphologic features in Figure 4.8 demonstrate the power of presence/absence identifications, judgment-laden as they are, in quantifying this distinction. The transition is defined by averaging diameters of craters containing the largest simple features and smallest complex features. This diameter, about 5 km on Mars,

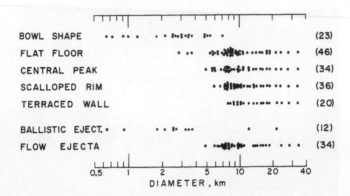

Figure 4.8 Qualitative criteria that quantify the morphologic transition from simple (bowl shape, ballistic ejecta) to complex (other five features) craters. Presence/ absence of features for 73 craters (205 dots) on Mars, from Viking Orbiter images.

differs from planet to planet according to gravity and rock materials and is critical to understanding controls on the impact process.[49,59]

Neglecting qualitative differences can lead to overgeneralization. The first quantitative relation to link craters on the Earth and its Moon, a continuous depth/diameter curve, did not separate simple from complex morphologies.[2] Making that distinction, however, revealed that the relation actually consists of two distinct, linear, segments—inflected at the transition.[39] This "dog-leg" break can be seen on page 99, in Figure 4.10(a). Similarly, concentric rings in impact basins on Venus are spaced at the 1.4 D interval described earlier.[58] They do not vary from this value as claimed by Alexopoulos and McKinnon,[1] who had combined three disparate types of craters and basins rather than plotting their data separately.[18]

Other types of landforms must be sorted. The author subdivided over 650 volcanoes by eruptive process and rock type before deriving metric profiles to compare their shapes with those on planetary images.[43] Profiles for the 20 classes in Figure 4.9 were computed from averages of the four dimensions in Figure 4.6 plus the circularity index. Assignment of a volcano to a class was based on the author's evaluation of descriptions in the literature. There is no "correct" number of these classes, which grew from the initial four[41] as volcanoes were added to the sample and larger classes were judged excessively mixed in geometry and geology. Success in subdividing large classes was confirmed by reduced variance in descriptive statistics for the five parameters. Because erosion rates on Earth differ widely in their effects, these volcanoes could not be stratified further by age or degree of degradation.

4.7.2   *Stratifying the sample*

Subdividing impact craters by age on the Moon where erosional changes in landform are more predictable was not only possible, but led to inferences of surface-shaping processes. Baldwin's[2] depth/diameter graph for the first

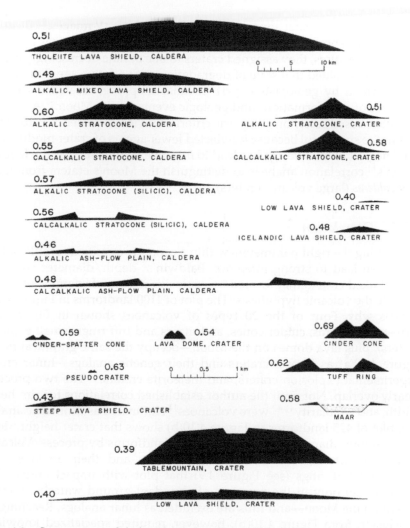

Figure 4.9   Geometric models for 20 volcano classes from measurements on maps and images. See text for explanation. Numbers give circularity of crater rim. Vertical exaggeration 2×; scale of lower nine profiles 10× that of upper 12 (low shields shown at both scales).

time linked lunar craters with terrestrial meteorite craters and craters formed by experimental explosions. Contributing to Baldwin's success was his inclusion of only the freshest-appearing landforms. Although subjective, his five age groups reflected the judgment of a keen observer. This deliberate winnowing excluded old, eroded craters that would have violated the cardinal rule of fitting an equation only to like phenomena.

Stratification by crater age also was instrumental in deciphering the geology of the Moon. Pohn and Offield devised an ordinal ranking of large craters from their visual appearance on Lunar Orbiter IV images.[53] By noting presence/absence or degree of preservation of rim-wall terraces and other secondary features, they assigned craters to one of nine decreasingly pristine classes and equated that state of degradation with relative age. This system, implemented by geologists expert in lunar mapping, created a workable sequence of rock formations and geologic events for the Moon.[67] A model of crater age based solely on geometric criteria, by a less experienced observer,[40] was not as successful because it reflected fewer agents of crater modification. Total neglect of relative age has lead to negative results, such as the failure of Green's[14] correlation analysis to distinguish the Moon's craters from terrestrial *calderas* (large volcanic craters).

4.7.3   Correlation

Correlating the right parameters within a properly stratified sample of landforms can lead to strong inference. Baldwin's[2] depth/diameter curve correctly linked craters that formed by explosive release of energy, but did not exclude the volcanic hypothesis. The plot of 1100 landforms in Figure 4.10(a) reveals why. Four of the 20 types of volcanoes shown in Figure 4.9—terrestrial calderas, cinder cones, and maars and tuff rings (small explosion craters), plus lava domes on the Moon—occupy the same graphical field in Figure 4.10(a) as impact craters and their genetic analogs—lunar craters, experimental explosion craters, and meteorite craters.[41] The two processes clearly overlap. Not until the author established correlations for rim height, width, and circularity[41,42] were volcanoes[14] eliminated as geometric analogs. The plot of 425 landforms in Figure 4.10(b) shows that crater height/depth, unlike depth/diameter, does discriminate landforms by process. Volcanoes occupy a different field than impact craters and their analogs.[41] The maars and tuff rings (see Figure 4.9) that plot with impact craters form (explosively) only in the presence of abundant ground water[62]—virtually absent on the Moon—and thus are excluded as lunar analogs. Reaching this conclusion from Figure 4.10(b), however, required specialized knowledge beyond the plotted data.

   Landform correlations established from remote data tend to be revised as sensing technology improves with each mission. New, higher-resolution information may add nothing new, or it can force reexamination of earlier conclusions.[2,39] The author's revision of the simple-to-complex transition for craters on Mercury, for example, was so substantial that it led to the establishment of a basic correlation between crater morphology and surface gravity for the rocky planets.[49] Eventually, however, diminishing returns set in. Data will attain sufficient accuracy that no further revision of measures is justified from incrementally better information. Recognizing when this has occurred is one of the finer judgment calls in the remote study of landforms. Another fine point is the uneven quality of descriptive data.

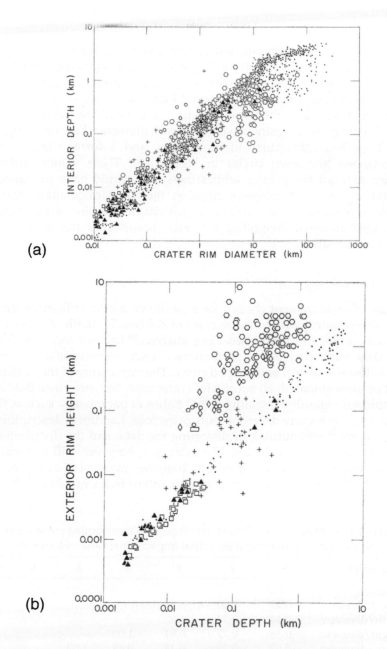

Figure 4.10 Good and bad discriminants of landform process. **(a)** Depth diameter fails to separate craters formed by different agents. Terrestrial calderas (hexagons), cinder cones (circles), maars and tuff rings (crosses), explosion craters (squares), meteorite craters (triangles), lunar craters (dots), and lava domes (diamonds). **(b)** Height/depth successfully divides volcanoes (upper cluster) from impact craters (lower cluster). Two rectangles are volcanic domes on Earth.

4.7.4 Weighting

Some landform measurements and parameters are superior to others, but whether to weight the data accordingly is seldom addressed. Weighting, when it is attempted, always hinges on human judgment. In systematizing the analysis of basin rings on the Earth, Moon, Mars, and Mercury through correlation, Pike[47] and Pike and Spudis[52] addressed the uneven quality of their 300 rings by assigning a weight to each diameter: 3 for unambiguous rings, 2 for less satisfactory identifications, and 1 for the least certain interpretations (the open circles in Figure 4.3). These values, although arbitrary, reduced the greater arbitrariness that would have prevailed by including cryptic with obvious rings in the same calculation. Another example of weighting is given later in this chapter, in discussing principal components analysis. Weighting the data, however, is the only way to improve a correlation.

4.7.5 Transformation

The scale of measurement chosen for a landform metric influences correlation. Further contributing to the success of Baldwin's[2] depth/diameter plot was his use of logarithmic scales. Prior analyses[28] had not corrected for the severe skew in the frequency distributions of crater dimensions, very few of which follow the normal bell-shaped curve. The importance of this difference cannot be overestimated; all successful crater morphometry since Baldwin's has employed logarithmic scaling.[45,59,68] Ratios of parameters, such as those in Table 4.1, may require different transformations. Landform descriptors are not transformed without risk of distorting the data, and the distribution of each measure must be evaluated. The extra care, however, will be repaid by improved correlations (as in Table 4.1), narrower margins of error, recognition of sub-categories of features, and more robust index numbers.[42,43]

Table 4.1 Correlation coefficients (r) for pairs of transformed parameters that describe 402 lunar and terrestrial impact craters and volcanoes*

Variables	1	2	3	4	5	6	7
1. Circularity	1.00						
2. Height/depth	−0.47	1.00					
3. Width/diameter	−0.44	0.73	1.00				
4. Height/diameter	−0.38	0.77	0.84	1.00			
5. Depth/diameter	0.07	−0.19	0.29	0.48	1.00		
6. Height/width	−0.01	0.29	−0.01	0.52	0.41	1.00	
7. Depth/width	0.46	0.79	−0.68	−0.40	0.46	0.31	1.00

*Absolute values of $r < 0.25$ not significant at 0.01 confidence level. Parameters were transformed, respectively, to x^3, $\log x^{-3}$, $\log x^{-2}$, $\log x^{-3}$, $\log x$, $\log x$, and x^{-3}. Parameters defined in Figures 4.1(b) and 4.6 and in the text.

4.7.6   Index numbers

The ratios in Table 4.1 exemplify combinations of measures that carry greater descriptive power than individual measures. Derivation of these index numbers from remotely sensed data is a heuristic process entailing familiarity with the landforms and a flair for experimentation. Figure 4.10(b), which shows that the ratio of landform height to depth separates most volcanoes from most impact craters, originated in trial plots of a few parameters that might prove more diagnostic than depth/diameter. From this tentative start the author recognized that the main difference between volcanoes and impact craters could be quantified: a broad form with a small summit crater located well above the surrounding landscape vs. a low and narrow rim surrounding a large depression excavated in the precrater terrain. This contrast is revisited below in combining all seven index numbers in Table 4.1,[42,44] where tests for parameter redundancy played an important role.

4.7.7   Data sifting and redundancy

Decisions to retain or discard landform descriptors are subjective and not always determined by statistical testing. One guideline is redundancy. Two or more parameters can express much the same basic attribute of form; if very similar, one of them may be extraneous. Including similar parameters in an analysis can reduce its descriptive or discriminating power by giving undue weight to one attribute. Two such metrics, the hypsometric integral [(mean elevation − minimum elevation)/(maximum − minimum elevation)] and skewness of elevation, characterize continuous terrain as well as discrete landforms.[7] Figure 4.11 shows that these quantities, computed from 1:24,000-scale maps, describe the same attribute of form for 14 small river basins in the U.S. According to the statistics for this correlation, 95% of the variance in one parameter is accounted for by the other—probably sufficient to drop one measure with little loss of information.

Redundancy is an ambiguous property, in that some correlated measures differ enough in their descriptive capability to warrant retaining both. Local relief (highest minus lowest elevation within a defined area) and slope angle are two vertical constituents of terrain roughness (spacing is its horizontal constituent). Because slope traditionally is measured over short distances, whereas relief is computed over a large area, one metric characterizes fine-scale roughness and the other coarse-scale roughness—a distinction worth preserving. Thus, it is not always desirable to pare down a data set to strictly uncorrelated descriptors. Where an exhaustive description of form is required, it may be wise to include as many metrics as practicable. Much of the art in screening variables for landform characterization lies in knowing which course to follow.

Expertise in exploratory data analysis, an intuitive process, is helpful in sorting descriptors. There are many ways, for example, to compare

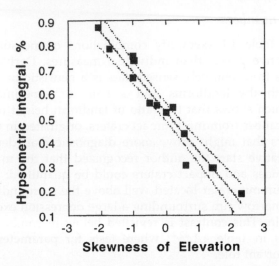

Figure 4.11 Redundancy in landform description. Inverse correlation of two similar parameters, skewness of elevation and hypsometric integral, for 14 river basins (see text).

parameters by arranging the correlation coefficient **r** in tables or diagrams.[7,33] In Table 4.1, correlations among seven index numbers computed for impact craters and volcanoes show that only variables 2, 3, 4, and 7 are closely related—albeit not to the point of redundancy. Large tables of this type[18] defy such a ready grasp of the interrelations, but a large number of variables can be sorted visually by color-coding the **r** magnitude (>0.90, 0.80–0.89, 0.70–0.79, etc.), arraying the coded rs for each variable in columns from highest to lowest, labeling the r-value that indicates statistical significance of the correlation, and finally rearranging the columns in order of diminishing number and strength of the correlations.

While nominally more "objective" than visual inspection in evaluating redundancy, multivariate techniques also require informed judgment. Principal components analysis (PCA), illustrated in Table 4.2, has reduced the matrix of **r** values for the seven measures in Table 4.1 to just four independent components—which express, in descending order of explanatory capability, the four fundamental attributes contained in the data.[42,44] The relative order of the PCs, while reasonable, should be accepted cautiously, for it depends as much on the number of contributing variables as on their intrinsic variance. In Table 4.2 the five high-scoring variables 1–4 and 7 dominate PC–1 (49%), depth/diameter and depth/width (measures of terrain slope) comprise much of PC–2, while rim-crest circularity is the only important constituent of the weak PC–4. Not all PCs are easily understood in terms of constituent variables; PC–3 has no clear-cut interpretation. One of the objectives of reducing redundancy by these procedures is to converge on a signature.

Table 4.2 Principal components (PC) analysis of seven parameters, based on correlation coefficients in Table 4.1, for 402 craters and volcanoes*

Variables	PC-1	PC-2	PC-3	PC-4	Variance
1. Circularity	−0.61	0.19	−0.01	0.77	1.000
2. Height/depth	0.93	−0.12	0.31	0.16	0.995
3. Width/diameter	0.91	0.05	−0.39	0.13	0.996
4. Height/diameter	0.88	0.46	−0.02	0.10	0.996
5. Depth/diameter	0.09	0.87	−0.47	−0.07	0.995
6. Height/width	0.21	0.76	0.61	−0.02	0.997
7. Depth/width	−0.76	0.61	0.02	−0.16	0.978
Variance	3.46	1.98	0.85	0.67	6.959
% total variance	49.4	28.3	12.1	9.6	99.4

*Values are PC scores of each parameter on first four components. PCs 1–4 yield nearly complete solution (99.4%). PCs 5–7 (not shown) add < 1% of total variance.

4.7.8 The geometric signature

Enzmann's concept of a signature, "a set of measurements sufficient to identify unambiguously an object or a set of objects,"[6] has adapted well from remote sensing to landform analysis. The geometric signature is a suite of measures · ufficient to distinguish a landform or its formational process(es) from all others.[48] No specifications exist for a signature, which is arrived at by intuition and experiment. It invokes four postulates:

1. The perception of landforms in a scene can be abstracted by discrete measures
2. The measures must represent the attributes that give a landform its unique character
3. This character is inherently multivariate; no one "magic number" suffices to "fingerprint" a feature or interpret its origin
4. Characterizing landforms is a statistical problem

Signatures such as the set of seven parameters in Tables 4.1 and 4.2 provide the operational tool for classification.

4.7.9 Classification

Grouping or separating remotely sampled features by a signature can furnish clues to landform process, but classification procedures rely on the analyst's expertise at every step. The first of two experiments described here retested, from more extensive data, the hypothesis that origin of the Moon's craters could be inferred from their geometry alone. To do this, the author compared 400 landforms—from 23 classes of lunar craters, meteorite craters, and terrestrial volcanoes—across the seven ratios in Tables 4.1 and 4.2 by cluster analysis.[42,44] This two-step procedure is *unsupervised:* "training samples" are not used to specify a desired outcome.

Principal components analysis first reduced the seven parameters, properly transformed (see Table 4.1), to four PCs that provide a less redundant signature (see Table 4.2). A clustering algorithm then sorted the scores (correlations of each landform with each PC), weighted by the percent variance explained by each PC. These scores determined a measure of similarity, the distance function by which an algorithm sorted the landforms into a hierarchical array. Although interpreting these arrays can be subjective, the resulting classification shown in Figure 4.12 is unambiguous. This

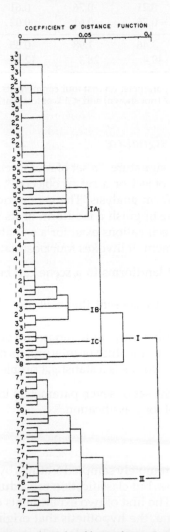

Figure 4.12 Inference of process from landform shape, I. A seven-parameter classification groups lunar craters with Earth's impact craters (I) not volcanoes (II). See text for explanation; 402 craters (numbers 1–9, every fourth shown). Classes 1–5 and 8 are lunar, meteorite, and explosion craters; classes 6, 7, 9 are volcanoes. Distance function is low for similar craters; horizontal lines show value at which each crater joins group.

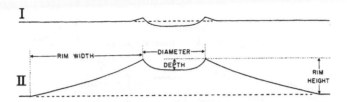

Figure 4.13   Geometric models contrasting "excavational" (I) with "constructional" (II) landforms, from classification in Figure 4.12. See text for explanation. Scaled to same rim diameter; respective mean values of crater circularity are 0.78 and 0.64; vertical exaggeration 2×.

dichotomous outcome reveals how dramatically lunar craters resemble Earth's meteorite craters, but differ from all of its volcanoes save the maars and tuff rings explained earlier. Cluster I (classes 1–5, 8) consists of lunar, meteorite, experimental, and explosion craters; cluster II (classes 6, 7, 9) includes volcanoes on Earth, the Moon, and Mars.

Contrasting profiles in Figure 4.13—computed from averaged values of height, depth, diameter, and width (see Figure 4.6)—summarize the results in Figure 4.12. The "excavational" (impact) processes that created the landforms in cluster I (275 samples) have been correctly distinguished from the "constructional" processes that built the volcanoes in cluster II (125 samples).[42,44] The higher circularity for cluster I reflects the radial symmetry imparted by the point-source release of impact energy. Judgment and intuition were essential to the success of this experiment. Classifications based on untransformed ratios or raw dimensions rather than ratios, for example, were inconclusive. Weighting the clustering required evaluation of the components. PC-1, with half the total variance, expresses the key discriminant: proportion of crater volume to that of the raised rim or volcanic construct. This attribute, evident in individual variables 1–4 in Tables 4.1 and 4.2, is so diagnostic that unweighted PCs would have invalidated the analysis.

A second experiment in multivariate classification compared over 700 volcanoes to infer the eruptive style of planetary volcanoes from the morphometry of terrestrial features. The seven-parameter signature that clearly distinguished impact from volcanism in Figures 4.12 and 4.13 did not discriminate well among eruptive styles. Nor did it display the full range of morphologic variation that the author knew existed in the 31 classes of volcanoes (increased from the 20 shown in Figure 4.9). Plotting PC scores for components on two- and three-axis diagrams (not shown) grouped most volcano classes fairly well, but the author's familiarity with volcanoes suggested that a key attribute was still missing.

Further experimentation revealed the missing descriptor to be volume of the landform. Average volume was computed for each class from the topographic profile of one fresh, well-formed volcano. The author's choices of examples so clarified morphometric relations that the simple plot of volume against rim-crest circularity shown in Figure 4.14 sufficed to array the

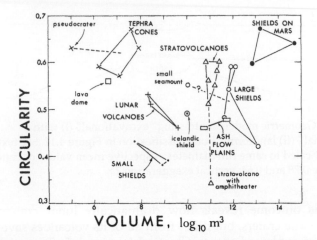

Figure 4.14 Inference of process from landform shape, II. Two parameters classify 31 volcano types into many fewer "process groups." Two of these groups resemble lunar and Martian volcanoes (see text). Symbols and solid lines group related styles of eruption; dashed lines show affinity of classes that form under unusual conditions.

31 classes in just a few groups, which correspond to the major eruptive processes and products. Four large groups—tephra (ash) cones, small lava shields, large constructs of ash and lava (stratovolcanoes), and large lava shields—account for 18 of the 25 terrestrial classes. (Discussion of the remaining seven classes lies beyond the scope of this chapter.) Adjusting volumes for differences in planetary surface gravity, moreover, moved the three Martian and three lunar classes to the left to exactly align, respectively, with large and small terrestrial shields. This alignment (not shown in Figure 4.14) suggests that volcanoes on Mars and the Moon do not form in exotic ways, but rather develop by two of the mechanisms that create Earth's chief types of volcanoes: the building of large and small lava shields. The interrelations among landforms described by the classifications in this section constitute an important type of model.

4.7.10 Modeling

Models are numerical or conceptual abstractions that aid in understanding natural phenomena. "Model" is an elastic concept, embracing interpretation and explanation as well as description and experimental analog. Human decision making colors all attempts to model landforms from remotely sensed information. Geometric models, which structure relations among descriptive measures, are the least subjective.[24,33,52] They include the 3-D abstraction of craters in Figure 4.1(b), the statistical order of basin-ring spacing in Figure 4.3, and the morphologic transition defined in Figure 4.8.

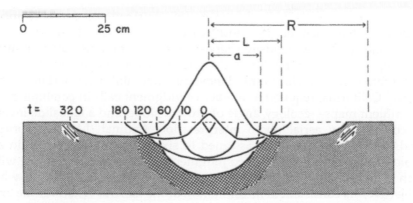

Figure 4.15   Analog model of a cratering process. Filmed experiment of impact into water shows growth of excavation cavity. See text for explanation of distances **a**, **L**, and **R**. Profiles at same scale and location in target chamber, at times **t** in msec after impact. Ejected material and raised rim omitted for clarity.

Landform classifications, such as the bivariate plot of volcanoes in Figure 4.14 and the multivariate parsing of craters in Figure 4.12, are taxonomic models.

Laboratory experiments are attempts to scale the formation of surface features, but such analog models do not necessarily simulate physical processes. They only imply. Figure 4.15 shows a model of impact cratering that scaled the strength of the target rocks as a fluid. Successive stages in the growth of a liquid-impact crater mimic the sequence thought to excavate a sombrero-shaped transient (temporary) cavity during formation of a meteorite crater.[46] The crater in water reaches its greatest depth at **t** = 60 msec (radius **a**) and then grows laterally at **t** = 120 to uplift the central peak and disrupt an inner region at radius **L**. Inertial recoil of the crater center drives late-stage growth. Uplift of the crater floor *before* gravitational collapse of the rim is consistent with the observation of central peaks and flat floors before (i.e., in smaller craters than) rim-wall terraces in the simple-to-complex transition on Mars (see Figure 4.8) and elsewhere.[49] Radius **R** at t > 320 marks the location of the final rim crest (not shown), which collapses in analogy to the terracing and faulting in meteorite craters (arrows).

Physically based calculations have mathematically simulated impact cratering and other surface-forming agents.[22,29,62] While more sophisticated than geometric models and more quantitative than analogs, such process models build on complex assumptions of their own and are no less the product of human decision making.[23,32] None of the several models proposed for the origin of concentric basin rings, for example, has achieved widespread acceptance.[31,52] Either they explain only rings within or outside of the main crater rim (rank IV in Figure 4.3), or require too many leaps of faith or logic, or are insufficiently quantitative.

Landform models derived from remote data can address more applied objectives. Newman et al.[35] and Nilsen et al.[36] translated the spatial distribution of discrete landslide deposits into a continuous statistical surface showing relative vulnerability to slope failure over a large area. Their semi-quantitative model, which ranks landslide vulnerability for part of northern coastal California, required a number of judgment calls in combining three constituent maps—geology, angle of ground slope, and a landslide inventory compiled by aerial photo interpretation. Ordinal (I-VI) categories of landslide vulnerability were assigned to six intervals of slope within each geologic unit, based on informed judgments of landslide prevalence within each slope interval. The map resulting from this model, while not wholly "objective," is consistent in its estimation of the hazard. Whatever the origin or purpose of the various types of models, however, most of them lead to a better understanding of surface-shaping agents.

4.8   Interpretation

Of the issues considered in this chapter, it is the inference of landform process that leaves the widest latitude for human judgment. Impact cratering illustrates this uncertainty. For such distant features as the rings of planetary impact basins, experts have yet to forge a strong link between form and process. The existence of multiple rings is admitted by former skeptics,[31] for example, but until the physics responsible for the 1.4 D spacing is understood, it cannot be known whether the rings formed—or perhaps were only located—by a wave mechanism,[52] a tectonic process,[32] or a scenario not yet proposed. On the other hand, the impact origin of smaller craters is no longer at issue,[2,42,45,62,67] and interpretations of the process now focus on details.[10]

Figure 4.16 is a general interpretation for complex impact craters based on the model in Figure 4.15 and other observations. Figure 4.16 is scaled to the averaged dimensions of Martian craters; its geologic detail summarizes field data from four well-studied meteorite craters.[45] The transient cavity of excavation (compare Figure 4.15) comprises the broad shallow zone above layer

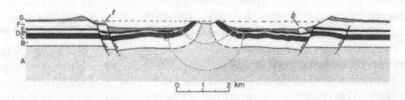

Figure 4.16   Interpretation of complex impact craters. Profile from measurements of Martian craters; geologic cross-section from terrestrial field data. Upper dotted arc is inner excavation cavity. See text for explanation and significance of rock strata A–G; arrows show faults.

E plus the deep central zone (small dotted arc). The large dotted arc marks the deep inner zone of total fragmentation and perhaps fluidization of the target rocks[29] (compare Figure 4.15). Uplift of the crater center has exposed and steepened rock strata **A–C** and distorted strata **D** and **E**; layer **F** has been stripped out of crater and forms slump block **b** and terrace **t** (by faulting: arrows); layer **G** is ejected material or fractured rock within the crater. Although Figure 4.16 explains many features of complex craters, it is not the sole interpretation.[29] Whether uplift of the crater floor or collapse of the rim is the dominant mechanism driving the transition from the simple to the complex morphologies shown in Figures 4.7, 4.8, 4.15, and 4.16 continues to be debated.[18,31,49] These uncertainties remain despite the field evidence from Earth's meteorite craters and the cumulative experience of many experts.

4.9   Conclusions

Human subjectivity in the task addressed by this chapter—imposing geometric order on landforms from remotely sensed information—can be reduced by developing expertise to make better operational decisions. Guidelines to more informed decision making include the following:

1. Define rules for identifying and measuring surface features
2. Reduce landforms to basic elements of shape (facets and lines)
3. Choose measurable elements common to many forms
4. Devise quantitative descriptions for qualitative features
5. Avoid incomplete samples
6. Expect landforms to vary in shape with size and age
7. Anticipate non-normal distributions of descriptive measures
8. Plot data to screen them visually before making calculations
9. Avoid inapt "apples/oranges" correlations
10. Explore the information: examine old data in new ways and new data in old ways
11. Avoid losing insights into data through their uncritical manipulation by computer

Sound judgments in landform quantification clearly relate to expertise in image interpretation, but who qualifies as an expert? One theme of this chapter has been disagreement among authorities, whose expectations commonly reflect the ruling paradigms of their respective fields. Disputes start at a low level: experts may not agree on what constitutes a valid observation, let alone "evidence." At a higher level, experts may reject results reached by analytical practices that differ from those of their own discipline; for example, theoretical vs. empirical modeling. These problems are embedded in the sociology and psychology of science and not easily resolved. Developing the expertise is more readily achieved, for landform quantification is a skill that can be learned.

In outlining a formal course of instruction, the author identified ten general topics:

1. *Conceptual framework*—philosophy of landform quantification, theory, perception and cognition
2. *Enabling technology*—image-processing, geographic information systems (GIS), knowledge-based feature recognition
3. *Elevation sampling*—map contours, profiles, DEMs
4. *Data structures*—spatial arrangements of points, lines, and areas for height derivatives
5. *Z measures*—relief, slope, profile curvature, hypsometry, other height derivatives
6. *X, Y measures*—location, extent, direction, arrangement, texture
7. *X, Y, Z measures*—3-D attributes, scale variance, self-organization (fractals)
8. *Analysis*—sampled in this chapter
9. *Synthesis*—landform taxonomy, parsing a scene, combining with non-topographic data, etc.
10. *Dynamic morphometry*—simulation and interpretation of processes to model landscape evolution[51]

Excepting theory, all these areas are fields of active research.[51] While it is capable of prediction, landform quantification is largely empirical and lacks unifying principles. Enough empirical relations may now have accumulated on which to base a general theory, but the direction remains unclear. An obvious path to theory lies through geomorphology, the established science of landforms. Alternatively, a scale- and process-independent theory based on mathematical geography might be more flexible. It would rely less on physical processes and laws than on spatial properties of relief and topologic relations derived from graph theory.[51] But, would a stronger theoretical foundation reduce the operational subjectivity described in this chapter?

Despite the uncertainties introduced by human factors, surface quantification from remotely sensed information has progressed steadily in the 200 years since Johann Schröter measured craters on the Moon. This chapter has described only a few of the discipline's recent achievements. Driven by current needs to accelerate the processing of remote imagery,[4,19,20] landform quantification is poised to make its most valuable contributions yet from the terrain data generated under such programs as the 2000 Shuttle Radar Topography Mission. Among these prospects are improved defense capabilities, more accurate appraisal of water resources, real-time warning of natural hazards, a deeper understanding of changes in the Earth's surface through time, and more refined criteria for guiding urban development and locating transportation facilities.

References

1. Alexopoulos, J. S. and McKinnon, W. B., Large impact craters and basins on Venus, with implications for ring mechanics on the terrestrial planets, in *Large Meteorite Impacts and Planetary Evolution*, Special Paper 293, Dressler, B. O., Grieve, R. A. F. and Sharpton, V. L., Eds., Geological Society of America, Boulder, CO, 1994, 29–50.
2. Baldwin, R. B., *The Face of the Moon*, Chicago, University of Chicago Press, 1949.
3. Breed, C. S. and Grow, T., Morphology and distribution of dunes in sand seas observed by remote sensing, in *A Study of Global Sand Seas*, McKee, E. D., Ed., U.S. Geological Survey, Professional Paper 1052, 1979.
4. Brodley, C. E., Lane, T., and Stough, T. M., Knowledge discovery and data mining, *Am. Sci.*, 87, 54–61, 1999.
5. Dence, M. R., A comparative structural and petrographic study of probable Canadian meteorite craters, *Meteoritics*, 2, 249–270, 1964.
6. Enzmann, R. D., Introduction to the section on signatures, *Ann. N. Y. Acad. Sci.*, 140(2), 154–156, 1966.
7. Evans, I. S., General geomorphometry, derivatives of altitude and descriptive statistics, in *Spatial Analysis in Geomorphology*, Chorley, R. J., Ed., Harper and Row, New York, 1972, 17–90.
8. Evans, I. S. and Cox, N. J., Geomorphometry and the operational definition of cirques. *Area*, 6, 150–153, 1974.
9. Fielder, G., The measurement of lunar altitudes by photography–I. Estimating the true lengths of shadows, *Planetary Space Sci.*, 9, 917–928, 1962.
10. Garvin, J. B. and Frawley, J. J., Geometric properties of Martian impact craters—preliminary results from the Mars Orbiter Laser Altimeter, *Geophysical Res. Lett.*, 25, 4405–4408, 1998.
11. Gelautz, M., Frick, H., Raggam, J., Burgstaller, J., and Leberl, F., SAR image simulation and analysis of alpine terrain, *ISPRS J. Photogrammetry Remote Sensing*, 53, 17–38, 1998.
12. Gibson, J. J., *The Perception of the Visual World*, Houghton–Mifflin, Boston, 1950.
13. Gilbert, G. K., The Moon's face, *Bull. Philos. Soc. Wash.*, 12, 241–292, 1893.
14. Green, J., Tidal and gravity effects intensifying lunar defluidization and volcanism, *Ann. N. Y. Acad. Sci.*, 123(2), 403–469, 1965.
15. Grieve, R., Terrestrial impact: the record in the rocks, *Meteoritics*, 26, 175–194, 1991.
16. Hartmann, W. K., Discovery of multi-ring basins: Gestalt perception in planetary science, in *Multi-Ring Basins, Proceedings Lunar and Planetary Science*, 12A, Schultz, P. H. and Merrill, R. B., Eds., Pergamon Press, New York, 1981, 79–90.
17. Hartmann, W. K. and Kuiper, G. P., Concentric structures surrounding lunar basins, *Commun. Lunar Planetary Lab.*, 1, 1962, 51–66.
18. Herrick, R. R. and Phillips, R. J., Implications of a global survey of Venusian impact craters, *Icarus*, 111, 387–416, 1994.
19. Hoffman, R. R., What's a hill? Computing the meaning of topographic and physiographic terms, in *Linguistic Approaches to Artificial Intelligence*, Schmitz, U., Schutz, R., and Kunz, A., Eds., Peter Lang Verlag, Frankfurt, 1990, 97–128.
20. Hoffman, R. R. and Pike, R. J., On the specification of the information available for the perception and description of the natural terrain, in *Local Applications of*

the Ecological Approach to Human-Machine Systems, Hancock, P., Flach, J., Caird, J., and Vicente, K., Eds., Erlbaum, Hillsdale, NJ, 1995, 285–323.

21. Horn, B. K. P. and Brooks, M. J., Eds., *Shape From Shading,* MIT Press, Cambridge, 1989.

22. Horton, R. E., Erosional development of streams and their drainage basins, hydrophysical approach to quantitative morphology, *Geol. Soc. Am. Bull.,* 56, 275–370, 1945.

23. Janes, D. M., Squyres, S. W., Bindschadler, D. L., Baer, G., Schubert, G., Sharpton, V. L., and Stofan, E. R., Geophysical models for the formation and evolution of coronae on Venus, *J. Geophysical Res.,* 97, 16,055–16,067, 1992.

24. Jarvis, R. S. and Clifford, N. J., Specific geomorphometry, in *Geomorphological Techniques,* Goudie, A. et al., Eds., Unwin Hyman, London, 1990, 63–70.

25. Johnson, G. G. and Vand, V., Application of a Fourier data smoothing technique to the meteoritic crater Ries Kessel, *J. Geophysical Res.,* 72, 1741–1750, 1967.

26. Knight, J., Morphological and morphometric analyses of drumlin bedforms in the Omagh Basin, north central Ireland, *Geografiska Annaler,* 79A, 255–266, 1997.

27. MacDonald, T. L., On the determination of relative lunar altitudes, *J. Br. Astronomical Assoc.,* 41, 367–379, 1931a.

28. MacDonald, T. L., The distribution of lunar altitudes, *J. Br. Astronomical Assoc.,* 41, 172–183 and 228–239, 1931b.

29. Melosh, H. J., *Impact Cratering—a Geologic Process,* Oxford University Press, New York, 1989.

30. Melosh, H. J., Missing rings, *Nature,* 368, 24, 1994.

31. Melosh, H. J., Multi-ringed revelation, *Nature,* 390, 439–440, 1997.

32. Melosh, H. J. and McKinnon, W. B., The mechanics of ringed basin formation, *Geophysical Res. Lett.,* 5, 985–988, 1978.

33. Melton, M. A., Correlation structure of morphometric properties of drainage systems and their controlling agents, *J. Geol.,* 66, 442–460, 1958.

34. Neuenschwander, G., Morphometrische Begriffe, eine kritische Übersicht auf Grund der Literatur, Universität Zürich, Inaugural-Dissertation, 1944.

35. Newman, E. B., Paradis, A. R., and Brabb, E. E., Feasibility and Cost of Using a Computer to Prepare Landslide Susceptibility Maps of the San Francisco Bay Region, California, U.S. Geological Survey, Bulletin 1443, 1978.

36. Nilsen, T. H., Wright, R. H., Vlasic, T. C., and Spangle, W. E., Relative Slope Stability and Land-Use Planning in the San Francisco Bay Region, California, U.S. Geological Survey, Professional Paper 944, 1979.

37. Nowicki, A. L., Lunar Topographic Mapping at the Army Map Service, U.S. Army Map Service, Washington, D.C., Technical Report 37, 1961.

38. Oreskes, N., *The Rejection of Continental Drift—Theory and Method in American Science,* Oxford University Press, New York, 1999.

39. Pike, R. J., Schroeter's rule and the modification of lunar crater impact morphology, *J. Geophysical Res.,* 72, 2099–2106, 1967.

40. Pike, R. J., Meteoritic Origin and Consequent Endogenic Modification of Large Lunar Craters—A Study in Analytical Geomorphology, U.S. Geological Survey, Open-file report 1158, 1969.

41. Pike, R. J., Geometric similitude of lunar and terrestrial craters, in *Proc. 24th Int. Geological Congr.,* 15, Montreal, Canada, 1972, 41–47.

42. Pike, R. J., Craters on Earth, Moon, and Mars—multivariate classification and mode of origin, *Earth Planetary Sci. Lett.,* 22, 245–255, 1974.

43. Pike, R. J., Volcanoes on the inner planets: some preliminary comparisons of gross topography, *Proc. 9th Lunar and Planetary Sci. Conf.*, Lunar and Planetary Institute, Houston, 1978, 3239–3273.

44. Pike, R. J., Apollo 15–17 Orbital Investigations—Geometric Interpretation of Lunar Craters, U.S. Geological Survey, Professional Paper 1046-C, 1980a.

45. Pike, R. J., Formation of complex impact craters: evidence from Mars and other planets, *Icarus*, 43, 1–19, 1980b.

46. Pike, R. J., Comment on "A schematic model of crater modification by gravity" by H. J. Melosh, *J. Geophysical Res.*, 88, 2500–2504, 1983.

47. Pike, R. J., Some morphologic systematics of complex impact structures, *Meteoritics*, 20, 49–68, 1985.

48. Pike, R. J., The geometric signature—quantifying landslide-terrain types from digital elevation models, *Mathematical Geol.*, 20, 491–511, 1988a.

49. Pike, R. J., Geomorphology of impact craters on Mercury, in *Mercury*, Vilas, F., Chapman, C. R., and Matthews, M. S., Eds., University of Arizona Press, Tucson, 1988b, 165–273.

50. Pike, R. J., Machine visualization of synoptic topography by digital image processing, Selected Papers in the Applied Computer Sciences 1992, Wiltshire, D. A., Ed., U.S. Geological Survey, Bulletin 2016, 1992, B1–B12.

51. Pike, R. J., Geomorphometry—progress, practice and prospect, in *Z. f. Geomorphologie N.F. Supple.-Bd.*, 101, Pike, R. J. and Dikau, R., Eds., 21–238, 1995.

52. Pike, R. J. and Spudis, P. D., Basin-ring spacing on the Moon, Mercury, and Mars, *Earth, Moon, Planets*, 39, 129–194, 1987.

53. Pohn, H. A. and Offield, T. W., Lunar Crater Morphology and Relative Age Determination of Lunar Geologic Units—Part 1, Classification, U.S. Geological Survey, Professional Paper, 700, C153–C162, 1970.

54. Pritt, M. D., Phase unwrapping by means of multigrid techniques for interferometric SAR, *IEEE Trans. Geoscience Remote Sensing*, 34, 728–738, 1996.

55. Rackham, T. W., Measurements and reductions of relative lunar altitudes, in *Measure of the Moon*, Kopal, Z. and Goudas, C., Eds., Gordon and Breach/Science Publishers, New York, 1967, 414–423.

56. Rodríguez-Iturbe, I., and Rinaldo, A., *Fractal River Basins: Chance and Self-Organization*, Cambridge University Press, Cambridge, 1997.

57. Sarnthein, M. and Walger, E., Der äolische Sandstrom aus der W-Sahara zur Atlantikküste, *Geologische Rundsch.*, 64, 1065–1087, 1975.

58. Schaber, G. G., Strom, R. G., Moore, H. J., Soderblom, L. A., Kirk, R. L., Chadwick, D. J., Dawson, D. D., Gaddis, L. R., Boyce, J. M., and Russell, J., Geology and distribution of impact craters on Venus—what are they telling us? *J. Geophysical Res.*, 97, 13,257–13,301, 1992.

59. Schenk, P. M., Crater formation and modification on the icy satellites of Uranus and Saturn—depth/diameter and central peak occurrence, *J. Geophysical Res.*, 94, 3813–3832, 1989.

60. Schröter, J. H. *Selenotopographische Fragmente zur genauern Kenntniss der Mondfläche, ihrer erlittenen Veränderungen und Atmosphäre*, 1, self-published, Helmstädt: Carl Gottfried Fleckeisen, Lilienthal, Germany, 1791.

61. Sharpton, V. L., Burke, K., Camargo-Zanoguera, A., Hall, S. A., Lee, D. S., Martin, L. E., Suarez-Reynoso, G., Quezada-Muneton, J. M., Spudis, P. D., and Urrutia-Fucugauchi, J., Chicxulub multi-ring impact basin: size and other characteristics derived from gravity analysis, *Science*, 261, 1564–1567, 1993.

62. Shoemaker, E. M., Interpretation of lunar craters, in *Physics and Astronomy of the Moon*, Kopal, Z., Ed., Academic Press, London, 1962, 283–359.
63. Spray, J. G. and Thompson, L. M., Friction melt distribution in a multi-ring impact basin, *Nature*, 373, 130–132, 1995.
64. Spudis, P. D., Comment concerning the review by W. B. McKinnon and R. Korotev of P. D. Spudis' book, *The Geology of Multi-Ring Basins*, *Geochimica Cosmochimica Acta*, 59, 2633–2635, 1995.
65. Watters, T. R. and Robinson, M. S., Radar and photoclinometric studies of wrinkle ridges on Mars, *J. Geophysical Res.*, 102, 10,889–10,903, 1997.
66. Welch, R., Jordan, T., Lang, H., and Murakami, H., ASTER as a source for topographic data in the late 1990s, *IEEE Trans. Geoscience Remote Sensing*, 36, 1282–1289, 1998.
67. Wilhelms, D. E., The Geologic History of the Moon, U.S. Geological Survey, Professional Paper 1348, 1987.
68. Williams, K. K. and Zuber, M. T., Measurement and analysis of lunar basin depths from Clementine altimetry, *Icarus*, 131, 107–122, 1998.
69. Zebker, H. A., Farr, T. G., Salazar, R. P., and Dixon, T. H., Mapping the world's topography using radar interferometry—the TOPSAT mission, *Proc. IEEE*, 82, 1774–1786, 1994.

Figure 2.1 A perspectival display illustrating the incorporation of multiple data types. From Treinish, L. A., and Rothfusz, L., *Proceedings of the Thirteenth International Conference on Interactive Information and Processing Systems for Meteorology, Oceanography and Hydrology,* 31-34, 1997. With permission.

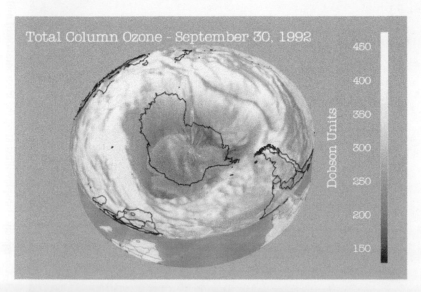

Figure 2.2 A perspectival display demonstrating a warping transformation. From Treinish, L. A. and Rothfusz, L., *Proceedings of the Thirteenth International Conference on Interactive Information and Processing Systems for Meteorology, Oceanography and Hydrology,* 31-34, 1997. With permission.

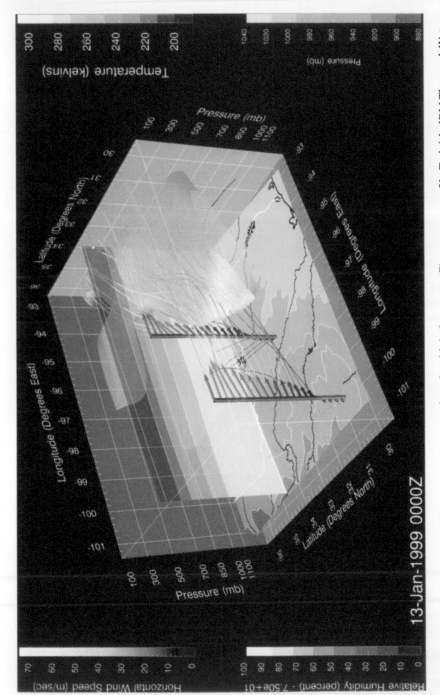

Figure 2.3 A perspectival display illustrating the incorporation of multiple data types. (Figure courtesy of L. Treinish, IBM Thomas J. Watson Research Center.)

Figure 2.4 An aerial thermogram of a suburban area. Indiana State University Thermography Project. With permission.

Figure 2.5 An aerial thermogram of a rural area. Indiana State University Thermography Project. With permission.

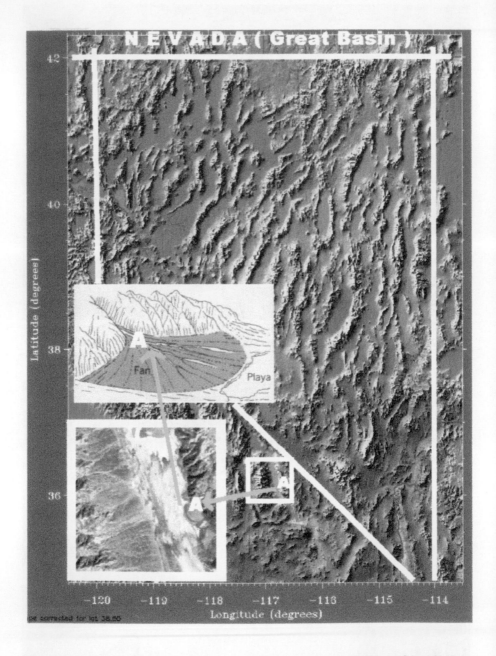

Figure 3.1 Study area. The state of Nevada as it appears in the color landform Atlas of U.S.A. [27]. The Death Valley Intermontane Basin is pointed out and an enlarged view of the basin in a Landsat TM image is provided. A block diagram showing an alluvial fan (A) is included. (From Sterner, R., 1999, http://fermi.jhvapl.edu/states/maps1/nv.gif. With Permission.)

Figure 5.1 A light-amplified scene showing forested area including a workshed (background) and a rock pile (foreground). (Image courtesy of American Technologies Network Corporation.)

Figure 6.3 Three color-fused versions of the nighttime scene shown in Figure 6.1. Fusion by the NRL method (top), the UCB method (middle), and the MIT-LL method (bottom). See text for details of fusion methods. The color images from all three methods appear to lose some of the detail apparent in the image-intensifier image of Figure 6.1. (The UCB image was provided by Frank Werblin and the NRL and MIT-LL versions are reprinted with permission from Steele and Perconti (1997), SPIE.)

Figure 6.4 Nighttime imagery taken with a visible daylight camera (top left), an IR camera (bottom left), and the sensor fused versions of the same scene (grayscale fusion top right, color fusion bottom right). (Images courtesy of Frank Werblin.)

Figure 6.5 An example of color-fused imagery created from three input bands rather than two. The visible image is shown on the top left, the long-wave IR image on the bottom left, and the mid-wave IR image on the top right. The three-color fused image created from these three sensor bands is shown at the bottom right. (Images courtesy of Dean Scribner.)

Figure 6.6 A nighttime scene taken with a visible camera (top left), an IR camera (bottom left), and the sensor fused versions of the same scene (gray-scale fusion, top right; color-fusion, bottom right). See text for details. (Images courtesy of Lex Toet.)

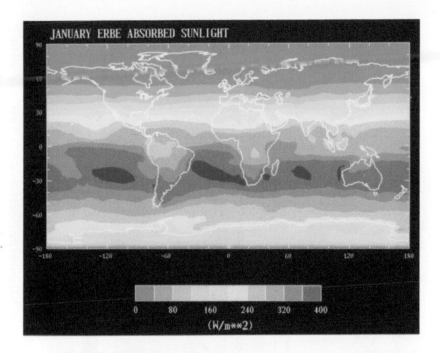

Figure 8.1 False color contour map of the five-year mean values of solar radiation flux absorbed by the Earth in January (in units of watts per square meter), derived from satellite measurements made by the Earth Radiation Budget Experiment (ERBE).

Figure 8.3 A false-color composite image of the clouds of Jupiter taken by the Voyager 1 imaging system. The Great Red Spot is visible in the upper right. (Photo courtesy of NASA.)

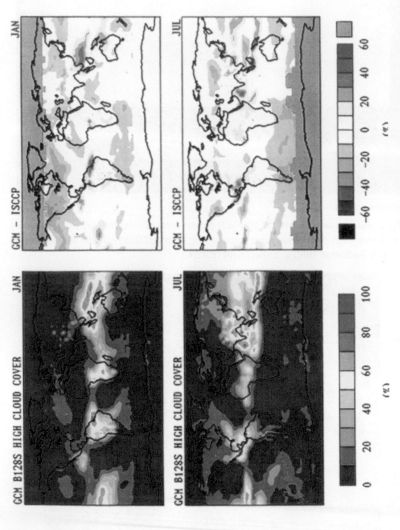

Figure 8.4 Left: Color contour map of monthly mean cirrus cloud coverage (%) simulated by the NASA Goddard Institute for Space Studies global climate model for (upper) January and (lower) July. Right: Differences in cirrus cloud coverage (%) between the simulations at the left and data acquired from visible and infrared satellite imagery by the International Satellite Cloud Climatology Project (ISCCP). The color contour resolution of 10 (%) is comparable to the accuracy of the ISCCP satellite retrieval of cloud cover. (Photos courtesy of NASA.)

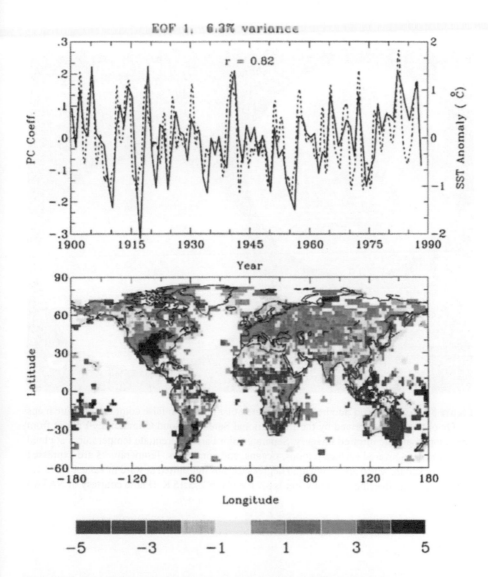

Figure 8.7 Top: the first PC of the record of observed monthly precipitation variations over land for the twentieth century (solid line), and the time series of SST anomalies in the equatorial east Pacific, an indicator of El Niño (dashed line). Bottom: the corresponding first EOF of the twentieth century land precipitation record, with blue indicating wetter than normal conditions at times when the PC coefficient is positive, and orange/red indicating drier conditions at these times. From Dai, A., et al., *J. Climate,* 10, 2943-2962, 1997. (Photos courtesy of NASA.)

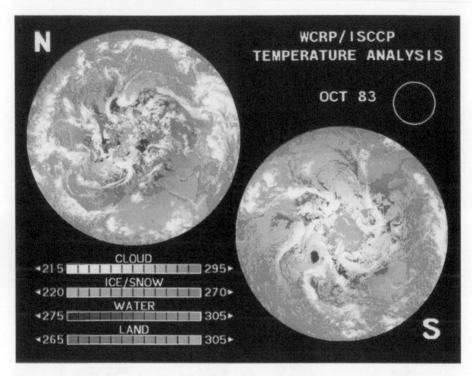

Figure 8.8 Northern and Southern Hemisphere polar projection false color temperature maps for October 1, 1983, derived by the International Satellite Cloud Climatology Project from operational satellite infrared imagery. Separate color bars differentiate temperatures at cloud tops, ice/snow-covered surface regions, oceans, and continents. Temperatures are expressed in units of kelvin, which are identical to degrees Celsius but shifted upward in value by 273.15. For example, the freezing point of water is 32°F = 0°C = 273.15 K. (Photo courtesy of NASA.)

Observed Sea Surface Temperature (°C)

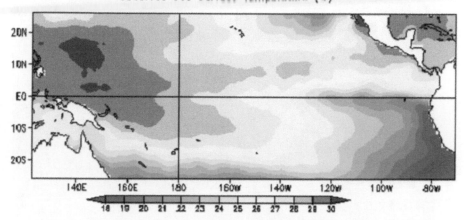

Observed Sea Surface Temperature Anomalies (°C)

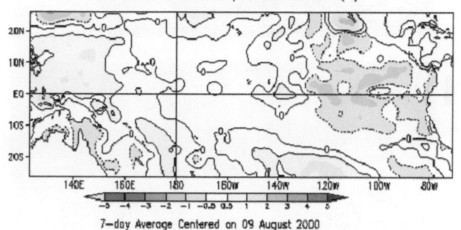

7-day Average Centered on 09 August 2000

Figure 9.10 Using satellites, ships, and data buoys, NOAA scientists create maps showing sea surface temperatures and departures from average in order to monitor the onset and demise of events such as El Niño and La Niña. (Maps courtesy of NOAA's Climate Prediction Center — http://www.cpc.ncep.noaa.gov/products/analysis_monitoring/lanina/.)

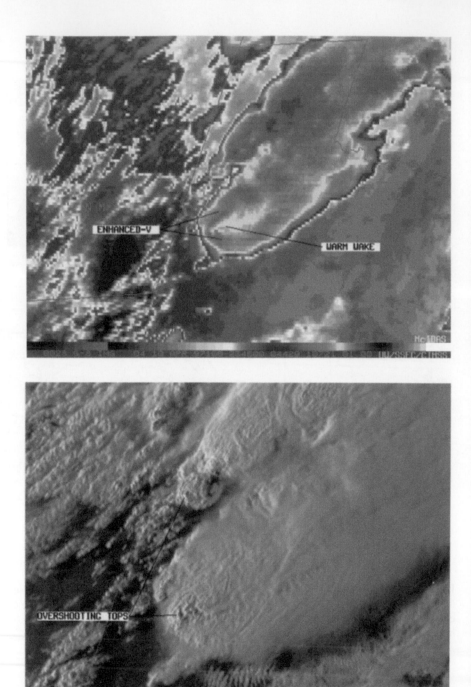

Figure 9.15 (Top) A color-enhanced infrared image showing the temperature pattern associated with an enhanced-v cloud-top signature. (Bottom) The corresponding visible image. (GOES images courtesy of the University of Wisconsin — http://cimss.ssec.wisc.edu/goes/misc/warm_wake.html.)

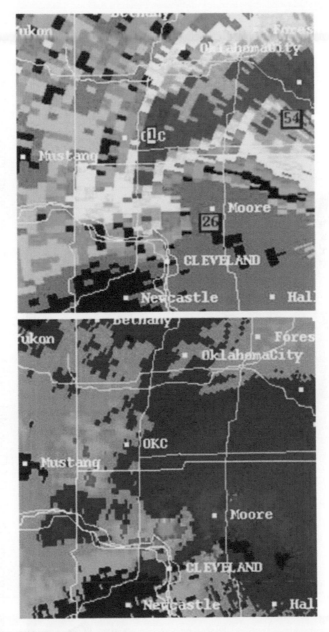

Figure 9.16 NEXRAD base reflectivity and velocity images for a major tornado event on May 3, 1999. Base reflectivity shows the classic "hook-shaped" image associated with a tornado just west-southwest of Moore, Oklahoma. Velocity data show a corresponding gate-to-gate (or pixel-to-pixel) shear of velocity inward toward the radar (green) and outward from the radar (red). This wind shear couplet shows two parts of a corresponding complete circulation pattern. (Image courtesy of NOAA's National Severe Storms Laboratory (http://www.nssl.noaa.gov/~tsmith/may3/0017-8panel.gif.)

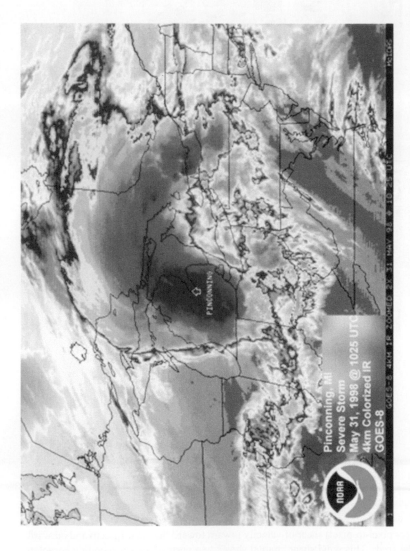

Figure 9.18 A large mesoscale convective complex (MCC) over Michigan on May 31, 1998. In this enhanced infrared image, the coldest and highest cloud tops (and the clouds likely producing the heaviest rainfall) are indicated by purple. Reds also show heavy rainfall. The rounded pattern of this weather feature makes it easy to identify. (GOES image courtesy of NOAA's National Climatic Data Center – http://www.ncdc.noaa.gov/pub/data/images/storm-pincon-19980531-g8ir.gif.)

section three

Seeing the Invisible

chapter five

On the Psychophysics of Night Vision Goggles*

William R. Uttal and Randall W. Gibb

Contents

Keywords: *light amplification, psychophysical methods, visual noise, contrast sensitivity, form detection, form recognition, visual acuity*

---

*This chapter contains material that has been abstracted and updated from previous publications (Uttal, Baruch, and Allen, [17]; Gibb, [7]).

5.1   Introduction

Perhaps more than any other of the remote sensing systems described in this book, the most intimate and personal is the night vision goggle (NVG). This device literally sits on the face of the observer and acts as an extended and immediate transducer of the physical stimulus in a way that is not too different from the transduction mechanism of the human eye. As such, the NVG can be considered an "extension" of the visual system and can be studied in terms of its fundamental psychophysics.

Scientific psychophysics is not a familiar concept for many engineers and other physical scientists. Psychophysics is the science responsible for the study of the relationship between human psychological responses and the physical aspects of stimuli. For over a century, a set of highly structured experimental methods (see [6,13,14,16]) has been developed that are designed to minimize experimenter and procedural bias to produce both reliable and valid measures of human performance. The discussion of our experimental results in this chapter has the additional role of introducing psychophysical methodology to our readers.

The results obtained when using the methods of psychophysics are particularly precise and valid in the study of the sensory processes. We now have very accurate measures of the sensory effects of wavelength, contrast, luminance, and many other parameters of visual perception. We know the dynamic range of vision as well as the other senses. Readers interested in these topics will find them fully described in two of our earlier books.[14,15]

The application of the highly structured psychophysical methodology to NVG technology has not been used as often as less formal experimental designs. There has been considerable study of NVGs in complex visual settings; it is only in recent years that highly controlled laboratory studies have been carried out in which the quantified parameters of the situation have been carefully manipulated and precisely measured.[2] In most earlier studies, simple comparative tests were made between situations in which NVGs were used and when they were not. Typical of the traditional approach was the work of Wiley, Glick, Bucha, and Park[18] in which the effect of NVGs on depth perception was studied using a modified Howard-Dohlman apparatus (a simple device that tested the limits of depth perception by the alignment of two vertical sticks). The basic independent variable in this case was only the presence or absence of the NVG device. Other applied problems such as the compatibility of aircraft cockpit lighting (e.g., [3]), the adjustment procedures for setting up the NVG for optimum use (e.g., [1]), or even the biomechanics of helmet loading when a NVG is attached (e.g., [5]) are still the targets of most contemporary investigations.

There is, however, another direction not often taken in this applied field, in which the goal is to consider the variables of the NVG to be continuous— to define independent and dependent variables, and then to manipulate one and measure the other. This is the classic psychophysical approach and the one we pursue in this chapter. To show how this can provide important insights into NVGs that may be obscure, we present the results of two series of experiments, both of which explore the fundamental differences between unaided normal vision and NVG enhanced vision.

5.2   A brief tutorial on NVGs

To understand the substantial effects of NVGs on human visual perception, it is necessary to understand the engineering underlying these devices that permits humans to see in nearly total darkness. NVGs provide an intensified image of scenes illuminated by ambient light in the red and near infrared part of the electromagnetic spectrum, with wavelengths varying from approximately 600 to 1000 nm. The level of ambient light in which an NVG can operate is surprisingly small. Scenes become visible in situations that may seem to be totally dark to even a moderately dark adapted eye. Reflected star light is sufficient illumination to produce a bright image. An example of a light-amplified image appears in Figure 5.1.

It should also be appreciated that NVGs work only because they are used at night. During the daytime, the huge amount of red and near infrared light produced by the sun would swamp the devices. It is only when the amount of this radiation is small that the device will work; fortunately, that is also only when it is needed. The near infrared region is also a desirable range to work in because it greatly simplifies the engineering complexity of the device. Longer wavelengths of infrared radiation would require refrigerated sensitive media.

Figure 5.1   A light-amplified scene showing forested area including a workshed (background) and a rock pile (foreground). See color version of this figure in the color section following page 114. (Image courtesy of American Technologies Network Corporation.)

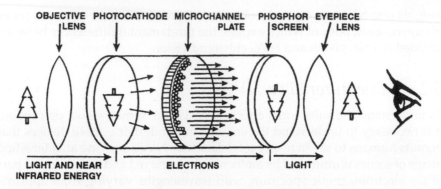

Figure 5.2   A diagram of a typical night vision viewing device.

NVG technology depends upon principles of photoelectric emission and multiplication that are well known. As shown in Figure 5.2, ambient light enters the goggle through an objective lens that brings the image into sharp focus on a photocathode—a source of photoelectric electrons. The relatively small number of electrons emitted from the photocathode is then amplified and accelerated by an ingenious device called a microchannel plate. It is this device that mainly accounts for the fine resolution of the scene achieved by an NVG. The microchannel plate maintains the spatial focus of the image but greatly increases the number of electrons that were originally generated by the infrared light. The enhanced output of the microchannel plate is then pro- jected, under the influence of an accelerating voltage, onto a phosphor screen which converts the stream of electrons into a perceptually useful luminance level. The final image is viewed directly through an eyepiece lens.

The emitted visible light, typically of a greenish hue, varies only in inten- sity and, thus, although not literally monochromatic, mimics a black and white colored image more than it does a fully colored one. The key factor, however, is that the increase in both the total number of photoelectric elec- trons and their velocity results in an intensified image on the NVG that can be 3000 times or more brighter than the original scene. Output luminances from a typical NVG can be as high as 5 or cd/m^2 (candles per square meter). Image resolution is diminished compared to a daylight scene but can be improved by placing the objective lens, the photocathode, the microchannel plate, and the phosphorescent screen close together. The entire system may be only a couple of inches long in a well-designed modern system such as the F4949 or the AN/PVS-7.

NVGs employ an automatic brilliance control (ABC) feature that acts to maintain a constant overall image luminance by decreasing the gain across the microchannel plate when the total input light level exceeds a pre- determined threshold. This helps to minimize the blooming or veiling when an intense light source emits energy in that portion of the electromagnetic spectrum in which the goggle is sensitive. Otherwise, the details of the image would be obscured or (occasionally) the display phosphor burned.

The main advantage of NVG devices is that they raise scene luminance sufficiently to allow the observer to see in what would otherwise be visually a completely dark situation. Unfortunately, this enormous advantage is counterbalanced by a number of image distorting and degrading visual effects that pose serious challenges to the human perceptual system. It must be clearly understood that NVGs do not provide anything close to normal visual conditions. These distortions must be understood by the user if these devices are to be used in effective ways and to avoid demanding more from the technology than should be reasonably expected. These distortions are not always understood by the user. A common problem is that the user may get overconfident when using these image enhancing devices, creating a feeling of invincibility. In reality, the typical NVG provides a visual experience that is drastically deficient compared to normal daylight vision.

Understanding the perceptually relevant properties of existing devices is also important for the design of future generations of NVGs so that they can be progressively improved. All too often, the design engineers responsible for improving these devices are oblivious to the implications of engineering changes for these primarily visual devices.

The list of visual distortions introduced by the use of NVG is not long, but includes some parameters that are familiar to vision scientists, if not to engineers. It includes:

1. Monochromatic (typically greenish) images
2. Low contrast (especially at high luminance levels because of the ABC)
3. Low resolution
4. Nonlinear luminance changes
5. Scintillation interference
6. Geometrical artifacts (Honeycomb patterns)
7. Susceptibility to interference from other sources of ambient light other than that which is desired such as lightning
8. Image persistence effects due to the long decay time of the phosphors used in NVGs; this distortion can lead to trails as the field of view of the NVG is swept across point sources
9. Reduced depth perception, both because of a reduction in monocular cues and binocular cues such as stereopsis. (There is still uncertainty in the literature concerning the impact of NVG on stereoscopic viewing. It is not yet agreed that it is possible to have good stereopsis with this viewing device, but it is clear that the absence of this cue to depth perception has played a role in some formation flying accidents, particularly with helicopters.)

Clearly, NVGs do not provide anything like normal views and extensive basic research is needed to understand the fundamental limits and aberrations that are introduced into this very different kind of visual task. In this chapter, we report two series of psychophysical studies that we carried out to study NVG vision. The first used a model display in which we simulated the distortions that were introduced by NVG so that they could be studied under well controlled laboratory conditions. It was aimed at gauging the effects of the luminance, contrast, and scintillation distortions just mentioned. The second series was concerned with contrast sensitivity and the influence of colored ambient light, a common problem in aircraft cockpits. The second series, unlike the first, used a real, rather than a simulated NVG. Because of the application of precise psychophysical techniques, both series led to an enhanced understanding of how a human perceives when using these devices.

5.3   Experiment Series I: psychophysical studies using an NVG simulation

It is difficult to manipulate the parameters of actual NVG devices in a way that permits controlled psychophysical studies. For example, the ABC overrides any effort to manipulate contrast or luminance by the experimenter. Therefore, we developed a simulation of the device. An important issue when one substitutes a model for the reality is, how close does the model we use fit the actual system? There will be some obvious discrepancies. For example, the "greenish" appearing emission spectrum of night vision displays is different from that of the black-and-white computer display used in this study. The critical issue, however, is that both the model and the actual devices display images that vary only in luminosity and are essentially constant in their respective chromaticity.

The range of luminosity values (2 to 14 cd/m^2) used in the experiments reported here overlapped the maximum luminance range required for night vision devices by the U.S. Air Force (USAF) (2.77 to 5.54 cd/m^2). [Values obtained from USAF specifications document MIL-A-49425(CR).] Direct measurements were made with a Tektronix J17 photometer of the luminance of an ITT ANVIS model 6(4) night vision system. Luminance values varying between 4.0 and 4.5 cd/m^2 for a white field and 3.3 to 3.7 cd/m^2 for a field containing high contrast gratings were obtained. Since our experimentally controlled luminance values (2 to 14 cd/m^2) bracketed these empirically measured values, our model system both conforms to and exceeds the actual photometric luminance levels obtainable displayed by NVGs. Since the light levels of the NVG are technically constrained, it would not have been possible to use them as the experimental tools for exploring the luminance variable.

The viewing region defined by the visual interference was 512 × 480 pixels and 10.9 × 12.2° of visual angle in extent on the face of an Apollo 3000 graphic work station. As a general calibration procedure, the luminance of a test pattern consisting of fully illuminated screen (i.e., all pixels set to white) was regularly adjusted to 36 cd/m^2 with the Tektronix photometer in the presence of the ambient veiling light.

There is one major way in which our simulation differed from the real viewing situation. We chose to use a brief exposure (100+ msec) rather than the continuous observation time typical of real NVG usage. Brevity of exposure is traditionally used as technique to separate the psychophysical proportion of preattentive visual processes from the processes involved in long term attentive scrutiny or search within a complex visual scene. Unless this form of temporal degradation is used, it would be impossible to distinguish the immediate psychophysical effects in which we were interested from those "higher level" and longer-term search processes.

5.3.1 Stimulus materials

A typical stimulus frame (one of two sequentially presented in the same position showing the appearance of the image presented in moderate amounts of visual interference) is shown in Figure 5.3.

The task required the observer to detect a simple geometrical form (e.g., a square, see Figure 5.3) outlined by illuminated pixels embedded in a background of variable amounts of randomly positioned illuminated pixels. The randomly illuminated pixels tend to degrade the image. As their density

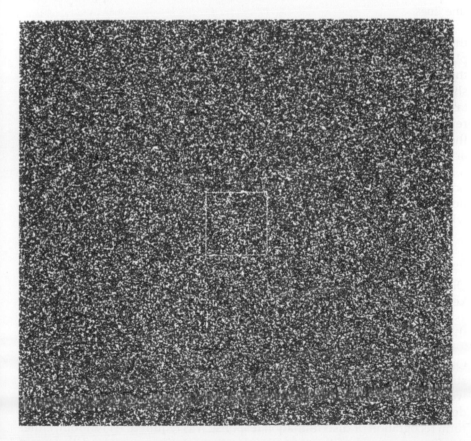

Figure 5.3 A typical stimulus frame showing one of the target stimuli embedded in visual interference with a density of 40%.

increases, these "visual noise" dots make the detection task more difficult in a manner that is analogous to the degradation of target detectability in night vision viewing devices when scintillation artifacts increase. The density of this visual interference is defined as the proportion of illuminated pixels (i.e., pixels set to the "white" level for each condition of this study). The visual interference was generated by applying a probabilistic rule that determined whether a white dot was placed in each of the 245, 760 pixel locations of the viewing region on the display screen. The higher the probability, the more pixels were present and the more difficult it is to detect the target stimulus. Of course, as the number of illuminated pixels increased, so did the overall luminance of the screen. As we shall see later, however, overall luminance has a negligible effect on this task.

The target stimuli usually consisted of samples chosen from a library of three different sizes of four outlined polygonal forms (i.e., a triangle, a square, a pentagon, and a hexagon). The outlines defining the forms were one pixel wide so the forms were constructed from what appeared to be fine lines.

In each trial, the target stimulus was placed at random anywhere within the region of the screen defined by the visual interference. A limit of displacement was used to avoid any stimulus being clipped as it extended over the edge of the visual interference-defined viewing region. The variations in shapes, sizes, and positions were utilized to add uncertainty to the observer's task and to avoid detection based on partial features or familiarity with a repeated location. Large differences were observed in the detachabilities of the different shapes. However, most of these differences were attributable to artifactual distortions due the staircase aliasing of diagonal lines. Outline forms of the kind used here do not, therefore, permit us to answer the question of the effect of form on detection. It should be noted that this is a distortion produced by our simulation and would not occur in the actual NVG where the resolution is somewhat finer.

5.3.2   General procedure

Observers signed into each session by typing their names on the computer keyboard. This initiated a sequence of actions in which the experiment assigned for that session was loaded and the computer configured to present the appropriate stimuli.

The experimental task utilized a two-alternative, forced-choice design. Observers were instructed to specify which of two sequentially presented stimuli in each experimental trial contained a target form. Since the observers were not required to specify which form had been presented, this was a detection task. Although the form of the target might affect detection, no form recognition or discrimination response was required. At random, either the first or second of the two stimulus presentations contained the target form. The other consisted solely of visual interference.

A trial consisted of a sequence of visual displays on the CRT. The observer was first presented with a fixation point at the center of the display. This was followed by a 500 msec blank period. The first stimulus display was then presented for 100 msec (plus the persistence time of the display). A blank screen was then presented for 1025 msec. It was followed by the second stimulus display; the temporal duration of which was the same as the first. Following another 500 msec blank period, the observer was presented with a question mark and was instructed to only then respond by pushing the left or right mouse button to indicate that the first or second display, respectively, appeared to contain the target stimulus. As soon as the observer responded, the fixation point for the next trial was displayed and the cycle repeated. Observers were instructed to rest as needed during the course of the experiment by simply delaying their response. The activity level of the observers was monitored in an adjacent room by means of another computer display.

The dependent variable in each case was the percentage of correct responses (i.e., the proportion of the time that the observers correctly specified in which of the two sequential presentations the target form had been inserted). Since this was a two-alternative paradigm, purely random behavior associated with total nondetectability would produce a score of 50%. Scores above 97% were considered to represent perfect detectability diluted by a few random response selection errors or flagging attention. Furthermore, since this was a forced choice procedure, variations in the observer's personal criterion level were tightly controlled. This is a very important advantage of this method—observers are forced to make a positive decision and, therefore, are not permitted any uncontrolled flexibility in deciding where their threshold for accepting or rejecting the perceptual existence of a stimulus lay.

5.3.3   Experiment 1

In the initial experiment, the density of the visual interference was the main independent variable. In our simulation, this interference is analogous to the scintillation artifact. The percentage of illuminated pixels varied from 20% to 60% in 10% steps. All twelve stimulus polygonal forms (3 sizes × 4 shapes) were used in this experiment and, as noted previously, presented in random positions in the field of visual interference.

Figure 5.4 plots the major results of this experiment averaged across sizes and for the three stimulus sizes separately. Observers are able to read through the visual interference virtually perfectly at low (20%) interference density levels. Performance at this interference level is in the high 90% range for the detection scores. As the visual interference density increased to 60%, there was a progressive decrease in performance to a detection score of 58%. Throughout Experiment 1, for the range of stimulus sizes we used, Figure 5.3 also shows that the larger the stimulus, the more detectable it was. We

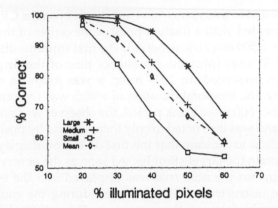

% illuminated pixels

Figure 5.4 The results of Experiment 1 of Experiment Series I, showing the effect of variations in the visual interference density on target detection for the three stimulus sizes separately and for the mean values of the scores for the three sizes.

believe, however, that this size effect is largely determined by the length of the component lines in each form rather than its overall geometrical form.

Long term learning effects on performance were not measured, but supplementary experiments did show improvements in performance in some, but not all, stimulus conditions. Since all conditions were present in each daily session, learning effects were controlled over the course of each experiment.

5.3.4   Experiment 2

In Experiment 2 we varied another of the variables specifically identified as being significant in the operation of amplified night vision viewing devices— the overall luminance of the image. We asked: "What is the effect of image luminance on the detectability of the outline polygonal target stimuli?" This is an important issue because it is often the case that when image luminance is increased, artifacts (e.g., the hexagons produced by the fiber optics of the microchannel plate and reductions in image contrast) are spuriously introduced. Although, some readers may have an *a priori* intuition that increasing the luminance of the screen should improve performance during amplified night vision tasks, this cannot be taken for granted. Luminance-related artifacts are countervailing conditions that suggest that simply increasing luminance should not be done indiscriminately.

It should be noted that our display did not insert any other of the artifacts that the actual night vision viewing devices do. Therefore, the results of this experiment are relatively "pure" estimates of the effect of variation in image luminance unencumbered by these other artifacts.

Luminance was varied in this experiment by adjusting the binary code for image gray-level scale within the computer program and indirectly calibrated with a Tektronix photometer. This luminance level was varied in random order between five binary coded pixel gray levels (112, 144, 176, 208, and 240). These binary codes corresponded to luminances of 1.6, 3.6, 6.4, 9.8, and 13.5 cd/m² , respectively, as measured on a static image of a 42% visual interference density field at each of the luminance levels. These values determined the luminance of both the pixels in the interference and the target stimuli. We did not use lower display luminance, in order to avoid floor effects with the smallest target stimuli utilized.

This means of controlling stimulus luminance (instead, for example, of using neutral density filters) was chosen to meet the needs of a subsequent experiment in which the luminance of the stimulus pattern and the visual interference would be manipulated separately.

The same 12 shapes and sizes of polygonal stimuli used in the first experiment were also utilized in the second experiment. A normative visual interference level of 42% illuminated pixels was used in this experiment to adjust the performance level to about 80% as described in the results of Experiment 1.

Figure 5.5 plots the averaged results for the three stimulus sizes utilized in this experiment for the three stimulus sizes. The main result is a gradual, but relatively slight, diminution of the detectability scores with decreasing luminance. The decline in detectability is not nearly as profound as that produced by increases in the visual interference density obtained in Experiment 1, nor, as we shall see, as that produced by contrast difference between the target stimulus and visual interference as obtained in Experiment 3. In fact, the total decline in detectability over the full range of luminance used in this experiment is comparable to that produced by only a few percent change in visual interference density, as shown in Figure 5.3.

The results of this experiment confirm that the human visual "gain control" mechanism is well adapted to accommodate wide ranges of stimulus

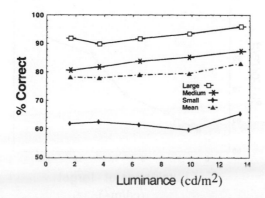

Figure 5.5 The results of Experiment 2 of Experiment Series I, showing the minimal effect of variations in overall display luminance for the three stimulus sizes separately and the mean values of the scores for the three sizes.

luminance with minimal effects on performance, at least in this simulated viewing situation. This human property is complemented by the automatic brilliance control (ABC) of the night vision devices to further mitigate any putative effects of display luminance on performance. In other words, there may be little to be gained by engineering higher luminance NVGs.

5.3.5   Experiment 3

Another major display image factor impacting on target stimulus detectability is the contrast between the target stimulus and the background.[2] The purpose of Experiment 3 was to measure the effect of contrast when the visual system was challenged by the presence of visual interference. We controlled this important contrast variable by using different coded gray-level values for the visual interference and the target stimuli, respectively. In this experiment, as previously, the visual interference density was kept at 42% illuminated pixels and was displayed with a coded gray-level luminance level of 240. The independent variable was the gray-level luminance of the target stimuli, a factor which was randomly selected in each trial from five coded pixel values (176, 192, 208, 224, and 240). These values correspond to photometric luminance measures of 6.4, 7.9, 9.8, 11.3, and 13.4 cd/m^2, respectively. These values were measured with the photometer from a static image consisting of 42% visual interference.

All four of the polygonal stimulus shapes were used, and sequential presentations plotted in random positions on the screen to add uncertainty. However, only the medium size stimuli were used in this experiment because of the proliferation of experimental conditions.

The results of this experiment are shown in Figure 5.6. Unlike the relatively modest effect of overall image luminance (over a wide range of 1.6 to

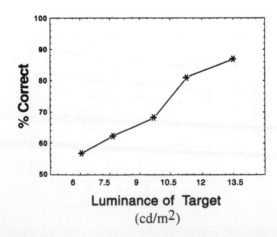

Figure 5.6   The mean values of the results of Experiment 3 of Experiment Series I, in which the luminance of the target stimulus was reduced to increase the contrast between the them and the visual interference.

13.5 cd/m^2), the effect of varying the contrast by reducing target luminance (over a narrow range of 6.4 to 13.5 cd/m^2) was profound. Performance declined from 87% to 57% over this reduced range of target stimulus luminance ranges.

This result is anomalous compared to the usual influence of contrast. Increasing contrast usually increases detectability. It may be that some new or secondary effect is overshadowing the usual kind of contrast effect. One possibility is that the bright visual interference pixels are disrupting the geometry of the stimulus lines. This disruption may overwhelm what would have been a more typical contrast-driven improvement in performance. Whatever the explanation, the result stands: with this stimulus type, reduction in target pixel luminance relative to the luminance of the visual interference definitely reduces detectability.

5.4 Experiment Series II: the effect of NVG viewing on contrast sensitivity

In the second series of experiments, we had two goals; one was general and the other specific. Our general goal was to demonstrate the value of a precise psychophysical methodology in understanding the function of complex display devices like the NVG. Our specific goal was to examine the effect of NVG viewing on the contrast sensitivity function and to evaluate the effect of colored ambient lighting on NVG viewing. Although visual acuity (VA) is the standard form of measuring visual performance among pilots in the U.S. Air Force, it has previously been noted that VA remains constant despite a substantial loss in visual contrast. Therefore, we hypothesized that contrast sensitivity (CS) might be a better measure of visual spatial acuity under degraded viewing conditions. Our research investigates and compares both NVG-aided CS and VA performance with two different kinds of incompatible cockpit lighting (and one baseline condition) used as a degrading parameter much in the same way we used the visual interference in the first series of experiments. By incompatible lighting, we refer to ambient lighting that interferes with the advantages gained when one uses an NVG, typically because of overlapping spectral curves. The fact that the green light used in this experiment was similar to that emitted by the NVG made it particularly important that its interfering effects be understood and the traditional VA measure obscures the performance decrement. We show that the combined assessment procedures in which both CS and VA were measured provided a superior assessment of NVG aided visual performance in conditions of ambient light.

5.4.1 Stimuli and apparatus

A modified Class B NVG filter was used on an ITT F4949D NVG. This combination yielded a 50% spectral response at 665 nm and 1% spectral response at 545 nm. Two charts were used to measure VA. The first was the standard

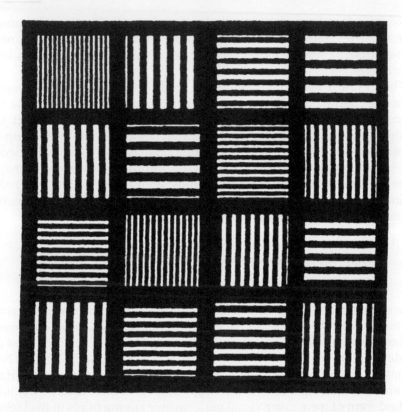

Figure 5.7 The standard NVG resolution test chart described by Reising, Antonio, and Fields.[12]

NVG Resolution chart described by Reising, Antonio, and Fields[12] used to assess NVG-aided VA. This is shown in Figure 5.7.

The second was the USAF 1951 Medium Contrast Resolution Resolving Power Target (otherwise known as the Tri-bar Chart). This is shown in Figure 5.8.

Both charts were positioned randomly in orientation but at a constant viewing distance of 6.1 m from the observer.

Because of the unsuitability of commercially available spatial contrast sensitivity charts, a special CS chart for NVG-aided vision was developed for this research. Two factors had to be considered in the design of this special chart—the ranges of the spatial frequencies and the contrasts suitable for NVG studies. The range of contrasts to be used should range from a qualitative "easily discernible" to "unable to see." The best NVG-aided VA chart previously reported had been in the Snellen eye chart range of 20/45 to 20/60 (equivalent to performance on 13 to 9 c/deg gratings). This value, therefore, defined the highest spatial frequency to be used. The sharp low-frequency fall-off in the standard (high illumination) CS response specified that 3 c/deg would be a satisfactory lower limit for our new chart. The final version of the

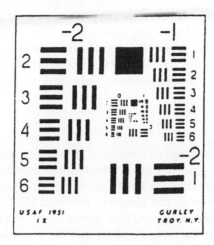

Figure 5.8 The USAF Medium Contrast Resolution Resolving Power Target. (The Tri-bar Chart.)

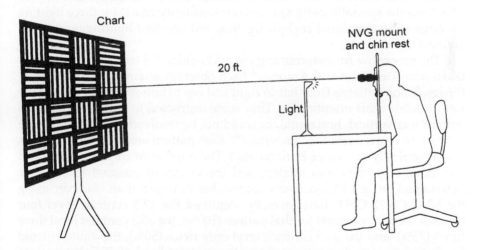

Figure 5.9 A diagram of the experimental apparatus used in Experiment Series II.

chart we developed consisted of 16 levels of contrast for each of the three test spatial frequencies we used—3, 6, and 12 cpd, respectively.

All visual performance charts were illuminated at the equivalent of starlight viewing conditions by a Hoffman Engineering Corporation LS-65-GS integrating sphere. The sphere provides near uniform light distribution on the charts. The illumination level was measured with a Photo Research PR-1530AR NviSpot radiometer fitted with a Class B filter.

The supplemental light source (simulating the ambient light from instruments in a aircraft cockpit) was positioned as shown in Figure 5.9, a diagram of the experimental apparatus. This supplemental light source was colored (in two of the three conditions) by inserting a filter in front of a calibrated incandescent bulb. The green filter that we used was a standard NVIS Green B(NV-2GB) and the red filter was a standard NVIS Red (NV6RC-10). A third lighting condition—no ambient lighting—was also used to establish a baseline condition.

5.4.2 *Procedure*

All observers were evaluated in a viewing lane that was approximately 10 m long and 2 m wide. Prior to dark adaptation, observers were instructed how to read the USAF 1951 Tri-bar Chart in normal room lighting. During this pre-adaptation period, the observer reported the minimum resolvable pattern from a distance of 6.1 m. This preliminary procedure ensured that each observer was familiar with the chart and also provided an unaided base-line VA score. The observer was then seated and the room lights extinguished in the viewing lane. Observers were then allowed 10 minutes to dark adapt and to set up and focus the NVG apparatus. Measurements were then made using all three of the test charts (the NVG Resolution Chart, the USAF Tri-bar Chart and the specially designed contrast sensitivity chart) for three lighting conditions (no simulated cockpit lighting; red ambient lighting; and green ambient lighting).

The procedure for determining the NVG-aided CS using the charts was taken from DeVilbiss and Antonio.[4] Each observer attempted to read all of the resolution patterns from left to right and top to bottom under each of the four possible chart orientations. They were instructed to indicate whether a pattern was vertical, horizontal, or could not be resolved (in which the case the pattern was reported as "uncertain"). Each pattern was viewed four times (twice vertically and twice horizontally). The number of correct vertical and horizontal responses was totaled, and the threshold contrast levels were determined using a 75% correct criterion. For example, if an observer using the NVG CS 12 CPD chart correctly identified the 42.3 contrast level four times of the four attempts for that pattern (100%), the 35.3 contrast level three times (75%), and the 31.5 contrast level only twice (50%), the value entered for that particular observer would be the contrast level of 35.5. If a pattern could not be resolved in any of the four trials, a score of 100 was entered, indicating 100% contrast was required for identification.

The two VA tests were assessed in a similar manner. However, the dependent measures were the Snellen values at which the 75% correct response criterion was achieved.

5.4.3 *Results*

First, we consider the results for the contrast sensitivity measurements. Table 5.1 lists the spatial frequencies and light condition contrast means and standard deviations.

Table 5.1 NVG-aided Contrast Sensitivity Means and Standard Deviations for a 75% Criterion*

	Baseline	Green light	Red light
12 cpd chart			
Mean Contrast	35.69	59.70	87.48
Standard Deviation	10.52	29.87	19.66
6 cpd chart			
Mean	9.48	11.13	14.96
Standard Deviation	2.94	5.31	7.04
3 cpd chart			
Mean	7.00	6.66	8.84
Standard Deviation	1.97	2.27	3.47

*Contrasts are determined by the values used in the special CS chart.

Table 5.2 NVG-aided Visual Acuity Means and Standard Deviations for a 75% Criterion Expressed in Snellen Scores*

	Baseline	Green light	Red light
NVG chart			
Mean	20/49.0	20/55.0	20/65.25
Standard Deviation	4.47	4.29	11.30
1951 Tri-bar chart			
Mean	20/48.50	20/55.45	20/65.43
Standard Deviation	4.23	5.74	8.56

*Standard Deviation values are calculated from the right hand side of the Snellen mean scores.

Table 5.2 lists the mean and standard deviation of the 75% criterion-meeting Snellen values for the corresponding six treatment combinations for the two VA charts and three ambient lighting conditions.

Table 5.3 compares the results for each of the five different charts for the green and red ambient light conditions, respectively. These values reflect the degradation from the baseline (no ambient light) condition. The comparison of the VA and CS results, of course, is being made between percentage difference of two different kinds of units—the Snellen measures and the contrast sensitivity scores. However, this procedure normalizes the scores in a way that permits us to carry out this comparison.

The substantially higher degradation (in terms of the percentage change) indicated in Table 5.3 for the CS tests indicates that the VA tests are not measuring the full effect of ambient lighting either in magnitude or in terms of

Table 5.3 Percentage Change from Baseline of the VA and CS Charts

	NVG chart*	Tri-bar chart*	12 cpd	6 cpd	3 cpd
Green Light	11.9	12.5	40.2	14.8	0
Red Light	24.9	25.9	59.2	36.6	20.9

*The values are obtained by averaging the right-hand side of the Snellen values.

changes with size—a variable closely associated with spatial frequency. Subtle differences appear that confirm the earlier anecdotal observation that visual perception could be seriously degraded without substantially affecting the VA scores. For example, where the VA tests showed approximately a 25% degradation in performance with red ambient cockpit lighting, high spatial frequencies resulted in greater than twice that level of deficit.

Our research clearly demonstrates, therefore, that CS is a useful additional assessment tool of NVG visual performance under conditions of ambient light degradation. Both the spatial frequency of the test chart and the ambient light conditions significantly affected visual performance, particularly at the higher spatial frequencies, in a way that was not evident in the VA tests. As Rabin stated,

> . . . acuity provides only the limit of resolution, while contrast sensitivity can provide a more comprehensive index of visual function over a range of stimulus sizes.[9]

This study supports the argument that CS charts sensitively assess a loss in visual performance that is not assayed by the VA tests. Thus, CS is more closely related to some of the most salient aspects of a stimulus that make it differentially detectable and recognizable. As such, it is an important supplemental measure of visual performance.

5.5 Discussion

The results of the two series of experiments in this study provide support for the main thesis of this chapter. That thesis is that classical psychophysics provides an important means of understanding complex visual behavior, one that is often overlooked by both engineers and users of devices like NVGs.

Above and beyond the specific details of the obtained results, we make two other general points in this chapter. The first is that it is necessary to simulate NVGs if we are to be able to study the specific effects on performance and to design better ones. Simulations of NVG viewing conditions are especially important simply because of the technological limitations of the NVG devices themselves. Using a real NVG would have made it impossible to study the effects of scintillation or contrast in the quantitative way that our first series of experiments did. Because of the simulation we used, we were able to demonstrate that the specific relations between luminance, contrast, and punctate interference in a precise manner that would have been impossible to demonstrate if we had used real NVG devices.

The second general point is evidenced by the stress we place on the CS measure in this chapter. The importance of the use of the concept of contrast sensitivity as a function of spatial frequencies cannot be overemphasized. Classical psychophysical researchers have long been aware of the sensitive nature of the CS as a predictor of detection, discrimination, and even recognition performance. For example, Ginsburg et al.[8] found that the higher spatial frequencies (8, 16, and 24 cpd) correlated with detection performance better than the lower frequencies. Rabin[10] and Rabin and McLean[11] stressed that the steep portion of the CSF is most vulnerable to a degraded visual scene. This is due to a small change in VA resulting in a large change in contrast threshold. Yet, for the most this part, it has been only recently that this fundamental idea in the study of vision has been applied to NVG operation and performance measurement. Our results make it clear that while a useful global measure, VA obscures many of the fine details of visual perception that are absolutely essential both for the design and use of NVGs and that the CS measure must be utilized as well in pilot training and evaluation.

References

1. Antonio, J. C. and Berkeley, W. E., Night Vision Goggle Model F4949 Preflight Adjustment/Assessment Procedures, (AL/HR-TR-1993–0111), Brooks Air Force Base, Air Force Materiel Command, Texas, 1993.
2. Berkley, W. E., *Night Vision Goggle Illusions and Visual Training,* Armstrong Laboratory, Higley, AZ, 1992.
3. Craig, J. L. and Purvis, B. D., Night Vision Goggles (NVG) Compatible Special Lighting for B-52 Special Operations (AAMRL-TR-88-028), Armstrong Aerospace Medical Research Laboratory, Wright Patterson Air Force Base, Ohio, 1988.
4. DeVilbiss, C. A. and Antonio, J. C., Measurement of night vision goggle (NVG) visual acuity under ideal conditions with various adjustment procedures, *Aviation, Space, Environ. Med.,* 65, 846–850, 1994.
5. Evans, L., *Fixed Wing Attack: In Helmet Mounted Displays and Night Vision Goggles,* (AGARD-CP-517), AGARD, Neuilly-sur-Seine, France, 1991.
6. Fechner, G. T., *Elemente der Psychophysik,* Breitkopf & Hartel, Leipzig, 1860.
7. Gibb, R. W., Night Vision Goggle Assessment Techniques with Incompatible Cockpit Lighting and a Modified Class B Goggle, Thesis, Arizona State University, Tempe, 1996.
8 Ginsburg, A. P., Esterly, J., and Evans, D. W., Contrast sensitivity predicts target detection field performance of pilots, *Proc. Human Factors Soc.—27th Annu. Meet.,* 269–273, 1983.
9. Rabin, J., Spatial contrast sensitivity through aviator's night vision imaging system, *Aviation, Space, Environ. Med.,* 64, 706–710, 1993.
10. Rabin, J., Time-limited visual resolution in pilot trainees, *Mil. Med.,* 160, 279–283, 1995.

11. Rabin, J. and McLean, W., A comparison between phosphors for aviator's night vision imaging system, *Aviation, Space, Environ. Med.*, 67, 429–433, 1996.
12. Reising, J. D., Antonio, J. C., and Fields, B., Procedures for Conducting a Field Evaluation of NVG Compatible Cockpit Lighting, Armstrong Laboratory, Aircrew Training Research Division, Mesa, AZ,AL/HR–TR–1995–0167.
13. Stevens, S. S., The psychophysics of sensory function, in *Sensory Communication*, Rosenblith W. A., Ed., MIT Press, Cambridge, 1–34, 1961.
14. Tanner, W. P., Jr. and Swets, J. A., A decision making theory of visual detection, *Psychol. Rev.*, 61, 401–409, 1954.
15. Uttal, W. R., *The Psychology of Sensory Coding*, Harper and Row, New York, 1973.
16. Uttal, W. R., *A Taxonomy of Visual Processes*, Erlbaum, Hillsdale, NJ, 1981.
17. Uttal, W. R., Baruch, T., and Allen, L., Psychophysical foundations of a model of amplified night vision in target detection tasks, *Hum. Factors*, 36, 488–502, 1994.
18. Wiley, R. W. Glick, D. D., Bucha, C. T., and Park, C. K., Depth Perception with the AN/PVS-5 Night Vision Goggle, (USAARL Report 76-25), U.S. Army Aeromedical Research Laboratory, Ft. Rucker, AL, 1976.

chapter six

Human Perception of Sensor-Fused Imagery

Edward A. Essock, Jason S. McCarley,
Michael J. Sinai, and J. Kevin DeFord

Contents

1-56670-413-8/01/$0.00+$.50
©2001 by CRC Press LLC

Keywords: *sensor fusion, image fusion, infrared, image intensification, color, texture, segmentation, detection, recognition, natural scenes, perceptual organization, psychophysics, nighttime, night vision*

6.1   Introduction

Remote sensing provides information about external stimuli that humans would not otherwise be able to perceive via their biological sensory systems. The electronic sensors used in remote sensing obtain a spatial mapping of external stimuli that is then converted to a type of stimulation that the human biological sensors *can* detect. Typically, the electronic sensor output is converted into a spatial mapping rendered in variations of light energy emitted by a cathode ray tube (CRT) visual display. A crucial yet often overlooked factor that determines the usefulness of a remote sensing system is the ability of the human perceptual system to extract useful information from the transformed rendering of the alternative sensor's information that has been recoded into the visible-light display that the human views.[21] In other words, such sensors provide ways to present spatial information to the human visual system for analysis even though that information is not originally perceivable by the human visual system. Human viewing of such imagery, often termed "nonliteral imagery," implicitly subjects the spatial information to the powerful processing of the human visual system just as if the image were originally an optical mapping on the retina of reflected/emitted visible light conveying spatial and dynamic relations in a natural visual scene. The image produced by remapping the alternative spatial information into a visually accessible format must be analyzed and perceptually organized by the visual system, just as if it were a conventional light image, in order for the human viewer to find the remapped information useful.

In this chapter we focus on one type of nonliteral imagery; nighttime imagery obtained by electronic sensors. Typically, these sensors are either infrared detectors or image intensifiers. (The latter sensor, typified by traditional night vision goggles, serves to electronically amplify the effect of the few photons in the nighttime outdoor environment.) In our review, we focus on imagery produced by combining or fusing imagery from multiple electronic sensors, a procedure performed in an attempt to capitalize on the advantages of each type of sensor. We present an overview of the research findings to date that bear on the question of the extent to which the sensors and fusion methods effectively convey spatial information that humans can perceptually organize and use functionally. Our goals in this chapter are to:

1. Explain the need for behavioral assessment of perceptual performance with artificial imagery
2. Summarize the findings of performance assessment to date with nighttime imagery

3. Emphasize the need for much more research that draws upon the expertise of the sensor engineers and scientists, on the one hand, and human factors psychologists and psychophysicists, on the other

In this introduction we also need to emphasize that this is an evolving and rapidly changing field with sensors and fusion techniques continually being altered and improved. As a consequence, reports of rigorous psychophysical testing will often lag behind advances in technology, reporting results with imagery of a method that has since been modified. The advantage to this however, is that it is beneficial to build up a body of psychophysical results with a variety of both sensors and methods that reflect different monetary and/or computational costs as these methods may find different applications. The data and images presented in this chapter should be viewed in this light. That is, they reflect the fusion method and imagers tried at a particular time and may not be necessarily the best end-products that a given lab can produce. In this regard, we thank all individuals who provided the images that we present in this chapter or who helped in other ways.

The chapter is organized into the following sections. In the remainder of this introduction, the types of nonliteral imagery and the processing of that imagery by the human visual system are characterized in general terms. The second main section of the chapter considers the nature of multiple-sensor systems. It includes the display of multiple-sensor images (both fused and non-fused), and addresses the complexities created by sensor fusion—including the potential loss of image information—and constraints placed on the effectiveness of fusion by the nature of human visual processing. The third main section provides an overview of some of the diverse approaches to fusing this type of imagery by various researchers. The fourth section addresses some of the special difficulties of testing perceptual performance with natural outdoor scenes. The fifth section catalogs the findings of studies conducting behavioral testing of perceptual ability with nighttime imagery and fused imagery, with the results grouped in subsections by type of perceptual ability evaluated: object recognition texture-based region segmentation, object/target detection tasks, preferences of human viewers, and miscellaneous tasks. The final section of the chapter offers a table summarizing the behavioral results, conclusions, and a look to the future.

6.1.1 Types of nonliteral imagery

Visual images from electronic sensors are encountered in a number of situations in contemporary life. They are seen routinely on television in the form of Doppler radar images on daily weather reports, and they are also seen in specialized situations such as MRI, ultrasound, or other types of medical imagery. One prominent use of nonliteral imagery is to allow visual perception when there is not adequate light to support human biological vision.

Two main types of alternative sensors have been used to assist human nighttime vision. One of these detects longwave infrared (IR) radiation, providing essentially a thermal image based on spatial heat differentials in the scene. The other, termed an image intensifier (I^2), detects primarily short-wavelength infrared light ("near IR") and relatively long-wavelength visible light (i.e., red, and to a lesser extent, orange), then amplifies the detected signal to create a visible display. Thus, the IR and I^2 devices rely largely on emitted and reflected electromagnetic radiation, respectively.

Images from IR or I^2 sensors, or images from their combination (i.e., fused images) are presently used in a number of applications to enhance night vision ability. Indeed, some commercial automobiles offer IR cameras and associated displays to help drivers look beyond the headlights when driving at night.[4,30,70] More common has been the use of IR or I^2 nighttime imagery by pilots or crews of helicopters, fixed-wing aircraft, and boats in military, Coast Guard, and police tasks to increase success of nighttime piloting, targeting, search and rescue, and surveillance.[9,13,47,58] In short, these images are used to increase situational awareness during night operations. In addition, IR sensors are also used by firefighters to perform visual tasks in conditions of dense smoke, and image intensifiers are used as visual aids in vision disorders involving rod dysfunction.[6]

6.1.2 Perceptual organization of nighttime imagery

Although the IR or I^2 images (see Figure 6.1) that are presented on the visual display offer a substantial improvement over the unaided human visual system in nighttime, these images are clearly inferior to unaided daylight vision or even to daylight artificial imagery presented on a visual display. When a human views any image, good visual performance is dependent upon the ability to make perceptual sense out of the image. This "perceptual organization" of a scene entails complex processing of the information that is conveyed to the retina by the scene (e.g.,[14,18]). For example, in the perceptual organization of any scene, the visual system must make use of correspondences of local properties in order to segment the image into regions and then organize the regions into meaningful objects.[5,14,25] In particular, image points with similar values of low-level image properties such as brightness/color and multipixel relations (texture) need to be linked together as an early step in perceptually forming regions and objects. The perceptual processes that form boundaries and regions are highly dependent upon the richness of low-level information in an image (e.g.,[5,14,18,40]).

When a sensor presents imagery that is degraded relative to normal daylight viewing, less low-level information is available in the scene, and satisfactory perceptual organization becomes an even more difficult task for the visual system. For example, when a scene is displayed in monochrome, as opposed to color, a strong cue for perceptual organization and preattentive processing is unavailable.[39] Similarly, information such as microtexture at

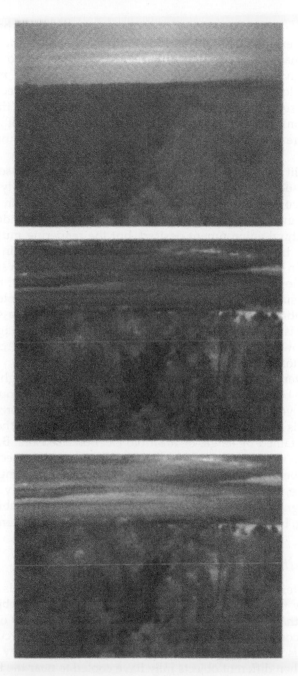

Figure 6.1   An example of a nighttime scene that has been imaged using a low-light, image-intensified CCD camera (top), an IR sensor (middle), and a gray-scale-fused version (bottom) where the two single sensor images have been combined (see text). (From Steele, P. M. and Perconti, P., *Proc. SFIE 11th Annu. Inter. Symp. Aerosp./Defense Sensing, Simulation and Controls*, 3062, 88–100, 1997. With permission.)

various spatial scales can also be lost in images produced via particular types of artificial sensors due to diminished contrast at various spatial scales. For example, small-scale spatial information can be lost due to the resolution limit of a given device and can also be lost in low-light images simply because of a low level of signal relative to the noise of the detectors. Thus, the imagery presented to the human visual system that displays the information from electronic sensors is not as rich as daylight imagery of natural scenes and therefore is expected to adversely affect the perceptual organization of the scene.

The ability of the human user to make good perceptual sense out of the resultant visual image from an artificial sensor is particularly critical in the case of sensor systems intended to improve human vision in real-world nighttime viewing conditions. Here, not only is a realistic rendering of a very complex natural environment desired, but the rendering must support the user in an interaction with the dynamic environment in which he is immersed. In comparison, medical imagery or imagery from satellites representing geologic or vegetative spatial information need not be as rich and realistic for successful use. With standard night vision technology, providing a crude spatial mapping on a display monitor is actually a simple matter. However, it is presently impossible to present a nighttime image on the monitor that allows the fidelity and richness of human visual perception in daylight conditions.

In an attempt to improve upon the perceptual utility of nighttime imagery, efforts have been made recently to combine imagery from multiple sensors. For several years, our group has been investigating the perceptual performance that is allowed by the display of spatial mappings of the natural environment obtained by single or multiple electronic sensors. Because human perception is very complex and multifaceted, defining the specific perceptual abilities to be evaluated in a naturalistic setting is a challenging endeavor. Furthermore, natural outdoor scenes are themselves extremely complex, making the design of rigorous psychophysical tests of perceptual ability even more challenging. In the following sections these issues are considered.

6.2   Multiple sensor systems

Because different sensors are sensitive to different wavebands of electromagnetic energy, they convey different information about distal objects. An imaging sensor that is optimal for one perceptual task, or under one set of environmental conditions, can be inadequate under different circumstances. For example, discrimination of details is difficult on IR imagery obtained near morning when different objects may have cooled to near the temperature of the background ("thermal cross-over"). Similarly, the reflectivity of two objects may be quite similar with respect to an image-intensifier sensor, or there simply may be little starlight/moonlight available to reveal their different reflectances. Because of the advantages and disadvantages of these single sensors, it may sometimes be beneficial to provide human operators with the output of multiple sensor systems.

In an attempt to improve the perceptual effectiveness offered by images from a single sensor, researchers have presented images from more than one type of sensor to a user. This has taken the form of multiple displays viewed successively or simultaneously, or images from multiple sensors fused into a single display.

6.2.1   Presentation on multiple displays

One obvious way of presenting views of a scene from different sensors is to simply present the output from each sensor within its own display, and to allow observers to alternate between displays electronically or by shifting their gaze. Unfortunately, the usefulness of such a set-up might be mitigated in several ways by demands created by the need for observers to alternate fixation and attention between displays. Because renderings obtained through different sensors are likely to differ in gross characteristics such as mean luminance and contrast, shifts from one display to another can demand changes of the adaptive state of the visual system and entail transient but substantial decrements in visual performance.[47] Furthermore, because multiple displays must be spatially or temporally separated, their combined utility might be limited by the difficulty of remembering and mentally integrating their contents.[24,46]

An alternative, dichoptic presentation (simultaneous presentation of different stimuli to the two eyes), could avoid these problems by allowing observers to view two distinct displays concurrently, but this too could be problematic. Though observers under some circumstances can process and combine information from both of two dichoptically presented images,[67] dichoptic displays of longer than 150 msec duration allow the possibility of binocular rivalry.[3] This phenomenon, in which portions of each dichoptically viewed stimulus perceptually mask portions of the other,[23] can lead to the perception of a patchwork stimulus in which portions of each image are alternately visible and hidden. Worse, observers have no volitional or conscious control over which portions of the images are visible at a given instant and therefore have no way of ensuring that information from either source will be available when needed.

6.2.2   Presentation via fused images

A more effective method of providing users with information gathered through two or more sensors might be through the process of sensor fusion. Sensor fusion seeks to obviate shortcomings of individual imaging sensors by combining the output of multiple single-band sensors to form a single multiband image. Fusion algorithms take as input two or more single-band views of a scene obtained from a common vantage point, and from these produce a single composite image.

This manipulation offers users two general types of potential benefits. First, it could allow observers to view and access useful information from multiple images simultaneously, without needing to alternate gaze and attention between displays and without the complications of dichoptic presentation (which can be thought of as biological fusion). Second, fusion algorithms can exploit differences between single-band images of the same scene to provide a fused rendering enhanced with new, *emergent*, information that is not present within either of the component images singly. That is, objects in the world will register differently with respect to the properties measured by different sensors and comparison of these spatial mappings will create different signatures across the spectral bands, or contrast between sensors (i.e., any differencing operation between sensors). Information derived from such intersensor contrast might augment the spatial information conveyed by individual component images.[66,73,76] Furthermore, intersensor contrast can be taken as the basis for color rendering of an image, much as differences in output of the retinal cones provide the basis for human color vision. To the extent that sharp changes in contrast between single-band images tend to occur at objects' edges, the emergent information derived through fusion would then appear in the image as color contrast between image regions that correspond to different distal objects.

For several reasons, however, many of these potential benefits might not be easily realized. Ultimately, an image is useful to a human operator only to the extent that it is interpretable. An observer's visual system, presented with a sensor-fused rendering, must parse, or segment, the image into a representation of distal surfaces and objects, extracting structure and meaning just as it would from a natural image. The potential utility of a sensor-fused image, like that of a natural image or an electronically sensed single-band image, will therefore be constrained by limitations in the observer's perceptual system. Information present within a sensor-fused image, and thus theoretically available to mathematical pattern analysis, could in actuality be of little value to a human observer. Emergent information, for example, might be of low salience and therefore of little perceptual utility even for trained observers. Worse, single-band information that is salient within a component image might not be easily perceptible within a fused image. Features of one input image might instead obscure details of the other, leaving the information conveyed by one single-band source degraded or even imperceptible within a dual-band rendering. Paradoxically, fusion could then impair visual performance. Finally, there is nothing to assure that sensor fusion, even if helpful under some circumstances, will be equally beneficial to visual performance in other circumstances. Visual perception is not the result of a single, monolithic process or mechanism, but represents the working of multiple channels and processing modules operating for various purposes on various aspects of a stimulus.[12,19,31,35] Thus, it is possible that sensor fusion might aid some aspects of visual performance while hindering others. Clearly, important issues are raised for human factors engineers in this realm.

6.2.3   Complications raised by sensor fusion

The aim of sensor fusion is to receive as input two or more images of a common scene and from these create a unitary, composite rendering. In principle, a fusion algorithm might receive input from any variety of sensors. For several reasons, however, research into sensor fusion has largely focused on the possibility of melding nighttime I^2 and IR imagery.[50,66,73,76] First, because I^2 and IR night vision devices are now in widespread use, algorithms for fusing their output could find diverse and ready application. Second, and more important, I^2 and IR sensors together provide information which might be optimal for exploiting sensor fusion.[73,76] As noted above, image intensified sensors respond to long-wave visible and short-wave IR light, typically collecting energy that has been reflected off the surfaces within a scene. Long-wave IR sensors, conversely, respond to thermal radiation, collecting energy emitted by objects within a scene. Figure 6.1 shows a nighttime outdoor scene imaged by both an I^2 sensor (see Figure 6.1, top) and an IR sensor (see Figure 6.1, middle). As seen in the figure, the information provided by these two classes of sensor is largely complementary, indeed formally so, related by Kirchhoff's Law, $\rho(\lambda) = 1 - \varepsilon(\lambda)$, where ρ is the spectral reflectance and ε is the spectral emissivity. Thus, an algorithm that effectively combines the sensors' output could create imagery that is of considerably enhanced utility by capitalizing on the differences of objects in terms of their emissivity/reflectivity ratios.

6.2.3.1   Potential problems with fused imagery

There are many ways in which sensor fusion could fail as an aid to human perception, however. Some of these are simple technical shortcomings which might eventually be overcome by developments in the construction of imaging systems. Sensor-fusion researchers, for example, have typically faced the difficulty of aligning or registering pixels in the single-band images to be fused. Because of various optical distortions, even sensors with matched fields-of-view can generate images that are not precisely registered spatially (see description in ref. [53]). Before image fusion is possible, therefore, preprocessing is generally necessary to map pixels in one image onto those pixels in the companion image that represent the same distal points. That is, one image must be stretched ("rubber-sheeted") into alignment with the other. This distortion can cause noticeable degradations, and can produce fused imagery that is aesthetically displeasing and disruptive of visual performance.[29] The problem of misregistration between component images, however, is being mitigated by the development of methods that allow sensors of different spectral sensitivities to be arranged vertically with perfect pixel registration[38] or directly by matching field of view, pixel number, and optical path.[1,74]

Other difficulties, however, are more fundamental and will not be so easily conquered. It is impossible to achromatically fuse nonidentical images without loss of physical image information. Within an achromatic image, pixels are constrained to vary along a single dimension. Achromatic fusion thus entails mapping multiple one-dimensional spaces of single-band pixel values onto a single one-dimensional space of multiband pixel values, and ensures that information within a fused image will be insufficient for full recovery of individual input images (thus, the task in achromatic fusion is to ensure that it is the perceptually less-important information that is lost; a task requiring considerable empirical psychophysical testing, as described in later sections). This loss of physical information can only be avoided through the use of a chromatic display rendered in a color space whose dimensionality is equal to or greater than the number of images being fused, such that one dimension can be dedicated to represent each input image (or transformations). Furthermore, such a display, would augment single-band stimulus information by making differences between component images explicit as chromatic contrast within the composite display.

6.2.3.2   *Constraints due to the human perceptual system*

It is at this point however, that characteristics of human visual perception become constraints on the utility of sensor fusion. One potential impediment to the use of color-fused imagery as an aid to human performance arises from the difficulty of achieving seminaturalistic color renderings from sensor-fusion. Because single-band images to be fused will generally be collected with sensors whose spectral sensitivities differ from those of the human photoreceptors, color-fused scenes will typically be rendered in colors different from those in which they appear during unaided daylight vision. To the extent that visual perception exploits stored color knowledge for recognition or other purposes, fused-color imagery might therefore be disruptive of visual performance. Fortunately, evidence indicates that the role of stored color knowledge in vision is secondary to the role of color in image segmentation, i.e., in the process of delineating objects' edges within the image [7,80], suggesting that the benefits of false-color rendering relative to achromatic rendering may outweigh its costs. Resolution of this specific issue requires future research specifically weighing costs and benefits of color rendering.

Another limit on the scope of sensor fusion, however, is clearer and more obviously insurmountable. Because the human visual system is trichromatic, the color space in which images are fused can be of no greater useful dimensionality than three. Thus, no more than three images can ever be fused directly and presented for analysis by a human observer without loss of physical information. Furthermore, the chromatic discrimination ability of the human visual system imposes an even more subtle limit, dictating that fusion of even three or fewer images will generally entail functional loss (i.e., perceptual, as opposed to physical, loss) of single-band information (see also ref. [22]). This is because equal physical steps in a physical "color" space are not equally discriminable to a human observer. Thus, the mapping of physical differences onto perceptual color space is nonlinear, and if performed blindly, could serve to make important physical differences *less* discriminable when rendered in false color.

Ultimately, the quality of a sensor-fused rendering is not measured by the information contained within the image, but rather by the *useful* information, in the sense of human factors constraints, that is truly conveyed by the image to an observer. Limits of visual acuity, of contrast and chromatic sensitivity, and of higher-level perceptual organization ensure that not all of the information within an image is perceptible. Indeed, it is unlikely that observers could perceptually recover component images from a composite rendering of a single scene[8], even if it were mathematically possible to do so. Thus, sensor fusion algorithms face the challenge of overcoming limits of human perceptual processing by selectively preserving and enhancing the single-band information that is necessary for accurate visual perception.

Fortunately, for a sensor-fused image to be useful, it is not essential that its component images be fully recoverable. Rather, it is important that the task-relevant distal structure perceptible within the component images remain visible, or become more visible, in the fused image. An observer typically has no need of reconstructing component images pixel-by-pixel from the information within a fused image, but must only recover the texture and contours necessary for perceptual organization of the depicted layout of surfaces and objects. For this purpose, much of the information between and within single-band renderings of a common scene will be redundant and thus, at least to some extent, expendable (i.e., in a physical sense). The goal of a sensor-fusion algorithm must therefore be to create a multiband image that *at worst* preserves information necessary for human perception of the distal structure visible within the single-band renderings, and that *at best* derives new information to improve veridical perception of the distal stimuli depicted in the imagery. In addition to this physical-level definition of information, perceptual/functional considerations abound[26] (e.g., issues of user training and experience with particular display formats, the use of particular colors or redundant information coding schemes, and the familiarity with nighttime imagery as well as certain types of scenes).

There have been several approaches developed to attempt to meet this goal of creating improved sensor-fused imagery. To give the reader a sense of the different approaches to fusion of night vision images employed to date, this literature is characterized in the next section.

6.3   *An overview of fusion approaches*

A variety of fusion algorithms have been developed (e.g.,[45,50,53,59,64-66,71-77]), and the diversity of the methods being developed indicates that no single ideal fusion method has been established. In this section, several fusion methods employing different basic approaches are described to provide an overview of the types of methods being pursued.

6.3.1 Monochrome fusion

The most direct method of fusion involves combining an image from each of two different sensors (e.g., IR and I^2) into a single composite grayscale image. For example, Toet and associates[60,61,65] developed a monochrome fusion method that uses a hierarchical image-merging scheme based on a spatial decomposition of the original imagery performed at several spatial scales. Thus, the original single sensor imagery is first decomposed into a contrast-based mapping at several spatial scales represented in a multiresolution pyramid. The amount of contrast present at each scale is compared for each single-sensor image, and the single-sensor image with the greatest contrast at that scale at a given location is chosen for the fused image. Thus, the fused image is a construction made from local patches of information in one or the other of the two sensors' images. Peli et al.[43] report a similar type of stratified fusion in which the fusion is based upon contrast calculated locally within spatial frequency bands[41]. An example of this type of monochrome fusion[43] is shown in Figure 6.2 (bottom) along with the initial IR (middle) and I^2 (top) images. Indeed, examples of image structure present only in one of each of the two single-sensor images can be seen in the fused image. Fusion stratified by spatial scale (i.e., spatial frequency bands) also occurs to some extent in the algorithm of Therrien, Scrofani, and Krebs[59], using two scales. Numerous other methods of monochrome fusion have been developed (e.g., [44,48,68,73]; also see ref. [33], for a review).

The approach of Waxman, et al.[1,2,71-76] differs, emphasizing intersensor differences (intersensor contrast) instantiated by shunting center/surround filter mechanisms, although center/surround filters also can be conceived of as the application of a band-pass filter as is done in the multiscale filter methods just noted. An example of results with this type of monochrome fusion[73] is shown in Figure 6.1 (bottom) resulting from the combination of the IR and I^2 images shown in Figure 6.1. Again, notice how the fused image appears to retain much of the image structure present in both of the component single-sensor images. It should be noted that this particular fusion method is best viewed as an intermediate step in the creation of a type of color-fused imagery.[73]

6.3.2 Color fusion

In addition to achromatic fusion, several labs have developed methods to perform fusion in either two- or three-dimensional color space (e.g., [45,50,66,73,76,77]). An obvious way to perform color fusion would be to simply send one image (e.g., IR), as the input to one of the display monitor's guns (e.g., red), and a second image (e.g., I^2) to another of the monitor's guns (e.g., green, or even green and blue jointly), thereby allowing the monitor's array of RGB phosphor dots and the human visual system to fuse the two monochromatic images into one color image. In a sense, this is another example of biological fusion, but instead of using the binocular neural pathway to biologically fuse dichoptic

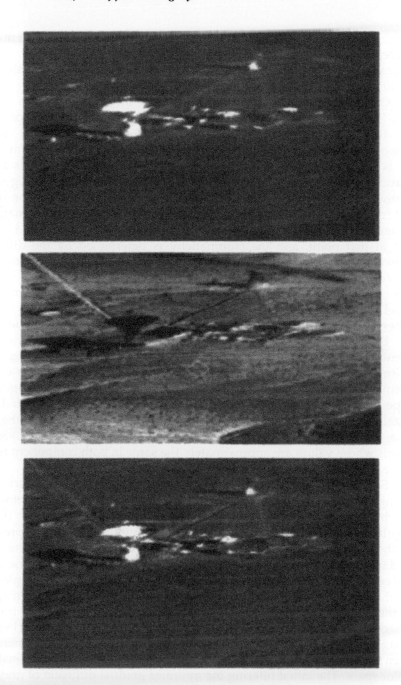

Figure 6.2   A nighttime scene of a large satellite dish, roads and various other structures. The normalized visible image (top), IR image (middle), and the gray-scale–fused version (bottom) are shown. (From Peli et al., *Proc. SPIE Conf. Sensor Fusion: Architecture, Algorithms, and Appli. III*, 3719, 1999. With permission.)

images, the neural color pathway is biologically fusing single-sensor maps in perceptual color-space. Several methods go beyond this type of direct (biological) color fusion to extract intersensor differences and to display them in a particular color format.

One method of color fusion, developed at the Naval Research Laboratory (NRL), is to create chromatic dual-band imagery by mapping pixel values from single-band I^2 and IR images into a two-dimensional space.[53] The output of this method applied to the I^2 and IR images shown in Figure 6.1 is shown in Figure 6.3 (top). Note that the fused image reveals a chromatically salient horizon while preserving other structure in the images. This method utilizes an intensity axis and a single color-axis (corresponding to red/cyan of various saturations) wherein intensity in the fused image at a given image point is determined by the sum of the two single-band intensities at that point, and the chromaticity is determined by the difference between the single-band intensities at that location. That is, saturation on a red/cyan color axis encodes intersensor contrast. This method uses a principal components procedure to enhance chromatic contrast by normalizing pixel values in the direction orthogonal to the principal component direction when plotting the raw I^2 value of each pixel against the raw IR value.

By using red and cyan as color primaries, the fusion algorithm implements a form of color cancellation, creating a flattened, or two-dimensional, color space (i.e., with chromaticity based on saturation of one pair of complementary colors). Rather than producing a variety of colors, colors in this type of imagery range from saturated red through gray to saturated cyan; pixels that are bright only in the IR component image appear red in the fused image, pixels that are bright in only the I^2 component image appear cyan, and pixels whose values are approximately the same in both component images appear achromatic.

Several researchers have taken two-band color fusion a step further utilizing a three-dimensional color space. For example, a method developed by Werblin and associates at the University of California, Berkeley (UCB)[77] combines single-band images through processing similar to that represented in their computational model of retinal processing, emphasizing the spatial and temporal diffusion of local neural responses (e.g., the time-course of retinal center/surround receptive-field spatial antagonism).[78] An example of this method's fusion is shown in Figure 6.3 (middle) in which it has been applied to the I^2 and IR images like those shown in Figure 6.1. Note that the resultant image shows good preservation of image structure from each single-sensor image. The algorithm first provides single-band image enhancement, and then fuses the enhanced single-band images within a three-dimensional false-color space. The initial filtering incorporates gradual diffusion of gray-scale values within homogeneous regions of the image, thereby "growing" regions in conjunction with region boundaries (Das, personal communication, 1997). A similar concept is seen in the method of Waxman et al.[73,76] incorporating region growing implemented by Grossberg's BCS/FCS model of human

Figure 6.3 Three color-fused versions of the nighttime scene shown in Figure 6.1. Fusion by the NRL method (top), the UCB method (middle), and the MIT-LL method (bottom). See text for details of fusion methods. The color images from all three methods appear to lose some of the detail apparent in the image-intensifier image of Figure 6.1. See color version of this figure in the color section following page 114. (The UCB image was provided by Frank Werblin and the NRL and MIT-LL versions are reprinted from Steele, P. M. and Perconti, P., *Proc. SPIE 11th Annu. Inter. Symp. Aerosp./Defense Sensing, Simulation and Controls*, 3062, 88–100, 1997. With permission.)

boundary and region formation.[20] In both methods this region growing serves to produce better segmented imagery with regions better filled in.

The color rendering in Werblin and associates' method also occurs through sending the output of the sensors differentially to the R, G, and B inputs of the color display monitor. In this method, the R, G and B values of each pixel are set to the corresponding pixel's intensity in the IR image (for the R input), the intensity of the corresponding pixel in the I^2 image (for the B input) and a combination of the intensity of the corresponding I^2 and IR pixels (for the G input). A considerable potential advantage of this method based on the analog processing within the retina is that it is being developed for implementation on an analog chip to support real-time processing (Kozek, personal communication, June 1999).

Very rich color rendering has been obtained by spreading the color mappings across a larger volume of three-dimensional perceptual color space. Although the earlier version of Werblin and associates' procedure produced a color mapping onto a rather flat three-dimensional color space, a more recent version produces a fuller three-dimensional color mapping. Figure 6.4 shows an example of this in which a scene, imaged by an IR sensor and a light (i.e., daylight) sensor, have been fused. The scene shows the use of daylight/IR sensor fusion for nighttime use when artificial lighting is present (e.g., automobile or building lights). Note how objects with different combinations (spectral signatures) of light and heat values (e.g., the person, window, trees and building) are distinguished in the color coding (bottom right) and to a lesser extent, in the monochrome fusion (top right) compared to the single-sensor images.

Another method of obtaining a richer color rendering is to employ three sensor bands of imagery, typically I^2, mid-wavelength infrared and long-wavelength infrared sensors types (e.g., ref. [52]). A method by Scribner and colleagues[52,53] uses images in these three bands as the input to the three color channels of the display, following conjoint application of the principal components scaling, to yield direct fusion of three-band imagery in three-dimensional color space with minimal processing. Figure 6.5 shows an example of this method in which long-wave IR, mid-wave IR and visible images have been fused. The scene contains a Jeep near shrubs before an agricultural field, with the Jeep, particularly the windshield of the jeep, most apparent on the fused image. Note that the prefusion imagery is of lower resolution than in some other examples (e.g., see Figure 6.4).

Two related color-fused methods that use this same general approach to fusion have been reported by Toet[64] which rely on splitting the output of a visible camera (400–900 nm) into a band of shorter wavelengths of the visible spectrum and a band of longer wavelengths. For one color-fusion method, the short wavelength image is used as the R input, the longer wavelength image as the G input, and the gray-scale image (from multiresolution pyramidal fusion) is taken as the luminance component in NTSC color space. The color-fused rendering is displayed after transformation to RGB color space.

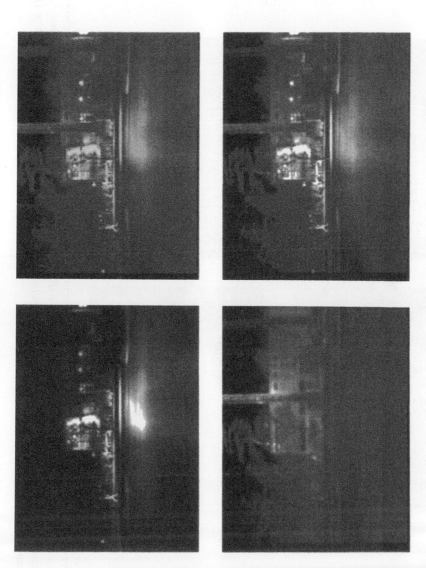

Figure 6.4 Nighttime imagery taken with a visible daylight camera (top left), an IR camera (bottom left), and the sensor-fused versions of the same scene (gray-scale fusion top right, color fusion bottom right). See color version of this figure in the color section following page 114. (Images courtesy of Frank Werblin.)

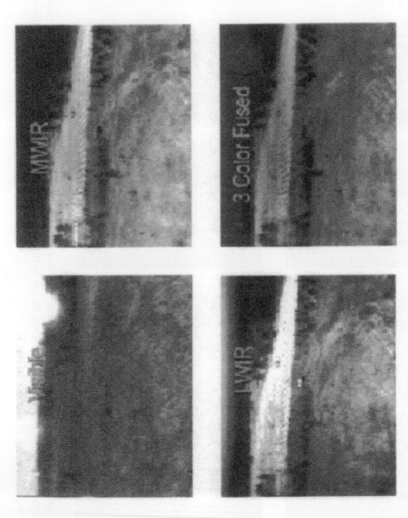

Figure 6.5 An example of color-fused imagery created from three input bands rather than two. The visible image is shown on the top left, the long-wave IR image on the bottom left, and the mid-wave IR image on the top right. The three-color fused image created from these three sensor bands is shown at the bottom right. See color version of this figure in the color section following page 114. (Images courtesy of Dean Scribner.)

The second method uses the IR image as the R input, the longer wavelength image as the G input and the shorter wavelength visible image as the B input and thus provides a type of fusion similar to three-band fusion.

Alternatively, one may use dual-band fusion with a processing method that more explicitly extracts new information from the comparison of the two images to provide the input for the third channel. For example, a method by Waxman and associates[1,2,72–76] developed at MIT Lincoln Laboratory (MIT-LL) provides rich false-color rendering (i.e., a less flattened three-dimensional perceptual color space) from dual-band imagery. An example of color-fused imagery from this method is shown in Figure 6.3 (bottom) in which the I^2 and IR imagery of Figure 6.1 has been fused. The fused image is particularly notable for the realistic colors appropriate for an outdoor scene. In this method, a center/surround shunting neural network is first used to enhance and to normalize image contrast and also to form the three center/surround spatial filters that provide the input to the three color channels (R, G, and B). In their initial reports, Waxman and associates produced the false-color images by using as R, G, and B input the output of the center/surround filtered IR image, the center/surround filtered I^2 image, and a third channel produced by contrasting I^2 input to the center with IR input to the surround. This third channel conveys intersensor contrast and also provides for a perceptually rich (i.e., not flattened) three-dimensional color space by providing a third input channel and it also can serve as a gray-scale–fused image (shown previously in Figure 6.1, bottom).

In more recent developments (e.g., ref. [1]), this group bases two of the three channels on intersensor contrast and one on the image-intensifier image; with each of the center mechanisms receiving I^2 input (from a single pixel in size) and the antagonistic surrounds contrasting this center input with either the I^2, the positive-polarity IR, or the negative-polarity IR signal. The resultant images are passed to the G, R, and B monitor inputs, respectively, to complete the color fusion after color remapping is performed to make the colorations look more realistic (i.e., vegetation colored green). A variation of this has been reported[62,63,72] for use when the IR image is of a resolution comparable to the I^2 image, in which case three differenced inputs are used. The authors[71,73,76] relate this method based on intersensor center/surround opponency to the spatial center/surround color-opponency shown in the primate visual system and the IR/visible mutual inhibition shown in the pit viper sensory system.

Other methods of obtaining dual-image color fusion based on intersensor contrast have also been developed.[62,66] An example of output from one of these methods[62] is shown in Figure 6.6 illustrating fusion of images from a visible-light CCD camera and a mid-wave IR camera. The TNO color-fusion algorithm of Toet et al.[62,66] is based on differencing operations and is in this sense, of the same genera as the method of Waxman et al.[71,72,74,75] In this method, first the minimum intensity value of the two images (CCD and IR) at each pixel is selected, resulting in a map termed the "common component"

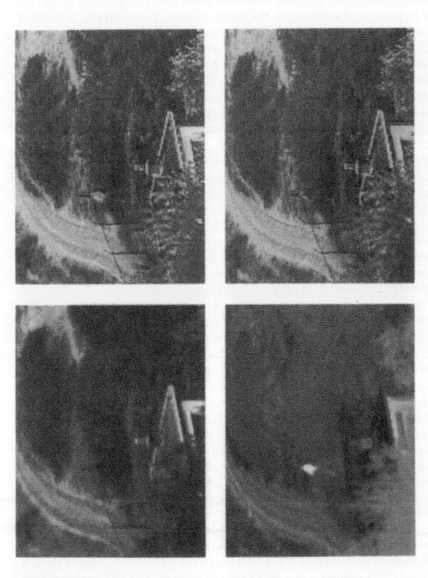

Figure 6.6 A nighttime scene taken with a visible camera (top left), an IR camera (bottom left), and the sensor-fused versions of the same scene (gray-scale fusion, top right; color fusion, bottom right). See text for details. See color version of this figure in the color section following page 114. (Images courtesy of Lex Toet.)

of the two images. Next, this common component is subtracted from both the CCD image and the IR image at each pixel to obtain the "unique component" of each sensor's image. Finally, the unique component of each sensor is then subtracted from the *other* sensor image and sent to the R input (IR − unique CCD) and the G input (CCD − unique IR). The B channel gets the differenced original images (CCD − IR)[63] or differenced unique images (unique CCD − unique IR).[66] (Gray-scale fusion is taken as a weighted sum of the three monitor inputs resulting from the color-fusion procedure.)

It is noteworthy that the concept of intersensor contrast (or differencing) is quite common in the satellite remote sensing literature (e.g., the "normalized difference vegetation index"). Thus, the areas share similar issues and hopefully this literature will become better integrated in the future, leading to more cross-pollination of ideas.

Finally, an alternative approach for the utilization of color in fused imagery is offered by Peli et al.[43] in which color is used as a means of increasing the distinctiveness of certain specific regions thought likely to be targets, somewhat analogous to "painting" targets with a salient color in a monochrome-fused image.

We anticipate that efforts for future improvements in the field of color-fusion in the near-term are likely to focus on several key issues. Possibly the most important is to support full processing and fusion in real time. Currently, simpler fusion methods, for example mapping three sensor bands with minimal processing directly onto R, G, and B inputs, can be performed in real time, but extremely computationally intensive methods cannot. Great strides in real-time processing are being made.[2,52] It would seem that hardware developments such as specialized processors, dual-band IR focal plane array sensor packages that obviate registration and scaling, and algorithms that are optimized for speed will contribute to this in the near future. Real-time processing will also lead the researchers to a consideration of temporal noise reduction and temporal processing aspects. Other issues likely to be investigated are those surrounding the color remapping that determines the specific coloration of particular types of object. Issues include whether use of more natural, as opposed to "unnatural," scene colorations are more useful in a functional (perceptual) sense; whether unique coloration of a particular type of scenic characteristic can offer a performance advantage; or whether false-color mapping is useful at all (cf. ref. [22]). A related issue concerns how to minimize the change in coloration from moment to moment as an object changes its reflectivity or emissivity (e.g., as when a helicopter passes through mist or fog) and how to minimize the perceptual consequences of this. Investigation of experience and training with color-fused imagery will surely be an active area. Another area in which we anticipate considerable efforts is the use of a greater number of spectral bands and research into the conditions in which various combinations of narrow or hyperspectral bands are particularly useful (e.g., [52]). Finally, we anticipate an increase in the evaluation of all of these hardware and algorithm implementations in *functional* terms, that is, the human factors assessment of perceptual performance as described in the next section.

6.4   Psychophysical testing with natural scenes

Typically in vision research, simple stimuli that can be exactly specified and varied on a single dimension are used for testing visual performance.[12,69] For example, a typical stimulus is a patch of a sinewave grating that might be varied in either orientation, spatial frequency, or contrast. Common stimuli for evaluating, visual search, for example, might consist of an array of identical bars with the target differing only in bar orientation or color. In the case of a texture segmentation test, a region containing bars of a second orientation or second color might be physically grouped within the field of bars of the first type.

Natural scenes, on the other hand, are incredibly complex compared to these simplified test patterns typically used for evaluating perceptual ability. Images of natural scenes contain regions such as grass or trees that are nominally or symbolically unitary, but are actually highly variable in terms of texture composition or local luminance/color composition from one part of the symbolically uniform region to another. That is, relative to the variations of stimuli typically tested in psychophysical experiments, regions of natural scenes that are nominally uniform (e.g., grass) are actually highly diverse. Specifying the texture present in only a small region of a natural scene is an extraordinarily difficult problem, approached in myriad ways in the computational vision literature.[14] (Even if viewed in the frequency domain where the power spectrum of natural scenes typically falls off linearly, exceedingly complex relations exist between the phase and power spectra as well as orientation.) Simply finding a suitable way to define contrast of a natural image is a challenging and controversial problem.[42] Due to this complexity, testing a particular perceptual ability with natural scenes may seem to be straightforward but is actually a quite complicated problem and one that is fraught with numerous potential pitfalls.

As an example, consider a test of whether the presence of an object is better detected by a human viewer when an IR or I^2 sensor is used to image the same scene. To have a reliable psychophysical measurement, the dependent measure must be based on a large number of trials, and hence requires a number of different stimuli so that the observer does not always know when and where the test object will appear. One approach is to manipulate the image using software in order to cut out a "target," say a truck, and paste it at different locations to make alternative stimuli. The problem that this introduces is that artificial edges or borders may be created between the cut-and-pasted target and its new background, with respect to some property (e.g., texture or even luminance). Just by chance, the target patch might be highly detectable or undetectable, depending on where in the image it was placed, and so the performance measured can actually be determined by

factors unrelated to the original quality of the image. Such edge-effect confoundings can be very pronounced perceptually. Indeed, even an apparently
small texture difference makes a highly salient emergent edge around the
patch, similar to a subjective contour. In this example, the extent to which the
IR or I^2 imagery conveys the background property (e.g., variations of grass)
determines how salient the emergent edge surrounding the target is, and
hence governs performance rather than performance being governed by how
well the target is conveyed by a given type of sensor.

Another problem associated with comparing the utility of alternative
sensors is that even if one target (again, say, a particular truck in the scene)
"pops out" perceptually and yields high detection performance on one type
of image (say IR), this alone is no indication that that image type mediates
better performance for other than artifactual reasons. For example, if a truck
is cut from one image and pasted into an image from a second sensor to serve
as a visual target, the truck could be highly detectable for the very reason that
the quality of the imagery is so poor. As an extreme example, imagine an IR
image of a grassy field that is so poor that all vegetation is a uniform value
(say black) with no texture details apparent at all. On such an image, the pasted truck would be highly detectable, mediating superior test performance
for the very reason that the imagery is so poor! However, it would require
additional testing with a different target stimulus (e.g., grass), or test of a
different perceptual ability, to reveal that the imagery supporting "good"
performance is actually of extremely poor quality.

Evaluating perceptual performance with real-world scenes, or even
naturalistic imagery,[79] requires special efforts to minimize confoundings (i.e.,
it is not even clear that confoundings can ever be avoided entirely). That special efforts to minimize confoundings are required is especially true when
alternative imaging methods or sensors are to be compared because the
experimenter must be concerned about equating several images.

In our work, we have tried a variety of methods to avoid problems such
as these. To avoid the spurious interactions at the target's boundary, we have
often cut patches from the images (i.e., from the I^2 and IR images at the same
pixel coordinates) and presented the target patch on a uniform background
field rather than on the imaged scene itself. We have presented patches to
be identified in this way, singly on a uniform gray field[15,16], and we have also
presented multiple small patches simultaneously on a uniform field to test
texture-based grouping.[17,57]

To make sure that the target patch cut out at a particular x-y location from
an image of one sensor type does not have any unique properties that make
it stand out from other patches cut out at the same location on other sensor
types (e.g., the mean brightness of a truck patch from different sensors),
we have used target *categories* (e.g., vehicles or buildings) with the exemplars
in the target categories and those in the nontarget stimulus set intentionally
chosen to be heterogeneous.[15,16] That is, by having a set of target patches that
vary considerably in terms of luminance and an equally broad overlapping

range of luminances for the nontarget patches, potential artifacts caused by differences from one image to the next in the portion of the natural scene selected to be a target can be minimized. Since it is essentially impossible to equate all properties of a natural image, this method seeks an approach that essentially randomizes the difference across *groups* of test stimuli and does not try to equate a single natural-scene target patch on all possible image properties. As summarized in the next section, several labs are currently working on other ways to improve psychophysical test methods for testing various aspects of perceptual performance with remotely sensed imagery of natural scenes.

6.5 *Psychophysical experiments*

The concerns discussed earlier raise at least two general questions that psychophysical study of sensor-fusion might address. First, what single-band and intersensor emergent information does a particular sensor-fusion algorithm convey? Specifically, does information provided by one component image perceptually dominate that provided by another and is the emergent information within fused images perceptible? Second, how useful is the information within a sensor-fused image for different aspects of human visual perceptual performance? Since sensor fusion can aid perceptual performance either by presenting multiple sources of single-band information concurrently, or by deriving information not available within component images singly, a single demonstration that fusion influences visual performance may provide ambiguous implications for development of fusion algorithms. A measure of both the perceptible single-band information and the perceptible emergent information conveyed by the sensor-fused imagery might eliminate this ambiguity, lending greater meaning to a finding that sensor fusion affects image quality in the sense of determining which aspects of the fusion algorithm are beneficial and what aspects are not. Because of the number of diverse fusion algorithms currently in use and because of the many aspects to visual performance, these are both important questions. With these questions in mind, we review the results of perceptual testing with night vision real-world imagery. In the next four sections we review studies of object recognition, texture-based region segmentation, object/region detection, and observer preferences.

6.5.1 *Object recognition*

We began our own psychophysical tests of human performance with night-time imagery using a recognition task that we developed.[10,15,54] Following the reasoning described above, this task was designed to use a set of target patches (e.g., buildings) and a set of nontarget patches (shown in Figure 6.7(a) for the category "buildings"), making sure that both sets overlapped in terms of mean and maximum (local) luminance, contrast and spatial frequency power

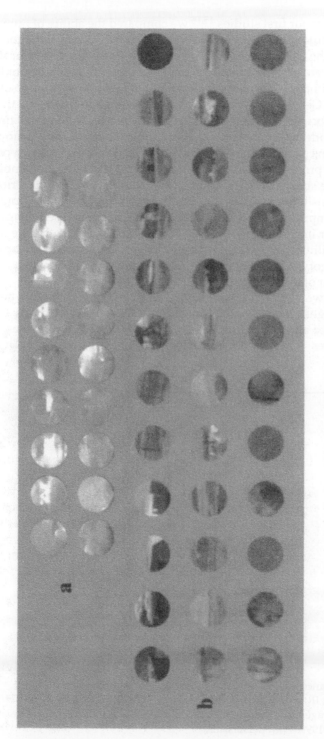

Figure 6.7 Patches of nighttime imagery used in the target category recognition task are shown. Part "a" shows patches used for the "buildings" target category for the I² imagery with target patches in the top row and nontarget distractor patches in the second row. Reprinted with permission from Essock et al., 1999, Human Factors Society. The three rows of panel "b" (from top to bottom) show the members of the target categories, "man-made objects," "sky/tree horizon" and "trees" for IR imagery from a similar category recognition task. (Part "b" imagery courtesy of Army NVESD and ONR.)

spectrum.[16] In one of our first studies [15,16] we compared the ability of human observers to perceptually organize low-level pixel and texture information in the 1.4° regions of the nighttime scene into recognizable patterns, specifically as examples of the categories of buildings, people, or tree/sky horizon, for IR, I[2] and, color-fused images. The imagery was obtained with a medium-resolution IR sensor and a Gen III I[2] sensor, and was color-fused by the earlier method of Waxman and associates.[73] Images were presented for a brief amount of time (100 msec) to preclude eye movements so that different patterns of eye movements and fixations could not be elicited by the different image types. Duration of visual processing was controlled and equated by use of a noise mask following the stimulus. Performance was measured by d′, a criterion-free estimator of sensitivity calculated from hits and false alarms.[34] We found clear evidence of improved perceptual performance for color-fused imagery with this particular imagery and task.[15,16] The results, shown in Figure 6.8, indicate that the ability to recognize an image patch as containing an exemplar of the target category was significantly better with color fusion than for imagery from either of the single sensors.

Subsequently we used this task with other imagery that had been obtained with a higher-resolution IR sensor and other fusion methods: one gray-scale and three alternative color-fusion methods (see ref. [58] for sensor details and Figures 6.1 and 6.3 for examples of the imagery). These

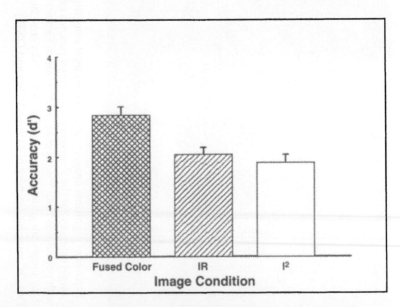

Figure 6.8 Performance for a region recognition task comparing overall performance with I[2], IR, and color-fused imagery. Results from various target categories were averaged together in this graph. (From Essock, E. A. et al., *Hum. Factors*, 41, 438–452, 1999. With permission.)

studies[10,54] used several additional target categories. They also increased the variability of the nontarget patches by drawing the distractors from the patches of the target categories not being used as target categories. Three target types, man-made, horizon, and trees, are shown in Figure 6.7(b). Again, we found that color fusion can improve human perceptual performance relative to monochrome fusion for certain types of targets, and that monochrome fusion can improve performance relative to performance with single-sensor images. The results are shown in Figure 6.9 for I^2, IR, gray-scale–fused, MIT-LL color-fused,[72–75] NRL color-fused[50–53] and UCB color-fused[77] image types.

These results were obtained for targets defined by contrasting regions, for example road next to grass or trees next to sky. However, while one method of color fusion may improve performance over that for single-sensor imagery, another method of color fusion may actually hurt percep-tual performance, underscoring the fact that sensor-fusion will not necessarily avoid the loss of perceptually important image structure. Using the same imagery, Steele and Perconti[58] also found this to be the case. Furthermore, they report-ed that while one color method (MIT-LL) mediated more accurate perceptu-al performance on one type of task (consisting of queries about objects and locations), the other color method tested (NRL) was better on another type of task (queries about geometrical relations). Using the same region recognition task developed previously,[10,15,54] Toet et al.[64] also report that performance is

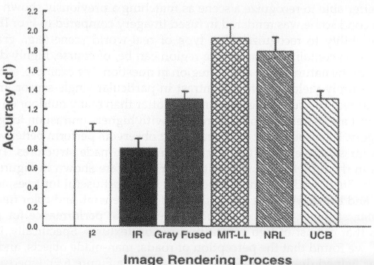

Figure 6.9 Region recognition performance for a second experiment using I^2, IR, and four types of fused imagery (see text). Data reflect average performance for target categories that consist of patches containing two contrasting regions within them, e.g., road next to grass or trees next to sky.

better with one color-fusion method for some region types, but better with another method for other region types. Indeed, another study[62] concluded that color rendering per se adds nothing beyond the information already contained in gray-scale–fused imagery for performing a spatial localization task.

Interpretation of the findings of the Steele and Perconti[58] study, like several of these studies of performance evaluation, however, is complicated by certain methodological problems. In their study, very few trials were run, a ceiling effect was apparent, and the results obtained were not consistent across the two dependent measures used. The long presentation time (i.e., allowing differential scan patterns and exposure) as well as the general notion of the test queries (differing single questions and varied scenes, as opposed to a specific and criterion-free psychophysical procedure with controlled stimuli and numerous trials), also make the results difficult to interpret for the reasons outlined in the other sections of this chapter. Rigorous psychophysical testing is difficult with natural scenes, and slow, but necessary, if the results are to be meaningful.

Finally, two other studies also bear on this issue. Although they did not evaluate region recognition per se, they involve similar aspects of perceptual organization. In a comparison of performance with imagery from single sensors and from a local contrast-based monochrome fusion technique, Ryan and Tinkler[48] found that pilots received higher ratings of piloting performance when using monochrome-fused imagery than when using imagery from either sensor alone. In another study, Sinai et al.[56] found that people were better able to recognize a scene as matching a previously shown scene if the second scene was rendered in fused imagery compared to I^2 or IR.

The ability to recognize what type of real-world scene (e.g., grass or buildings) is contained in an image region can be, of course, highly dependent upon the nature of the object/region in question. For example, some situations simply yield very high contrast in particular single-sensor images. People or recently run vehicles are much hotter than many outdoor environments and are therefore typically imaged with higher contrast on longwave IR imagery. It has been our experience that observers perform better with I^2 images for sky, trees, sky/tree horizon, and man-made structures. Typical data from the target-patch recognition paradigm are shown in Figure 6.10. Similarly, Steele and Perconti[58] report that I^2 is most useful for trees, terrain slopes, and brush. We have found that fusion in general, and color fusion in particular, strongly help some types of perceptual performance for image regions that consist of two contrasting region textures. Specifically, in one study[10] we found that the perception of roads, man-made objects, and horizon was helped dramatically by color fusion (see Figure 6.9), whereas perception of tree, sky, and grass regions was not aided when tested on a recognition task. Indeed, performance for the latter set was actually hurt significantly by color fusion relative to performance with single-sensor IR images. We suggested that this is because color-fusion methods improve the imaging of regions with contrasting textures (such as road next to grass or

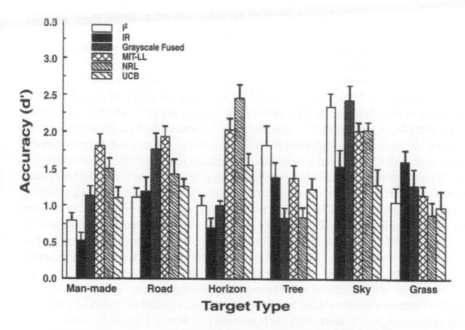

Figure 6.10   Region recognition performance shown for all target categories used, including both contrasting regions (man-made, road, sky/tree horizon, as shown in Figure 6.9), as well as homogeneous regions (sky, tree, and grass). A strong interaction between target category and image type can be seen where performance varies dramatically depending on the image format and the target category.

dirt, man-made objects against other structures or surrounding grass or vegetation, and regions of trees against sky), but hurt the imaging of regions of single homogeneous textures (regions consisting entirely of grass, trees, or sky). In other words, fusion helps most in making different types of scenic regions more differentiable in the perceptual organization of a scene.

6.5.2   Texture-based region segmentation

On a different type of task, the segmentation of regions based on texture, we have found that color fusion that would otherwise appear to be quite good upon informal inspection can hurt performance on some perceptual tasks.[17] In the early stages of perceptual organization, the human visual system links together locations with similar texture properties to begin to form perceptual regions and, eventually, surfaces and meaningful objects.[14,25] For example, locations (pixels) of a certain color or brightness need to be linked together to form a region. In "growing" these regions, the system must be able to account for (i.e., ignore) noise in the pixel values and also for actual image variations such as those due to shadows, gradients of texture size (change of texture-element visual angle with distance), and actual variations of the structure within the region itself (e.g., wood grain on a desktop, or patterns on tree trunks in a forest). If successful, this segmentation process will produce bounded regions that can be readily imparted with meaning (e.g., a road through a field of grass).

Human texture segmentation, sometimes called "texture discrimination" or "grouping," is typically measured by forming an array of simple texture elements within which the elements in one region are perturbed in some way. For example, a region of "T" shapes may be imbedded in an array of "+" shapes. To test image segmentation with natural scenes we formed arrays that consisted of copies of a sample of an image texture rather than copies of the typical type of texture element. The image texture was a small (0.6°) patch sampled from an image of an outdoor scene, for example, a small patch of imaged grass or trees. The texture patch was duplicated many times to form an array of this texture. To test segmentation ability, we rotated the individual patches of natural texture within one region of the texture array. Just as people can discriminate a region of vertical bars from a region of horizontal bars in a typical texture-grouping test array (shown in Figure 6.11(a)), if a given sensor was effective at imaging texture information in a way effective for the human visual system to use, then people should be good at performing texture segmentation with such stimuli (shown in Figure 6.11(b)).

This paradigm specifically tests texture-based segmentation as opposed to segmentation based on color or intensity differences (which are, in another sense, "texture" features themselves[14]). In other words, to detect a difference in two texture fields whose only difference is a 90° rotation of elements located within one side of the array, the spatial texture within the patch must be well conveyed since the texture elements differ only in the orientation of the spatial structure. The luminance, contrast, and color relations are all identical since the spatial structure of the patch is not changed (it is only rotated). To the extent that one sensor or fusion type provides the human visual system with more of this type of spatial texture information than another, the better performance should be on this segmentation task.

We measured performance on this texture-grouping task in two ways, both using a single-interval forced-choice paradigm. In one method, the texture difference was present on every trial, but it was arranged horizontally on half the trials and vertically on the other half. Observers had to demonstrate region segmentation ability by correctly identifying the orientation of the texture boundary (or, equivalently, the orientation of the regions formed by the grouping). In the other method, a vertical texture boundary was present on half the trials and was absent on the other half. Ability to segment the natural scene texture arrays was measured as the observers' ability to correctly respond "edge" or "no edge" to these trials.

Several different texture arrays made from several representative patches each taken from regions consisting of grass and trees were used. Results, shown in Figure 6.12, indicated that people were better able to perform this texture-based segmentation on the basis of the spatial structure within the IR

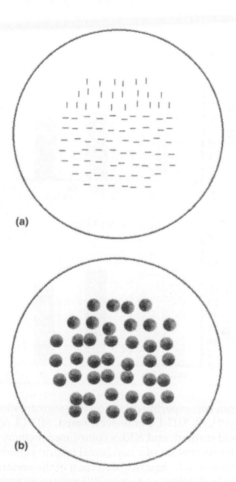

(a)

(b)

Figure 6.11 Two texture fields used to test region segmentation are shown. **(a)** An array of simple texture elements as commonly used in texture segmentation experiments (left side). **(b)** A similar array as in "a", but made with texture elements that consist of a small patch of a real-world scene rather than a line segment element (right side). The texture elements on the left side of both arrays (i.e., both "a" and "b") are rotated 90° with respect to the texture elements on the right side. If the real-world patch as imaged by a particular sensor or fusion method contains adequate texture information, the left and right sides will group readily into two distinct perceptual regions as in "a."

imagery than any other image type (I^2 or any of the four types of fused imagery). Indeed, we found that fusion actually *hurt* performance significantly for all types of natural texture tested relative to performance with IR imagery. Thus, again, we see that although gray-scale fusion or color fusion may very well help perceptual performance with one type of region or for one perceptual task, fusion most definitely can hurt performance for other perceptual tasks or for other particular region types. Presumably, this texture

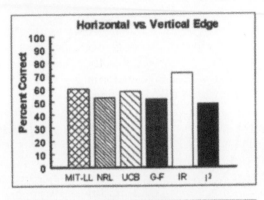

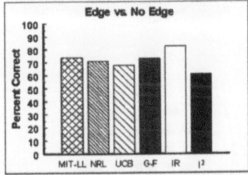

Figure 6.12 Results from two experiments on texture segmentation using six types of night-vision imagery (I^2, IR, MIT-LL gray-scale fused, MIT-LL color-fused method, UCB color-fused method, and NRL's color-fused method. Results are for (top) a task requiring discrimination of a horizontal texture boundary from a vertical boundary, and (bottom) a task requiring detection of the presence of a texture boundary as opposed to trials when no texture difference was present.

segmentation perceptual task relies upon image structure that is different from that required to perform the region recognition perceptual organization task[10] that found a different pattern of results (i.e., gray-scale fusion and color fusion helping performance for contrasting regions).

We pursued this issue further in a recent study in which we compared performance on three different types of texture-based image segmentation tasks.[11,57] The first task was the texture-grouping segmentation task just described. Thus this first task emphasized the grouping together of small regions of local texture into a larger region in order to distinguish this region from another region possessing identical structure, but with a different configuration (orientation) of the "emergent" texture contained in the small patches. In the second task, segmentation was performed on the basis of a difference in texture content in two relatively large regions. A texture boundary between the two regions was imposed within a scene (13.5° × 9°) by altering the spatial content within one region (one side of the images was filtered in the frequency domain to modify spatial content). The third segmentation task was based on detecting naturally occurring region boundaries in a fairly large scene (3° × 3°). The results further suggested that a given type of fusion may improve one aspect of perceptual performance (here, one type of segmentation performance) while hurting performance on other aspects. Specifically, we found that fusion did not help performance on the first two of these segmentation tasks (texture grouping and filtered-region detection), but did improve performance on the third segmentation task (detection of natural region boundaries). Furthermore, we demonstrated that the tasks for which fusion did not help performance were tasks whose performance was governed by the prevalence (power) of the middle spatial frequencies in the scene and that performance on the task for which performance was improved by fusion was governed instead by power at low spatial frequencies.

In addition to these specific findings about segmentation, more generally, this approach provides a way to assess the image structure required by humans to perform a specific perceptual task and, by extension, what scale a fusion algorithm should emphasize in order to maximize user performance on a specific type of perceptual task.

6.5.3   Object/region detection tasks

Our region recognition work utilizing target categories was similar to a target detection task, but emphasized the determination of membership in a target *category* rather than the detection of a specific target. As we described above, this procedure controlled for some of the problems inherent in performing target detection measurements with "real-world" imagery. However, there have been a number of attempts to test target detection ability more directly, in spite of the difficulties inherent in testing it with real-world images. Some attempts have used objects that are present in the actual images. Typically these studies pose questions to the observer that are tested one time each, asking, for example, about objects ("Is there a bridge present?"), or about position ("Is the sensor platform above the tree line?"). With movies of image sequences, observers can be asked to report when they first detect a certain object in the image sequence.[29,58] These methods offer the advantage that they are highly realistic, but have the associated disadvantage of being unable to conduct numerous repeated trials of the same task due to practical constraints on obtaining fused imagery and given the fact that the same image cannot be used repeatedly because of biases due to learning extraneous cues associated with the presence of the target. For example, if only one image sequence is available, after a single trial of asking "Is there a bridge present?" the image should not be reused to ask a question about another object (due to learning/memory bias favoring different target objects). Furthermore, repeated trials asking the same question cannot be asked to increase reliability and statistical confidence (and relatedly, to more easily avoid ceiling effects).

This inherent trade-off between realism (i.e., external validity) and psychophysical rigor is often encountered when employing real-world scene stimuli in psychophysical studies. However, by keeping this issue in mind when obtaining imagery, imagery for more rigorous psychophysical testing can be obtained.[37,55,62] We have used imagery choreographed to contain a varied number of people or vehicles allowing us to have an appropriately large number of trials in an object detection task. We had observers report whether people, vehicles or neither were present in a scene presented to them[55] and similarly, Krebs et al.[27,37] have tested with imagery obtained with pedestrians located at a predetermined set of positions. Results with these methods of implementing a target detection task using actual embedded targets suggest that fusion can, but does not always, improve performance over single-band imagery.

An additional approach for dealing with the confoundings and complexities of psychophysical testing with natural scenes is to model the presumed behavioral ability of observers. That is, rather than testing human performance, one can make up a mathematical detection rule and calculate detectability as defined by that rule.[28,53] With certain detection rules, color fusion is found to make pixels more distinctive and hence objects are more detectable when colored than when displayed in single-sensor monochrome.[53] However, at the present time, replacing the human perceptual system by a single calculation does not come close to capturing the complexity of human perceptual processing, particularly with respect to the effects of context and type of subject matter, the effect of various false-color relations, and the effects of complex texture variations.

Other efforts to implement a target detection measure in human psychophysical studies have included cutting out an object occurring naturally in an image to serve as a target,[32,49] and also perturbing a region of the image to create a target object.[57,76] These methods can be performed either before processing and fusion, creating an artificial target in the image that is then processed, or after processing and fusion when a portion of the processed image is cut out from the processed images. The cutout target patch may be then either placed into a scene processed in the same way or placed in a neutral homogeneous background. As described above, the first method, cutting and then pasting an image patch into a scene, is hampered by the perceptually powerful texture edges that can occur at the interface border. It is also hampered by the possibility that a patch moved from one area of an image to another will be highly detectable precisely because the sensor format does such a poor job at imaging features in various regions of the scene. For this reason, although we have tried the cut-and-paste method,[49] we have argued that forcing observers to *recognize* what *type* of region or object is contained in the image area is preferable methodologically.[15,16,54] Similarly, we have argued that the edge effects introduced by pasting the target into an image should be avoided, for example by presenting the cut-out image patches on a non-image background such as a uniform monochrome screen.[10,15,16,54] Results of our study with cut-and-paste targets[49] suggested that color fusion did not show a clear advantage over IR imagery.

The similar method of introducing an artificial perturbation into an image at various locations to serve as a target has also been tried. That is, rather than moving a real object into the scene, either by the cut-and-paste method or by actually moving the object at the time of acquiring the original imagery, the image has been manipulated. Waxman et al.[76] altered the image contrast in a small square region of the I^2 and IR images to serve as a target. They reported that target detection reaction times can be helped by color fusion, but performance can often be seen to be hurt at other contrast values (their Figure 5a, ref. [76]). Unfortunately, statistics to determine which trend predominates are not available.

Using objects placed in a scene Toet et al.,[62] found that the detection of the presence of a visual target (person) is increased with the two color-fusion methods tested (MIT-LL and TNO). As reported in the earlier discussion on region recognition, Toet et al. found that, the *position* of the person in the scene can also be best localized when using fused (color and gray-scale) images, but performance with gray-scale–fused images does not differ from that with color-fused images. They conclude that if enough achromatic spatial information is present, chromatic information is not used by observers to *localize* objects (rather, that color information aids in target *detection*). Our own target detection results with a similar method incorporating a physical translocation of objects during the recording of the imagery, also showed an improvement for the detection of the targets employed in that study in fused imagery,[37,55] but our results with the less rigorous cut-and-paste method indicated no advantage of fusion over IR.[49] Resolution of this conflict will require more testing to assess the limitations of the cut-and-paste method with the same types of targets and fusion methods.

Taken together, the results with these various approaches to testing target/object detection ability suggest that the ability of humans to detect specific region types or objects is often, but by no means always, improved by color fusion. It would appear that results depend upon the exact fusion method used, the type of target and background used, and the exact nature of the target detection task employed. More human factors perceptual testing is required to fully sort out these initial results.

6.5.4 *Observer preferences for imagery*

The crucial question in assessing color fusion is how well humans perform in methodologically rigorous perceptual tasks. Just as the image with the highest detail (contrast at high spatial frequencies) may not be the one that mediates the best performance on a given perceptual task, the observers' preference for one type of imagery or another may not correspond to best performance on a given task. With that important caveat in mind, it is still interesting to consider what type of imagery is preferred by viewers. In one such study comparing IR, I² and contrast-based local monochrome fusion, both experienced pilots and nonpilots vastly preferred the monochrome-fused imagery across a variety of thermal and illumination conditions.[48] In their study, Steele and Perconti[58] found that although Army helicopter pilots rating segments of video imagery found the imagery barely acceptable, one color-fusion method (MIT-LL) was preferred to another (NRL), but neither color-fusion method was preferred more than the IR imagery. In a second task, using a set of 25 still scenes, no preferences for any format were shown. In a study using a more rigorous scaling and preference mapping procedure[36] achromatic fusion generally was preferred, but single-sensor imagery, this time I², was preferred most. Indeed, most strikingly, there was a negative preference for color-fused imagery; that is, static color images were disliked.

In sum, single-sensor imagery is sometimes, but not always, preferred over fused imagery and no study has yet shown a strong preference for color-fused imagery on these types of preference measurements. Not surprisingly, some color-fusion methods are preferred to others. In light of the improved performance shown on certain perceptual tasks with color-fused imagery, the lack of a preference for this imagery is perhaps surprising. On the other hand, the color rendering in the fused imagery is frequently very different from natural daylight scenes; it often looks very unnatural. Thus it may not be surprising that it is often subjectively rated very low. Possibly, the low preferences are due to the lack of familiarity with the false-color renderings, in which case this dislike might be overcome with training. Alternatively, the low preferences might be because observers tend to weigh the appearance of spatial details, which are not perceptually salient in most color-fused imagery, heavily when making preference judgements. The answer to this question awaits further research.

6.6   Conclusion

In this review we have seen repeatedly that, compared to performance with the unfused single-sensor imagery, fusion may create imagery that helps human perceptual performance, but it also may create imagery that hurts performance. Sometimes the same fused imagery will yield increased human performance on one aspect of human perception yet decreased performance on another. Furthermore, we have seen that a given fusion procedure can lead to increased performance on a particular aspect of perception for one type of scene content, yet hurt performance on the same task for another type of scene content (e.g., recognition of grass and road). In sum, the single most compelling conclusion to be drawn from the research to date is that in assessing the utility of sensor fusion, the role of the human viewer must always be considered—the perceptual organization performed by the human visual processing is complex and multifaceted, and the effects of fusion on perception are not presently predictable without empirical psychophysical testing. To be useful, sensor fusion must create imagery that not only combines component images, but renders them in a format tailored for the multiple facets of human visual perception and for the demands of the perceptual task at hand.

From the studies in which human performance was carefully assessed by rigorous psychophysical methods, the inescapable conclusion is that sensor fusion in general, and color fusion in particular, *can* improve human visual perception and performance. This was seen numerous times in this literature review. In order to summarize studies that bear on this, we have tabulated the results of the studies that have assessed image fusion by behavioral means (see Table 6.1). We attempted to include as many studies as possible in the table and leave it to the reader to evaluate the methodological rigor and the import of the tasks utilized in the studies. For each perceptual task reported by each of these studies, a check mark is entered in the table to indicate whether fusion improved, was equal to, or hurt human performance, relative to the results from the unfused single-sensor imagery with the best perceptual performance of the tested single-sensor types. Where imagery from multiple types of fusion was tested in a single study, results from the imagery with best performance were used. In general, across all aspects of perception tested, fusion (either color or gray-scale fusion) was observed to help performance twice as often as it hurt performance. Fusion had no significant effect on performance about as often as it helped. In comparing performance with the various types of imagery (rightmost column of Table 6.1), performance with IR imagery beat performance with I^2 imagery as often as performance with I^2 imagery beat that with IR imagery (this finding alone explains the need for sensor fusion). In those studies that tested performance with both gray-scale and color-fused imagery, performance with color-fused imagery was almost uniformly superior; performance with gray-scale fusion only beat performance with color-fused imagery in a single case. Frequently, however, performance with color-fused and gray-scale–fused imagery was equivalent, with neither producing benefits relative to the other.

That performance with one type of imagery (say, color fused) does not always beat performance of another type indicates that the comparative utility of a particular type of imagery is dependent upon factors beyond image format. The conclusions drawn in the earlier sections of this chapter indicate that the utility of a type of imagery depends on the specific perceptual ability being considered, and the particular content of the scene (e.g., grass, sky, or man-made objects). Presumably it also depends upon sensor characteristics and quality for a given type of sensor and also upon the particular fusion method as well, although there is not enough data to indicate this yet.

What general conclusions can be drawn? From the literature it appears that (1) color fusion greatly helps to delineate image regions corresponding to contrasting regions of scenic content (e.g., road next to grass, or trees next to sky), (2) there exists strong agreement that color fusion can aid in target/object detection, and that color fusion specifically helps relative to gray-scale fusion, and (3) color fusion can aid in determining spatial relations in a scene and region classification, fundamental aspects of perceptual

Table 6.1 Summary of Results of the Psychophysical Testing to Fused Imagery (Fusion of Low-Light and IR Imagery)

Study	Task	Fusion helps	Fusion same	Fusion hurts	Complete results
Aguilar et al., 1999	Subjective rating of task difficulty for:				
	Tracking people		✓		$cf = ir > i^2$
	Identification of people		✓		$i^2 > cf > ir$
	Discrimination of people				$cf = ir > i^2$
	Identify activity	✓			$cf > ir > i^2$
	Detect vehicles		✓		$cf = ir > i^2$
	Identify vehicles		✓		$cf = i^2 > ir$
	Identify uniforms		✓		$cf = i^2 > ir$
	Discriminate uniforms		✓		$cf = i^2 > ir$
	Identify weapons				$cf > i^2 > ir$
	Discriminate weapons	✓			$cf > i^2 > ir$
	Detect camouflage				$cf > i^2 > ir$
	Obscurants: Vegetation		✓		$cf = ir > i^2$
	Obscurants: Smoke screen		✓		$cf = ir > i^2$
DeFord et al., 1997	Region recognition (uniform regions)			✓	$i^2 > cf = gf > ir$
See also Sinai et al., 1996	Region recognition (contrasting regions)	✓			$cf > gf > i^2 > ir$
DeFord et al., 2000					
Essock et al., 1996	Texture segmentation: Grouping			✓	$ir > cf = gf > i^2$
Essock et al., 1997	Texture segmentation: Filtered regions				$cf = gf = ir > i^2$
Essock et al., 1999	Region recognition	✓			$cf > ir > i^2$
	Texture segmentation: Grouping			✓	$ir > cf = gf > i^2$
	Region recognition				$cf > ir = i^2$
Krebs et al., 1998	Target detection in video sequence			✓	$ir > cf = gf > i^2$
Krebs et al., 1999a	Target detection of person	✓			$cf = gf > i^2 > ir$
Krebs et al., 1999b	Target detection of embedded object				$cf = lwir > mwir > gf > swir$

Reference	Task			Result
Ryan and Tinkler 1995	Subjective rating of image quality		✓	$gf > ir = i^2$
Sampson et al., 1996	Target detection of embedded object	✓		$cf = gf = ir = i^2$
Sinai et al., 1999a	Target identification (people and vehicles)	✓		$cf > gf = ir = i^2$
	Scene orientation	✓		$cf = gf = i^2 > ir$
Sinai et al., 1999b	Scene recognition	✓		$cf = gf > i^2 > ir$
Sinai et al., 2000	Texture segmentation: Grouping		✓	$ir > gf > i^2$
	Region discrimination	✓		$gf > ir = i^2$
Steele and Perconti 1997	Object identification/location queries	✓		$cf = gf = ir > i^2$
	Shape and orientation	✓		$cf = gf = i^2 > ir$
	Determination of level horizon	✓		$cf = gf = ir = i^2$
	Target detection in video sequence	✓		$cf = gf = ir = i^2$
	Subjective rating of image quality	✓		$cf = gf = ir = 2$
Toet et al., 1997a	Spatial relations in scene	✓	✓	$cf = gf > ir = 2$
	Detection misses in spatial relations task	✓		$cf > gf > ir > 2$
See also Aguilar et al., 1998 and Toet et al., 1997b				
Toet et al., 2000	Scene orientation	✓		$cf = i^2 > gf > ir$
	Horizon discrimination		✓	$i^2 > cf > gf = i^2$
	Region recognition (buildings)		✓	$ir > cf = gf > i^2$
	Region recognition (humans)		✓	$ir > cf = gf > i^2$
	Region recognition (road)	✓		$cf > gf = i^2 > ir$
	Region recognition (vehicle)	✓		$cf = gf > i^2 = ir$
	Region recognition (water)	✓		$cf > gf = i^2 > ir$
Waxman et al., 1996	Detection of embedded square	✓		$cf > ir = i^2$

organization. On the other hand however, color fusion seems to be detrimental for perceptual analysis for certain types of scene content, such as regions of uniform scenic content (e.g., trees or grass).

These instances of detrimental effect are, at present, somewhat unpredictable, in that the extent to which they may vary with the imagery (i.e., different sensors, environmental conditions, and fusion method) is not yet clear. Several studies have shown clearly that fusion utility interacts with type of scene content (e.g., trees vs. horizon). This issue, that the image content affects performance of a particular aspect of perceptual organization, needs to be addressed. For example, to optimize image segmentation for target search, research must determine what image structural content is important and therefore should be emphasized, and what content is irrelevant and should not have processing time devoted to it. We have begun this type of analysis for image segmentation and have found that for one aspect or another of general image segmentation, one particular band of spatial frequencies or another is more important. For example, fusion has been shown to help performance on scene segmentation if the segmentation is based on low spatial frequency content, but is detrimental to segmentation performance if segmentation is based on middle spatial frequency content. This type of finding raises the possibility of altering fusion algorithms to emphasize the particular spatial frequency scales most relevant to the perceptual abilities being utilized under given circumstances.

This review indicates that fused imagery, particularly color-fused imagery, offers considerable improvement to human perceptual organization and situational awareness in some situations. What can be done to ensure that fusion helps (and not hurts) performance more of the time is not yet known. This review of the present literature has suggested two general research areas that should be pursued to address this. First, the image content required to perform various fundamental aspects of perceptual organization should be determined and this knowledge incorporated into image processing and fusion algorithms. As noted above, fusion methods might then be "tuned" to emphasize perceptually relevant information for various perceptual applications. We have already shown by using band-pass filtered imagery in behavioral testing that one can begin to assess what types of spatial content may be important for a certain human task, and what information may be deemphasized in fusion without loss of perceptual performance. Further work along these lines is needed.

The second area of needed research concerns the selection of color mappings in the false-color imagery (and associated aspects of training of users). Color mappings need to be examined in more detail with respect to human color vision and human performance. First of all, the color space of the human viewing the false-color display should be considered. Since human color discrimination and also color salience in "preattentive" vision are not uniform with respect to physical color space metrics, it would seem more profitable to map the physical color space produced by the sensor fusion method linearly onto the appropriate perceptual color space rather than directly onto another physical (RGB) color space. In other words, something akin to histogram equalization needs to be performed in the three-dimensional space (rather than in one dimension) and it needs to be performed in *perceptual* space in order to spread out the false-color mapping such that the steps in this mapping are as perceptually useful as possible for the particular perceptual task facing the user. Secondly, the issues raised above related to whether it is more useful to use novel colorations of particular targets, use some particular unnatural color rendering of whole scenes, or use roughly natural colors for scenes, needs to be assessed. That is, whether natural coloration of outdoor scenes is optimal or desirable for a given perceptual task is not yet known. Finally, the benefits possible from the training of users with false-color imagery need to be investigated.

Future research on human perceptual ability with fused imagery also needs to investigate other issues. Performance with temporal sequences of imagery needs to be investigated, particularly as the quality of real-time fusion is ever increasing, and, of course, because of the dynamic nature of human visual processing and perceptual organization. Future research also needs to pursue issues concerning the use of alternative and additional bands of radiation including hyperspectral imagery. This research needs to address whether different sets of bands can be selected to create intersensor contrast, or "signatures" across bands, that are particularly effective for humans performing different perceptual tasks.

Color fusion is in essence biological fusion, computationally done by the human visual system. Like fusion of dichoptic images by the binocular neural pathway of the human visual system, human processing combines three one-dimensional displays into one three-dimensional (color) display. This is an incredibly powerful transformation leading to a much larger volume of realizable perceptual space. However there are problems: due to the processing of the human visual system, and due to the prior learning and experience in the visual world, color fusion does not presently necessarily improve visual performance of humans. Depending upon the characteristics of the particular images, the fusion and rendering method, the nature of the scenic content, and most importantly, the particular aspect of multifaceted human perceptual organization being considered, human performance may improve or may decrease due to color fusion. The challenge that now faces researchers is to determine whether fusion methods can be improved to be more broad-spectrum with respect to various aspects of human perceptual organization, or whether aspects of fusion and display need to be made selectable to emphasize the aspects of visual perception needed for a given type of task situation. Ideally, one fusion/rendering method will optimize numerous aspects of perception. Perhaps analysis of the image content required to mediate different human perceptual abilities can exploit knowledge of which types of image content to emphasize in fusion in different user situations. This exciting research is in its infancy and the answers to these questions await future research.

This work was supported by grant #N00014-99-1-0516 from the Office of Naval Research (ONR). We wish to thank ONR and Army Night Vision and Electronic Sensors Directorate (NVESD) for providing the imagery used in this research. We also thank ONR, Army NVESD, Tami Peli, Dean Scribner, Lex Toet, and Frank Werblin for providing the images reproduced in this chapter. Finally, we emphasize that all fusion was performed by the individuals/labs indicated in the text.

References

1. Aguilar, M., Fay, D. A., Ireland, D. B., Racamato, J. P., Ross, W. D., and Waxman, A. M., Field evaluations of dual-band fusion for color night vision, *Proc. SPIE Conf. Enhanced and Synthetic Vision*, SPIE-3691, 168–175, 1999.

2. Aguilar, M., Fay, D. A., Ross, W. D., Waxman, A. M., Ireland, D. B., and Racamato, J. P., Real-time fusion of low-light CCD and uncooled IR imagery for color night vision, *Proc. SPIE Conf. Enhanced and Synthetic Vision*, SPIE-3364, 124–135, 1998.

3. Anderson, J. D., Bechtoldt, H. P., and Dunlap, G. L., Binocular integration in line rivalry, *Bull. Psychonomic Soc.*, 11, 399–402, 1978.

4. Barham, P., Oxley, P., and Ayala, B., Evaluation of the human factors implications of Jaguar's first prototype near-infrared night vision system, in *Vision in Vehicles 6*, Gale, A. G., et al., Eds., Elsevier Science, Amsterdam, 1998.

5. Beck, J., Prazdny, K., and Rosenfeld, A., A theory of textural segmentation, in *Human and Machine Vision*, Beck, J., Hope, B., and Rosenfeld, A., Eds., Academic Press, New York, 1–38, 1983.

6. Berson, E. L., Night Blindness: some aspects of management, in *Clinical Low Vision*, Faye, E. E., Ed., Little, Brown and Co., Boston, 1976.

7. Biederman, I. and Ju, G., Surface versus edge-based determinants of visual recognition, *Cognit. Psychol.*, 20, 38–64, 1988.

8. Caelli, T. and Yuzyk, J., What is perceived when two images are combined? *Perception*, 14, 41–48, 1985.

9. Cameron, A. A., The development of the combiner eyepiece night vision goggle, *Proc. SPIE Conf. on Helmet-Mounted Displays II*, SPIE—The International Society for Optical Engineering, Bellingham, WA, 1290, 16–29, 1990.

10. DeFord, J. K., Sinai, M. J., Krebs, W. K., Srinivasan, N., and Essock, E. A., Perceptual organization of color and non-color nighttime real-world imagery, *Invest. Ophthal. Visual Sci. (Suppl.)*, 38, S641, 1997.

11. DeFord, J. K., Sinai, M. J., Purkiss, T. J., and Essock, E. A., Segmentation of nighttime real-world scenes, *Invest. Ophthal. and Visual Sci. (Suppl.)*, 41, S221, 2000.

12. DeValois, R. L. and DeValois, K. K., *Spatial Vision*. Oxford, New York, 1998.

13. Donderi, D. C., Visual acuity, color vision, and visual search performance at sea, *Hum. Factors*, 36, 129–144, 1994.

14. Essock, E. A., An essay on texture: the extraction of stimulus structure from the visual image, in Burns B., Ed., *Percepts, Concepts, and Categories*, Elsevier Science, Amsterdam, 1992, 3–35.

15. Essock, E. A., McCarley, J. S., Sinai, M. J., and Krebs, W. K., Functional assessment of night-vision enhancement of real-world scenes, *Invest. Ophthal. and Visual Sci. (Suppl.)*, 37, S517, 1996.

16. Essock, E. A., Sinai, M. J., McCarley, J. S., Krebs, W. K., and DeFord, J. K., Perceptual ability with real-world nighttime scenes: image-intensified, infrared, and fused-color imagery, *Hum. Factors*, 41, 438–452, 1999.

17. Essock, E. A., Sinai, M. J., Srinivasan, N., DeFord, J. K., and Krebs, W. K., Texture-based segmentation in real-world nighttime scenes, *Invest. Ophthal. and Visual Sci. (Suppl.)*, 38, S639, 1997.
18. Gibson, J. J., *The Perception of the Visual World*, Houghton Mifflin, Boston, 1950.
19. Goodale, M. A., The cortical organization of visual perception and visuomotor control, in S. M. Kosslyn and Osherson, D. N., Eds., *An Invitation to Cognitive Science*, 2nd ed., Volume 2: *Visual Cognition*, MIT Press, Cambridge, MA, 167–213, 1995.
20. Grossberg, S., *Neural Networks and Natural Intelligence* (Chapters 1–4). MIT Press, Cambridge, MA, 1988.
21. Hoffman, R. R., Remote perceiving: a step toward a unified science of remote sensing, *Geocarto Int.*, 5, 3–13, 1990.
22. Hoffman, R. R., Detweiler, M. A., Lipton, K., and Conway, J. A., Considerations in the use of color in meteorological displays, *Weather Forecasting*, 8, 505–518, 1993.
23. Howard, I. P. and Rogers, B. J., *Binocular Vision and Stereopsis*, Oxford, New York, 1995.
24. Irwin, D. E., Information integration across saccadic eye movements, *Cognit. Psych.*, 23, 420–456, 1990.
25. Julesz, B., Toward an axiomatic theory of preattentive vision, in *Dynamic Aspects of Neocortical Function*. Edelman, G. M., Gall, W. E. and Cowan W. M., Eds., Wiley, New York, 585–612, 1984.
26. Klein, G. A. and Hoffman, R. R., Seeing the invisible: perceptual-cognitive aspects of expertise, in *Cognitive Science Foundations of Instruction*, Rabinowitz, M., Ed., Erlbaum, Mahwah, NJ, 203–226, 1992.
27. Krebs, W. K., McCarley, J. S., Kozek, T., Miller, G., Sinai, M. J., and Werblin, F. S., An evaluation of a sensor fusion system to improve drivers' nighttime detection of road hazards, *Proc. 43rd Annu. Meet. Hum. Factors Ergonomics Soc.*, 1999a.
28. Krebs, W. K., Scribner, D. A., McCarley, J. S., Ogawa, J. S., and Sinai, M. J. Comparing human target detection with multidimensional matched filtering methods, *Proc. NATO Res. Technol. Conf. Search and Target Acquisition.* Amsterdam, The Netherlands, 1999b.
29. Krebs, W. K., Scribner, D. A., Miller, G. M., Ogawa, J. S., and Schuler, J., Beyond third generation: a sensor fusion targeting FLIR pod for the F/A-18, *Proc. SPIE-Sensor Fusion: Architectures, Algorithms, and Appl. II*, 3376, 129–140, 1998.
30. Krebs, W. K., Scribner, D. A., Schuler, J., Miller, G., and Lobik, D., Human factor test and evaluation of a low light sensor fusion device for automobile applications, Automotive Night Vision/Enhanced Driving Conference, Detroit, MI, June 5, 1996.
31. Livingstone, M. S. and Hubel, D. H., Segregation of form, color, movement, and depth: anatomy, physiology, and perception, *Science*, 240, 740–749, 1988.
32. Lowe, R. K., Components of expertise in the perception and interpretation of meteorological charts, in *Interpreting Remote Sensing Imagery: Human Factors*, Hoffman, R. R. and Markman, A. B., Eds., Lewis Publishers, Boca Raton, FL, 2001.
33. Luo, R. and Kay, M., Data fusion and sensor integration: state of the art in the 1990s, in *Data Fusion in Robotics and Machine Intelligence*, Abidi, M. and Gonzalez, R., Eds., Academic Press, San Diego, 7–136, 1992.
34. Macmillan, N. A. and Creelman, C. D., *Detection Theory: A User's Guide*. Cambridge University Press, New York, 1991.
35. Marr, D., *Vision: A Computational Investigation into the Human Representation and Processing of Visual Information*. W. H. Freeman, San Francisco, 1982.

36. McCarley, J. S., Krebs, W. K., Essock, E. A., and Sinai, M. J., Multidimensional scaling of single-band and sensor-fused dual-band imagery, unpublished data.
37. McCarley, J. S., and Krebs, W. K., Detection of road hazards in thermal, visible, and sensor-fused nighttime imager, *Appl. Ergonomics*, 31, 523–530, 2000.
38. McDaniel, R., Scribner, D., Krebs, W., Warren, P., Ockman, N., and McCarley, J., Image fusion for tactical applications, *Proc. SPIE—Infrared Technology and Applications XXIV*, 3436, 685–695, 1998.
39. Mollon, J. D., Tho' she kneel'd in that place where they grew . . . : the uses and origins of primate color vision, *J. Exp. Biol.*, 146, 21–38, 1989.
40. Nothdurft, H.-C., The role of features in preattentive vision: comparison of orientation, motion and color cues, *Vision Res.*, 33, 1937–1958, 1993.
41. Peli, E., Contrast in complex images, *J. Optical Society Am.* A, 7, 2030–2040, 1990.
42. Peli, E., in search of a contrast metric: matching the perceived contrast of Gabor patches at different phases and bandwidths, *Vision Res.*, 37, 3217–3224, 1997.
43. Peli, T., Ellis, K., Stahl, R., and Peli, E., Integrated color coding and monochrome multi-spectral fusion, *Proc. IRIS Specialty Group Sensor Data Fusion, Multi-Source Fusion Theory Applications*, 1999.
44. Peli, T. and Lim, J. S., Adaptive filtering for image enhancement, *J. Optical Eng.*, 21, 108–112, 1982.
45. Peli, T., Peli, E., Ellis, K., and Stahl, R., Multi-spectral image fusion for visual displays, *Proc. SPIE Conf. Sensor Fusion: Architectures, Algorithms, and Appli. III*, 3719, SPIE—The International Society for Optical Engineering, 1999.
46. Philips, W. A., On the distinction between sensory storage and short-term visual memory, *Percept. Psychophysics*, 16, 283–290, 1974.
47. Rabin, J. and Wiley, R., Switching from forward-looking infrared to night vision goggles: transitory effects on visual resolution, *Aviation Space, Environmental Medicine*, 65, 327–329, 1994.
48. Ryan, D. and Tinkler, R., Night pilotage assessment of image fusion, *Proc. SPIE Conf. on Helmet and Head-mounted Displays and Symbology Design Requirements II*, 2465, SPIE—The International Society for Optical Engineering, Bellingham, WA, 50–67, 1995.
49. Sampson, M. T., Krebs, W. K., Scribner, D. A., and Essock, E. A., Visual search in natural (visible, infrared, and fused visible and infrared) stimuli, *Invest. Ophthal. Visual Sci. (Suppl.)*, 37, S296, 1996.
50. Scribner, D. A., Satyshur, M. P., and Kruer, M. R., Composite infrared color images and related processing, IRIS Specialty Group on Targets, Backgrounds, and Discrimination, January, San Antonio, TX, 1993.
51. Scribner, D. A., Satyshur, M. P., Schuler, J., and Kruer, M. R., Infrared color vision, IRIS Specialty Group on Targets, Backgrounds, and Discrimination, January, Monterey, CA, 1996.
52. Scribner, D. A., Warren, P., and Schuler, J., Extending color vision methods to bands beyond the visible, *Proc. IEEE Workshop on Comput. Vision beyond the Visible Spectrum: Methods and Appl.*, June, Fort Collins, CO, 1999.
53. Scribner, D. A., Warren, P., Schuler, J., Satyshur, M., and Kruer, M. R., Infrared color vision, *Optics Photonics News*, 9, 27–32, 1998.
54. Sinai, M. J., Essock, E. A., and Krebs, W. K., Perceptual organization of real-world scenes, Annual Meeting of the Psychonomics Society, Chicago, IL, November, 1996.

55. Sinai, M. J., McCarley, J. S., Krebs, W. K., and Essock, E. A., Psychophysical comparisons of single- and dual-band fused imagery, *Proc. SPIE Conf. on Enhanced and Synthetic Vision*, Orlando, FL, 3691, 176–183, 1999a.

56. Sinai, M. J., McCarley, J. S., and Krebs, W. K., Scene recognition using infrared, low-light, and fused-color imagery, *Proc. IRIS Specialty Group on Passive Sensors*, February, Monterey, CA, 1999b.

57. Sinai, M. J., DeFord, J. K., Purkiss, T. J., and Essock, E. A., Relevant spatial frequency information in the texture segmentation of night-vision imagery, *Proc. SPIE Conf. on Enhanced and Synthetic Vision*, Orlando, FL, 4023, 2000.

58. Steele, P. M. and Perconti, P., Part task investigation of multispectral image fusion using gray scale and synthetic color night vision sensor imagery for heli-copter pilotage, *Proc. SPIE 11th Annu. Inter. Symp. Aerosp./Defense Sensing, Simulation and Controls*, SPIE—The International Society for Optical Engineering, Bellingham, WA, 3062, 88–100, 1997.

59. Therrien, C. W., Scrofani, J., and Krebs, W. K., An adaptive technique for the enhanced fusion of low-light with uncooled thermal infrared imagery, *IEEE Conference on Image Processing*, October, 1997.

60. Toet, A., Image fusion by a ratio of low-pass pyramid, *Pattern Recognition Letters*, 9, 245–253, 1989.

61. Toet, A., Multiscale contrast enhancement with applications to image fusion, *Optical Eng.*, 31, 1026–1031, 1992.

62. Toet, A., Ijspeert, J. K., Waxman, A. M., and Aguilar, M., Fusion of visible and thermal imagery improves situational awareness, *Proc. SPIE Conf. on Enhanced and Synthetic Vision*, 3088, 177–188, 1997a.

63. Toet, A., Ijspeert, J. K., Waxman, A. M., and Aguilar, M., Fusion of visible and thermal imagery improves situational awareness, *Displays*, 18, 85–95, 1997b.

64. Toet, A., Schoumans, N., and IJspeert, J. K., Perceptual evaluation of different nighttime modalities, *Fusion 2000: Proc. 3rd Inter. Conf. Information Fusion*, Paris, 2000.

65. Toet, A., van Ruyven, L. J., and Valeton, J. M., Merging thermal and visual images by a contrast pyramid, *Optical Eng.*, 28, 789–792, 1989.

66. Toet, A. and Walraven, J., New false color mapping for image fusion, *Optical Eng.*, 35, 650–658, 1996.

67. Uttal, W. R., Baruch, T., and Allen, L., Dichoptic and physical information com-bination: a comparison, *Perception*, 24, 351–362, 1995.

68. Vrahimis, G., Multisensor image fusion–a neural network based approach, *Progress in Connectionist-Based Information Systems: Proc. Inter. Conf. on Neural Information Processing and Intelligent Information Systems*, Springer-Verlag, Singapore, 1998.

69. Wandell, B. A., *Foundations of Vision*, Sinauer Associates, Inc., Massachusetts, 1995.

70. Ward, N. J., Stapleton, L., and Parkes, A., Behavioral and cognitive impact of night-time driving with HUD contact analogue infrared imaging, *Proc. 14th Inter. Technical Conf. on Enhanced Safety of Vehicles*, Munich Germany, May 23–26, 1994.

71. Waxman, A. M., Carrick, J. E., Fay, D. A., Racamato, J. P., Aguilar, M., and Savoye, E. D., Electronic imaging aids for night driving: low-light CCD, thermal IR, and color fused visible/IR, *Proc. SPIE Conf. on Transportation Sensors and Control*, 2902, 1996b.

72. Waxman, A. M., Carrick, J. E., Racamato, J. P., Fay, D. A., Aguilar, M., and Savoye, Color night vision—3rd update: realtime fusion of low-light CCD

visible and thermal IR imagery, *Proc. SPIE Conf. on Enhanced and Synthetic Vision*, 3088, 1997b.

73. Waxman, A. M., Fay, D. A., Gove, A., Siebert, M., Racamato, J. P., Carrick, J. E., Savoye, E. D., Color night vision: fusion of intensified visible and thermal imagery, *Pro. SPIE Conf. on Synthetic Vision for Vehicle Guidance and Control*, 2463, 58–63, 1995.

74. Waxman, A. M., Fay, D. A., Ireland, D. B., Racamato, J. P., Ross, W. D., Streilein, W. W., Braun, M., and Aguilar, M., Fusion of 2–/3–/4–sensor imagery for visualization, target learning, and search, *Proc. SPIE Conf. on Enhanced and Synthetic Vision*, 4023, 2000.

75. Waxman, A. M., Gove, A. N., Fay, D. A., Racamato, J. P., Carrick, J. E., Seibert, M. C., and Savoye, E. D., Color night vision: opponent processing in the fusion of visible and IR imagery, *Neural Networks*, 10, 1–6, 1997a.

76. Waxman, A. M., Gove, A., Siebert, M. C., Fay, D. A., Carrick, J. E., Racamato, J. P., Savoye, E. D., Burke, B. E., Reich, R. K., McGonagle, W. H., and Craig, D. M., Progress on color night vision: visible/ir fusion, perception and search, and low-light CCD imaging, *Proc. SPIE Conf. on Enhanced and Synthetic Vision*, 2736, 96–107, 1996a.

77. Werblin, F. S., Roska, T., Chua, L., Jacobs, A., Kozek, T., and Zarandy, A., Transfer of retinal technology to applications beyond biological vision, *Investigative Ophthalmol. Visual Sci.*, 38, S479, 1997.

78. Werblin, F. S., Roska, T., and Chua, L., The analogic cellular neural network as a bionic eye, *Int. J. Circuit Theory Appl.*, 23, 541–569, 1995.

79. Wolfe, J. M., Visual search in continuous, naturalistic stimuli, *Vision Res.* 34, 1187–1195, 1994.

80. Wurm, L. H., Legge, G. E., Isenberg, L. M., and Luebker, A., Color improves object recognition in normal and low vision, *J. Exp. Psychol. Hum. Percept. Performance*, 19, 899–911, 1993.

section four

Seeing the Dynamics

chapter seven

Components of Expertise in the Perception and Interpretation of Meteorological Charts

Richard K. Lowe

Contents

1-56670-413-8/01/$0.00+$.50
©2001 by CRC Press LLC

Keywords: *meteorologists, nonmeteorologists, expertise, perception, interpretation, knowledge, mental models, visuo-spatial, meteorological, domain-specific
knowledge, domain-general knowledge, weather maps, expert, novice, perceptual
salience, relationships*

7.1   Introduction

Meteorological charts, commonly known as "weather maps" are a form of
visual display that is used both as a specialized professional tool for practicing meteorologists and as a resource for teaching students of meteorology.
These two types of audiences bring very different levels of meteorological
expertise to their interactions with meteorological charts. The purpose of this
chapter is to explore the effects that such expertise differences may have on
the ways that meteorological charts are interpreted and perceived. The chapter reviews a set of research studies that investigated the way experts and
novices interacted with weather map information across a varied set of processing tasks. The underlying motivation for these investigations was to seek
expert/novice differences in the way weather maps are mentally represented, as a basis for helping beginning students of meteorology to develop
weather map interpretation skills more efficiently. However, the conceptual
frameworks and research approaches developed during this research
program also appear applicable more generally to studies of expert/novice
differences in the interpretation of a broad range of remote sensing data
displays.

This chapter begins with an overview of the theoretical foundations
supporting the set of research studies. It then presents a brief account of
each study that covers its specific theoretical framework, methodology,
and results. Finally, some overall conclusions are drawn, reflections
about training implications made, and recommendations for future research
given.

7.2   Theoretical foundations

A particular focus of this research is the role that knowledge plays in perception and interpretation of weather maps. What we perceive when viewing a
visual stimulus depends both on the characteristics of that stimulus (external
to the viewer) and on the knowledge we bring to that viewing experience
(internal to the viewer). Similarly, there are both external and internal influences on our ultimate interpretion of what we see. The extent to which perception and interpretation are shaped by each of these two influences is likely to depend in part on the nature of the stimulus involved. In the case of
visual displays, it seems reasonable to suppose that the less information a
display explicitly depicts, the greater would be the reliance on the existing

knowledge that a viewer brings to the processes of perception and interpretation. This knowledge is generally considered to be stored as structures in the mind that mentally represent information acquired as a result of an individual's prior experience.

Weather maps are abstract displays that give an economical representation of their referent situation. This representation is very selective in the content it includes, stylized in the graphic notation it employs to depict that content, and highly conventionalized in the way the markings constituting that notation system are used. Because weather map displays are in various respects a quite minimalist representation of information, it is likely that their perception and interpretation will be heavily reliant on the viewer's knowledge base.

There are two important classes of knowledge that could be involved here: everyday visual knowledge that can be applied broadly across a variety of subject-matter domains (i.e. domain-general), and more specialized domain-specific knowledge that characterizes a particular knowledge domain (in this case, meteorology). Two major components of everyday visual knowledge are (1) generalized visuo-spatial knowledge about aspects such as the size, shape, and apparent grouping of the entities we see that can be applied to any visual experience, irrespective of its content or format, and (2) visual knowledge about the content of our everyday experiences such as the materials, objects, systems, and events we routinely encounter as we interact with our environment. For successful perception and interpretation of visual information in a highly specialized domain such as meteorology, everyday visual knowledge should play a role that is subservient to that played by domain-specific knowledge. Some aspects of everyday knowledge may be irrelevant, unsuitable, or even misleading if directly and indiscriminately applied to a specialized domain.

Our perceptions provide the raw material upon which interpretation can operate, and so they determine what interpretations are possible. Incomplete or inappropriate perception of the information in a visual display can therefore derail interpretation processes. The research reported in this chapter focuses on how the external visual information presented in weather maps is represented in the minds of viewers with different levels of expertise in meteorology. The particular class of mental representation of interest here is the mental model, a type of representation that is assumed to be constructed on the basis of what has been perceived during viewing. Mental models are characterized as consisting of mental tokens and relationships that stand for the subject matter they represent. To be a useful basis for interpretation, a mental model should represent the meaning of the situation that is the depiction's referent, and not be merely a literal representation of the depiction itself. In the case of a weather map, this means the viewer's mental model would be of a particular meteorological situation in the real world, not merely a snapshot or image of a set of graphic elements arranged on a page.

However, it seems likely that this ideal would be difficult to achieve for viewers with a low level of meteorological expertise, because their mental model building capacities would be constrained by their lack of domain-specific knowledge. Without such a knowledge base, novices in the domain of meteorology could have little alternative but to invoke other types of knowledge to support their perception and interpretation of the highly parsimonious information presented in a weather map. Everyday visual knowledge of the type described above would appear to be a likely candidate. On this basis, we can speculate about the nature of the mental model that a nonmeteorologist could construct as a result. Perhaps the mental model would be based upon a mixture of (1) visuo-spatial information about the depiction itself, (2) tokens and relationships borrowed from everyday experience about how the world around us is constituted and works, and (3) any fragments of domain-specific knowledge (accurate or otherwise) that have been acquired from sources such as weather reports in the media.

If this were the case, domain novices—such as beginning students of meteorology—would be poorly equipped to process the weather maps they encounter. Providing maps to these students on the assumption that the maps themselves could make a significant contribution to the learners' understanding of meteorology would be useless if the students were not equipped to process them properly. This could help explain why those who teach introductory meteorology find that their students can have great difficulty with weather maps and seem initially to benefit little from their use as an instructional resource.

The research studies surveyed in this chapter formed the foundation for instructional interventions designed to help beginning students of meteorology use weather maps more effectively. The research aimed to explore differences between the knowledge that experts and novices appear to use in dealing with weather maps as a means of characterizing their mental representations of this class of depictions. The goal was to find ways in which novice meteorologists could be trained to perceive and interpret weather map displays more appropriately by taking account of, and dealing with, their initial knowledge structures then developing suitable support systems.

7.3   *Perceptual and meteorological significance*

The patterning of the set of markings on a given weather map can be considered from both domain-general (visuo-spatial) and domain-specific (meteorological) perspectives. In a domain-general sense, the shape, size, and arrangement of certain graphic elements may lead to their being perceived together as part of a broader visuo-spatial pattern. In some cases, these sets of elements also correspond to components of the underlying meteorological situation. So, a series of tightly spaced concentric closed-loop isobars is both a distinctive visuo-spatial feature and an indication of the presence of a cyclone. In addition, the visual significance of certain types of patterns (as signalled by how readily perceptible they are) may happen to correspond to their meteorological significance. For example, there is correspondence between high perceptual salience and a high level of meteorological significance for the series of concentric isobars that represents a cyclone. Similarly, the high perceptual salience of the barbed-line symbol that marks the location of a cold front is a good guide to its meteorological significance. However, there are other cases in which there is poor correspondence between meteorological significance and general perceptual salience. For example, troughs and ridges are often indicated not by isolated features but rather by patterning that is superficially quite unremarkable in a perceptual sense. In these cases, minor local convolutions that are echoed across a series of adjacent isobars indicate the presence of a meteorologically significant feature. However, this subtle patterning of isobars can be obscured to a large extent by their visually distracting context, and so these features are more likely to be overlooked unless given special attention. Examples of these less-perceptible aspects are shown in Figure 7.1 in which broad shaded lines have been added to a weather map to reveal the location of troughs and ridges that run across the component isobars.

The way in which a viewer processes a given weather map's specific markings is likely to be influenced by the basis upon which that viewer

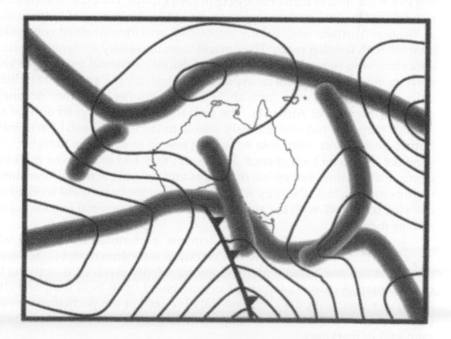

Figure 7.1 Australian weather map showing location of perceptually subtle patterns across markings indicating presence of troughs and ridges (gray shaded bands).

mentally represents weather map patterns in general. For example, if a viewer's mental representation of the weather map display genre is predominantly visuo-spatial in nature, that viewer's activity in processing a specific weather map could be expected to focus on the visuo-spatial characteristics of the display. Further, highly conspicuous aspects would be likely to receive most of the attention while more subtle aspects escape notice. Conversely, if a viewer's mental representation was predominantly meteorological in character, it would be more likely for processing activity to be dominated by the meteorological significance of the markings. Observable aspects of processing activity in both cases could include behaviors such as the order in which individual markings are dealt with in a weather map processing task, and the relative amounts of time devoted to the processing of the markings in different regions of the map. One of my experiments used such observations to explore the basis for meteorologists' and nonmeteorologists' mental representations.[2]

7.4   Copy-recall study

This study involved two groups of participants who were either experts or novices in the field of meteorology (16 in each group). The experts were experienced professional meteorologists employed by the Bureau of Meteorology in Western Australia whose daily forecasting activities involved concentrated work with weather maps. The novices were university students in teacher education who reported having only occasional, informal experience with weather maps, largely from newspapers and television. Participants individually copied the markings from an Australian weather map (the "original") onto a blank map of Australia. The task regime was designed so that the original map was not continuously visible to the experimental participant. Rather, participants were able either to view or to draw the markings but were not able to do both at once. This meant they had to copy the markings using an alternating succession of glances and drawing actions. After finishing this copying task, the copy was removed and the participant worked at a drawing recall task with the aim of regenerating the original markings onto a blank map.

Analysis of video records of participants' performance was made with respect to (1) the sequences in which markings were drawn, and (2) the duration of glances associated with the drawing activity involved in copying the original map. A cluster analysis procedure based upon local temporal clustering was used with the compiled data for each of the participant groups (meteorologists and nonmeteorologists) to assign a relational structure to the map's set of markings.

There was no direct attempt in this investigation to collect specific explanatory information, such as participants' characterizations of the particular element properties or relations upon which the clusters that emerged from the analysis were based. Nevertheless, there were indications of various differences between the two groups, including (1) the associations of graphic elements that emerged, (2) the sequence in which elements were processed, and (3) the effectiveness of recall. A discussion of selected findings illustrates some of the more important differences.

7.4.1 Results

The cluster analysis results suggested that meteorologists and nonmeteorologists have fundamentally different ways of grouping the meteorological markings comprising a weather map. For example, meteorologists' groupings indicated division of the map overall into a northern chunk and a southern chunk, which corresponds with the quite different meteorological influences that operate for these two halves of the Australian region.

This is shown in Figure 7.2 by the unshaded and shaded areas of the map. Such a subdivision is what would be expected if markings were treated in terms of the underlying meteorological situation represented by the map, not simply their visuo-spatial characteristics. In contrast, the nonmeteorologists' groupings divided the map into a western half and an eastern half. The shaded and unshaded areas in Figure 7.3 indicate these two chunks. This subdivision has no real meteorological foundation but is consistent with the fact that the markings on the west side of the map that was used formed a group of figurally similar elements in close proximity that are visually distinct from

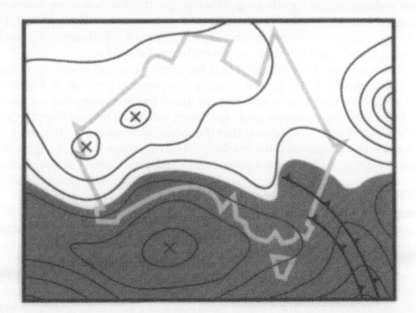

Figure 7.2 Meteorologists' north-south subdivision of meteorological pattern.

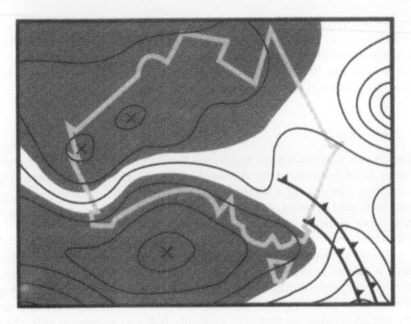

Figure 7.3   Nonmeteorologists' east-west subdivision of meteorological pattern.

the elements on the east side of the map. This explanation involves the low level visuo-spatial characteristics of the markings rather than their higher-level meteorological significance. (Further possibilities are other nonmeteorological influences such as the physical convenience of carrying out the drawing process during copying or the effect of habituated left-to-right patterns based upon the way people write English text.)

The sequence data indicated that meteorologists and nonmeteorologists used very different approaches during the copying process. In Figures 7.4 and 7.5 the outline of the Australian continent has been removed for the sake of clarity but the meteorological markings remain. The two superimposed pathways in Figure 7.4 indicate that the meteorologists typically used a two-stage strategy for copying the markings. The first stage (path 1) begins at the bottom right (cold front) then progresses via the high center and low centers to the cyclone. The meteorologists distributed several key elements around the map in positions that marked the location of major meteorological features. In effect, a general skeleton was initially set out for the whole map. The second stage (path 2) was then to pass through the map again in order to fill in subsidiary elements around this overarching framework. This pathway began with the cluster of isobars on the western edge, then progressed through the major features, adding isobars associated with each feature in turn. This approach was interpreted as evidence that the meteorological significance of markings plays a dominant role in the meteorologists' processing and that they characterize weather map markings in a structured fashion.

Figure 7.4 Meteorologists' two-stage strategy for copying weather map markings.

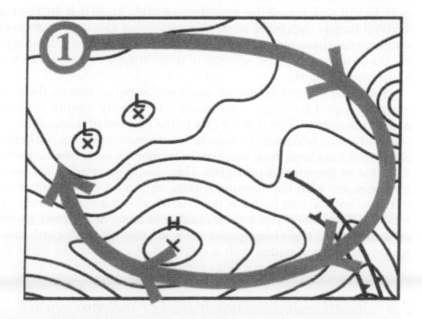

Figure 7.5 Nonmeteorologists' one-stage strategy for copying weather map markings.

In contrast, Figure 7.5 shows that the nonmeteorologists tended to use a one-stage strategy involving a single continuous pass around the map. Typically, this entailed starting from the top left of the map then working gradually around it in a clockwise sweep, exhaustively filling in all elements in each region as they progressed. Their sequencing of elements during this process was confined to a quite local focus and appeared to be influenced by the figural similiarity of elements and their spatial proximity. For the nonmeteorologists, approaches based upon superficial visuo-spatial characteristics of the map and habituated reading-writing processes suggest themselves as explanations, rather than a regard for the meteorological significance of the markings.

The meteorologists were significantly more successful overall than the nonmeteorologists at recalling the map's markings, both in terms of the proportion of elements recalled and the accuracy of recall. This suggests that the mental representation of the weather map constructed by the meteorologists during the copying task was generally more effective in terms of either or both storage and retrieval. These results are consistent with the meteorologists' ability to combine the many individual markings on the weather map into a richly interconnected and coherent array because of the multilevel meteorological relationships that they can invoke to bind these markings strongly together. The wealth of domain-specific meteorological knowledge possessed by the meteorologists could provide a basis for forming relational structures that facilitate storage and retrieval. In contrast, the nonmeteorologists' lack of such knowledge would presumably mean that their storage and retrieval largely depended on weakly connected low level domain-general visuo-spatial characteristics. This is unlikely to provide anything approaching the same multilayered network of relationships that would be available to the meteorologists.

Although the meteorologists' recall was superior overall, there was one revealing aspect for which their recall was actually inferior to that of the nonmeteorologists. This was the case of the number of triangular barbs that occurred on the cold front symbols. While the meteorologists had better recall of the cold front lines, their recall of the number of barbs was actually worse than that of the nonmeteorologists. This was interpreted as the meteorologists' concern with the meteorologically important component of the cold front symbol (the cold front line itself) while glossing over the more optional aspect of the symbols (the precise number of barbs on the line). By this type of explanation, the visuo-spatial basis of nonmeteorologists' processing would not have provided such a differentiation and so the barbs share as much status as the other markings comprising the map.

7.5   Relationships: visuo-spatial or meteorological?

Results from the first study indicated a need to gather more specific information about the nature of the relationships involved in structuring meteorologists' and nonmeteorologists' knowledge of weather maps in general.

Although the copy recall study had identified ways in which markings were clustered into groups, it did not directly investigate the basis for these groupings. Nevertheless, there were some indirect signs that the processing differences observed could possibly be explained by meteorologists' capacity to characterize a weather map in terms of powerful meteorological relationships, whereas the nonmeteorologists were largely confined to using superficial visuo-spatial relationships.

7.6 Element sorting study

The basis for the groupings that had emerged was investigated in a study that required experts and novices to make explicit decisions about how elements were related to each other and to provide explicit information about the nature of the relationships involved.[6] The experts were eight professional meteorologists while the novices were eight university teacher education students. The study used a card-sorting task during which participants grouped the graphic elements comprising a weather map in three stages and generated explanations for the basis of their groupings. Participants were given a randomly ordered set of cards, all of which showed the same weather map printed in black and white. Although all cards were otherwise identical, each card had a different element of the meteorological pattern highlighted in color.

Figure 7.6 shows two examples of these cards, each with a different graphic element highlighted. The first stage of the task involved participants freely sorting the card set into groups which they considered to contain related elements (elements that belonged together). In the second stage, they divided these original groups into smaller groups while in the third stage they returned to their original groups and combined them into larger groups. At each stage of the grouping process (original, subordinate, and superordinate), participants were required to give a verbal explanation for each group formed as to why its component elements were related to each other.

Figure 7.6 Examples of cards used for sorting task with different elements highlighted.

Records of the groupings' constituents were submitted to a cluster analysis that generated patterns of hierarchical organization involving groups, subgroups, and elements. In addition, a qualitative analysis of the grouping explanations was carried out to determine the extent to which domain-general or domain-specific relationships were used to account for the groups produced.

7.6.1   Results

The cluster analysis indicated that at a broad level, weather map markings were organized for the meteorologists according to large-scale patterns that corresponded to the locations of extended zones of regional meteorological significance.

The tree-diagram in Figure 7.7 summarizes the results of the cluster analysis and shows that each of these regions is comprised of a number of visually distinct but meteorologically related features. The overall clustering patterns for the meteorologist group as a whole were structured into the features found in the northern and southern halves of the map, a result consistent with that from the cluster analysis in the copy-recall study described above. This subdivision was further broken down into those in the extreme south, those in the midlatitudes, and those in the tropics. These zones differ from each other in terms of their meteorological environments due to the specific nature of the local and global influences involved. Each zone has its own particular climatology and is inhabited by a distinctive set of meteorological features.

As with the copy-recall study, the meteorologists' clusterings appeared not to be primarily based upon superficial visuo-spatial characteristics of the

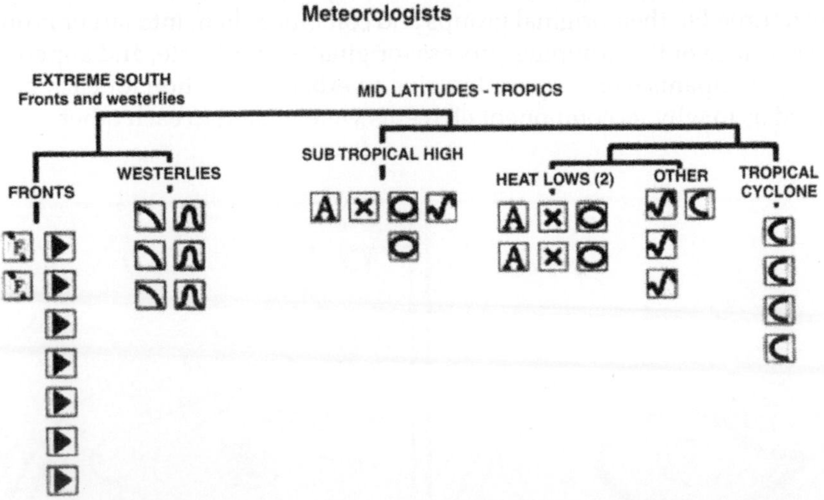

Figure 7.7   Summary of cluster analysis for meteorologists' results in card-sorting task.

markings but rather upon the deeper meteorological relationships in which they were involved. This conclusion is supported by the nature of the meteorologists' explanatory statements, which were highly domain-specific and indicated that the meteorological relationships involved ranged across multiple levels.

Example meteorologists' statements:

"Isobars showing the trough in which the fronts are embedded; frontal trough."

"(This marking is) . . . associated with a high in the Pacific to the south of the tropical cyclone; related to weather system not appearing on the weather map; Tasman high."

Meteorologists appeared to have a coordinated, hierarchical knowledge structure in which graphical information about markings was subservient to multilayered meteorological information about the atmospheric situation captured in the weather map. Further, there were indications in the meteorologists' statements that they used contextual knowledge to link markings shown within the map's boundaries to more global influences associated with meteorological zones that extended beyond those boundaries.

In contrast, Figure 7.8 shows that results of the cluster analysis for the nonmeteorologists' suggest an organization of elements that is primarily based on their appearance and proximity. Thus, the elements comprising the visually distinctive cold fronts were quite separate from those constituting the much less perceptually salient set of isobars in the two bottom corners of

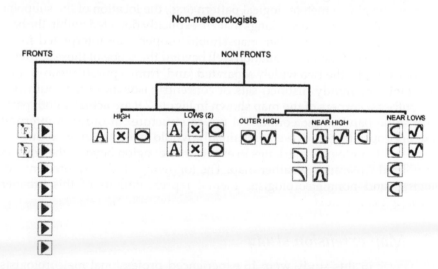

Figure 7.8 Summary of cluster analysis for nonmeteorologists' results in card-sorting task.

the map. However, this is a quite inappropriate distinction to make from a meteorological viewpoint, because these very different looking features all belong to the same southern meteorological zone. The nonmeteorologists' explanatory statements confirmed that they used a low-level visuo-spatial basis for combining the weather map markings into groups. In addition, these statements gave no indication that anything beyond the boundaries of the map was considered in making decisions about how markings were to be grouped.

Example nonmeteorologists' statements:

> "Curved lines or a second circle outside an inner circle; such as number 18 or 22; wavy lines or circular."
> "The cold front; threatening lines that move across at right angles to the other lines of pressure; only two so put together; lines of cold front."

7.7   Scope of representation

The processing behavior of nonmeteorologists was not only largely visuo-spatial in character; it also appeared to be based solely upon information which was depicted within the borders of the map. This latter constraint did not seem to apply for meteorologists, whose processing of within-map markings appeared to be modulated by consideration of the wider meteorological context. A normal Australian weather map covers a region only slightly larger than the Australian continent itself. However, a substantial proportion of the markings comprising such a map reflect broader-scale phenomena that contribute to the global meteorological pattern (e.g., the location of the subpolar jet stream). Therefore, the markings that are explicitly depicted within the borders of an Australian weather map should properly be interpreted in an implied context of their continuation well beyond the scope of those borders.

For example, the two widely separated (and, from a purely visuo-spatial viewpoint, apparently distinct) sets of concentric isobars in the southwest and southeast corners of the map shown in Figure 7.9 are actually both parts of the same band of meteorological macro structure. In order to interpret these appropriately, a viewer presumably would need to know about the types of meteorological markings to expect in the region beyond the borders of a normal Australian weather map. The following study explored meteorologists' and nonmeteorologists' mental representations of this broader meteorological context.

7.8   Map extension study

The experts in this study were 16 experienced professional meteorologists (forecasters with the Bureau of Meteorology in Western Australia) while the novices were 16 university students in the field of education who had no

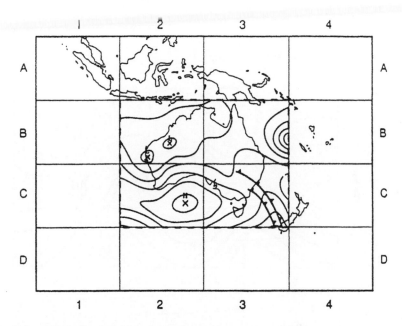

Figure 7.9 Australian weather map plus extension to region beyond that covered in standard regional map (used as basis for map extension study).

specialist training in meteorology. Participants were provided with a map that had been extended on all sides to cover an area far beyond that normally encompassed by an Australian regional weather map.[3] The central part of the full display was a normal Australian weather map (complete with meteorological markings) but the surrounding extended area was blank, except for land outlines where appropriate. Participants were asked to draw the meteorological markings that would be expected in the extended region.

7.8.1 Results

The two illustrative examples given in Figure 7.10 reflect the typical differences between meteorologists and nonmeteorologists in the sets of markings drawn in the extended region around the original map.

As well as producing significantly fewer markings in the extended region, the nonmeteorologists' markings appeared to have been derived quite directly from the visuo-spatial characteristics of the existing original markings. Typically, their new markings could be readily accounted for by assuming markings to result largely from the application of simple domain-general processes (such as extrapolation or interpolation) to the original markings. It was inferred that one of the nonmeteorologists' main frameworks for applying these processes was a visuo-spatially based "completion" strategy. In some cases, this strategy seemed to involve an attempt to turn as

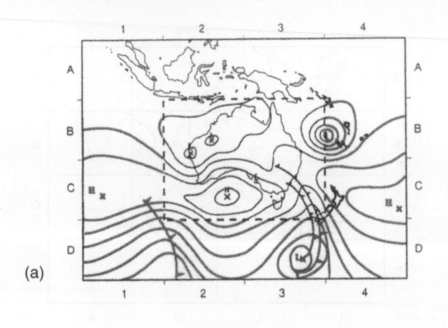

(a)

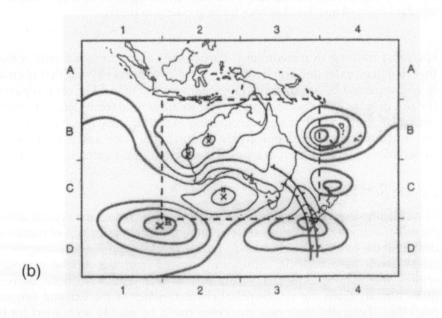

(b)

Figure 7.10   **(a)** Meteorologist's completion of the map extension task (illustrative example). **(b)** Nonmeteorologist's completion of the map extension task.

many simple curves as possible into closed figures (for example, closing arcs in the southwest corner to produce a figure resembling a pressure cell). In other cases where the curve was too complex for this simple conversion, the motivation appeared to be to continue existing patterns (for example, by extending open isobars that finished at the original map's border until they reached the extended region's border). The strategy can be interpreted as a reliance on internal, domain-general relations that were local in their scope and quite firmly anchored in the original map.

In contrast, the meteorologists' use of existing markings for generating markings within the extension area appeared to based upon far more than their literal visuo-spatial characteristics. Rather, their approach indicated they were operating in accordance with superordinate constraints involving a variety of external relations that integrated the original map area with the wider meteorological context. The resulting patterns in markings suggested the progressive clustering of lower-level weather map elements into high-level composite structures that correspond to meteorologically significant features and systems of wider significance. The superordinate constraints provided by relations involving the context of the Australian weather map region can be interpreted as a powerful framework that drives the meteorologists' interpretation of markings within that region.

The findings of this map extension study support the indications in the previous studies that meteorologists' and nonmeteorologists' mental representations of weather maps differ both in their fundamental basis (meteorological vs. visuo-spatial) and their extent (contextually situated vs. decontextualized). They also raise the issue of the temporal dimension of weather maps that is involved both in the way meteorological features change within a map's boundaries over time and in the way features enter and leave the weather map area as time passes.

7.9   Weather map dynamics

The investigations discussed thus far have been limited to single static depictions and so do not directly address weather map dynamics. However, one of the most important uses of weather maps is in making forecasts. These have traditionally relied heavily on reviewing past and current weather maps to predict the future pattern of meteorological markings, then interpreting that prognosis in terms of its real-life meteorological consequences. A well-rounded investigation of the mental representation of weather maps requires that this dynamic aspect be addressed. The next study compared the way experts and novices made predictions from a given weather map as a means of investigating their mental representations of weather map dynamics. It was based on the assumption that when meteorologists were given a weather map for a particular day, their efforts to predict the pattern of meteorological markings likely appear on the following day would be based on running a mental model of the current situation forward by a day.

Using the information on a given weather map to predict the pattern of markings expected on a later map is a direct test of the efficacy of the mental model constructed from the original map. For example, the indications from other studies that meteorologists' mental representations of weather map diagrams included contextual elaboration (that was largely absent from non-meteorologists' mental representations) should be supported by evidence from the type of predictions produced by these different participant groups. The running of a mental model built upon the basis of a well-contextualized domain-specific mental representation would be expected to produce a different prediction from that produced by running a model derived from a contextually impoverished domain-general representation.

7.10   Prediction drawing study

The experts in this study were 16 experienced professional meteorologists (forecasters with the Bureau of Meteorology in Western Australia) while the novices were 16 university students in the education field who had no specialist training in meteorology. Participants were given both a typical midsummer Australian weather map (including the main meteorological markings) and a blank map that showed only the outline map of Australia.[4,8] The blank map was printed on tracing paper so that the initial meteorological markings were visible when the blank map was superimposed on the original. Participants drew on the blank map the markings they expected to appear one day later than those shown on the original map.

7.10.1   Results

For the nonmeteorologists, markings on the forecast maps could be largely accounted for as the results of simple graphic manipulations of the original markings. Overall, these participants tended to move markings *en masse* from west to east without regard to meteorological dynamics. However, near the borders of the map, this general approach of translation could be modified to some extent by (1) stretching markings on the western edge to fill empty spaces that would have otherwise appeared, and (2) reducing the relative movement of markings close to the eastern edge so that they were retained on the map.

A more detailed examination of the nonmeteorologists' prediction markings revealed that the approaches described above were accompanied by problems with inter-isobar spacing and coordination. For example, there were irregularities in the isobar gradient pattern drawn by the nonmeteorologists across the prediction map as a whole that are inconsistent with the fluid nature of the atmosphere. There were also deficiencies at a more local level with the contouring and coordination of intra-isobar convolutions (such as would indicate the presence of a trough). For example, a major trough on the west coast of the continent that the meteorologists either maintained or deepened between the original and forecast maps tended to be reduced or to disappear completely in the nonmeteorologists' predictions.

In contrast, the meteorologists' predictions showed a much greater differentiation in the way the various markings on the map were treated. Rather than moving markings *en masse*, most of the displacement in the meteorologists' predictions was confined to markings in the southern half of the map and was quite differentiated according to feature type. Although this shift was in the same overall west-to-east direction as that produced in the nonmeteorologists' predictions, there was no evidence of the stretching or delaying of markings near the edges of the map as was found with the nonmeteorologists. Rather, completely new markings were added entering the western edge of the map (presumably having been moved in from the region beyond the map's boundaries). Markings near the eastern edge of the original map tended to disappear or become cut off at the border (as if they had continued their movement to take them beyond the map's boundaries). The markings in the meteorologists' forecast maps showed quite extensive changes from their original form, whereas those from the nonmeteorologists tended to retain much of their original form. Despite these changes in form made by the meteorologists, the overall isobar gradient patterns for the forecasts were adjusted to preserve the fluid-like character of the display.

The results of this investigation supported the earlier findings that nonmeteorologists' mental representations of a weather map are essentially confined within the boundary of the map while for the meteorologists they extend into the surrounding meteorological context. In addition, it seems that the nonmeteorologists' mental models of dynamic aspects of weather maps are highly simplistic and lacking in appropriate constraints on the form and movement of markings. These deficiencies are likely to be the result of nonmeteorologists' lack of experience with the temporal changes that occur across a sequence of weather maps. In contrast, professional meteorologists would have built up rich knowledge structures about weather map dynamics as a result of their long experience in daily forecasting activities.

If beginning students of meteorology are to obtain more instructional benefit from the weather maps they meet in their studies, perhaps they need to develop mental representations that are more consistent with the fundamental aspects of those possessed by professional meteorologists.

7.11   Summary and implications

The investigations reported here studied perceptual and interpretative processing from which inferences were drawn regarding the mental representation of weather maps. The results provided evidence that the nature of this mental representation varies greatly with meteorological expertise. The representational differences found between meteorologists and nonmeteorologists were indicated consistently across different types of tasks (copying, sorting, extending, and predicting), suggesting that they are not methodological artifacts. Knowledge appeared to play a dominant role in participants' performance on weather map processing tasks, which is as would be expected, considering the abstract nature of this type of depiction. A contrast between the dominance of either meteorological (domain-specific) knowledge or visuo-spatial (domain-general) knowledge with meteorologists' and non-meteorologists respectively was consistently indicated across the various studies. Another major difference was in the far more elaborate knowledge structuring that was apparent for the meteorologists, with rich, hierarchical, and extensively interconnected networks linking basic visuo-spatial information through to high-level meteorological structures. The meteorologists' structuring extended to include the wider context beyond the weather map area itself. The nonmeteorologists' knowledge structures were impoverished, decontextualized, and lacking in an appropriate temporal dimension.

Although the studies reviewed here focussed upon questions about the processing of weather maps, it should be important to ask similar fundamental questions across a whole range of remote sensing domains. This is because there are many characteristics shared by remote sensing displays as a class due to the nature of their referents, the way information about these referents is depicted, and the perceptual/interpretative tasks required of those who use these displays. Both the theoretical framework supporting this program of weather map research and the novel methodologies developed to address the questions raised appear quite broadly applicable, even to remote sensing domains that are superficially very different from those of weather maps. A recent example of adaptation of these approaches is the work of Hoffman[1] who applied methodologies formerly used with weather maps to the study of expertise in processing meteorological satellite imagery. This is a significant step because weather maps and satellite images are superficially very different in terms of their graphic characteristics. Despite these differences, the investigations with satellite images have produced findings that are generally consistent with the theoretical frameworks developed during the studies of weather maps.

As was mentioned in the introduction to this chapter, the underlying motivation for this program of research was the desire to improve the efficiency with which students of meteorology develop weather map interpretation skills. The consistent and complementary pattern of findings that emerged from this research suggested possible training interventions that could help students develop these skills more rapidly than via conventional university instruction. Such interventions would target the specific knowledge differences found between experts and novices with a view to providing students with a more extensive, powerful, and meteorologically appropriate mental representation of weather maps. The anticipated benefit from this type of training is that it would provide students with a short cut whereby they could partly bypass the traditional route to development of expertise (i.e., the type of experience-dependent component of expertise that practicing meteorologists currently acquire only as a result of years of working in their profession). However, beyond its specific potential to improve students' weather map skills, we can speculate that there could be much broader application of this type of research to in-service training of professionals in a whole variety of domains that already use remote sensing displays. This would be especially valuable when new display types are introduced or when more advanced interpretative techniques are developed.

As a result of the studies, interactive animated training was developed to address the fundamental differences found in the way meteorological experts and novices dealt with static weather maps.[7] It portrays temporal changes that occur across a sequence of weather maps and was developed to help meteorological novices build more sophisticated meteorological knowledge structures. The intention was to improve the way they conceptualized individual static weather maps to better equip them for performing interpretative tasks such as prognosis.

The animation provided novices with opportunities to explore the behavior of meteorological features and so confront their simplistic preconceptions about meteorological dynamics. Underlying this approach was the assumption that it would provide a route by which they could improve the quality of their meteorological knowledge structures via an upgrading process that worked through a series of intermediate mental models.[5] Because the training was designed to promote free exploration of weather map sequences, it allowed each user of the animation to follow an individually appropriate pathway for upgrading his or her mental representations of this domain.

Making the dynamics of weather maps explicit via an animation has the potential to supply nonmeteorologists with the information they need to build more effective mental models. However, a recent study of the information that students extracted from the animation mentioned above suggests that it is not enough simply to supply the dynamic information that is absent from nonmeteorologists' mental representations.[9] It appears that animated material introduces perceptual and cognitive processing factors that may actually work against the development of a high-quality mental model of weather map dynamics. Because it depicts a situation that involves a high level of visual complexity, a weather map animation is also capable of imposing a taxing processing load on the viewer. When the information extracted by students interacting with the animation was examined, it was found that they were highly selective in their approach, tending to extract material that was perceptually conspicuous, rather than thematically relevant to the domain of meteorology. This selectivity involved attention to aspects that were readily noticed because of their distinctive visuo-spatial characteristics or their temporal nature. The extraction of information about visually obvious features such as pressure cells dominated, whereas that involving more subtle features such as troughs was missed.

Over and above these visuo-spatial characteristics, the dynamic properties of features provided a factor that appeared to influence the type of information extracted. For highly mobile features such as high pressure cells, trajectory information was extracted while information about internal changes to the form of the feature tended to be lacking. In contrast, for less mobile features such as heat lows, more information about internal changes tended to be extracted. This suggests that the dynamic nature of the more mobile features acts to mask the more subtle intrinsic characteristics that may nevertheless be of particular meteorological significance. There is clearly more research required to tease out the complexities involved in addressing ways to help meteorological novices become more adept at weather map interpretation. In particular, we need to know more about the ways in which they interact with both static and dynamic displays.

As previously mentioned, there are indications that the theoretical frameworks and research methodologies used in these studies of weather maps have the potential for much wider applicability. However, thus far investigations of this type have been largely confined to the domain of meteorology (and even then, to a very limited range of the display types used in that domain). It is therefore important both to probe the generalizability of these findings in other remote sensing domains as well as to investigate the many as yet unresearched aspects of the perception and interpretation of meteorological displays. Further, it is vital to extend these investigations to address the potentially far greater demands made on users by the increasingly sophisticated display types that are evolving with the rapid progress in remote sensing display technologies.

Without a principled basis for designing powerful, appropriate training, skill development in the interpretation of images will remain a slow process that requires many years to develop. With the diverse and growing range of imaging technologies at meteorologists' disposal, it is becoming increasingly impractical to rely on this gradual accretion of skills in the future.

References

1. Hoffman, R. R., *Revealing the Reasoning and Knowledge of Expert Weather Forecasters*. Paper presented at the 4th International Conference on Naturalistic Decision Making, Warrenton, VA, May 1998.
2. Lowe, R. K., Constructing a mental representation from an abstract technical diagram, *Learning and Instruction*, 3, 157–179, 1993.
3. Lowe, R. K., Selectivity in diagrams: reading beyond the lines, *Edu. Psychol.*, 14, 467–491, 1994a.
4. Lowe, R. K., Diagram prediction and higher order structures in mental representation, *Res. Sci. Educ.*, 24, 208–216, 1994b.
5. Lowe, R. K., *Supporting Conceptual Change in the Interpretation of Meteorological Diagrams*, Paper presented at the 6th European Conference for Research on Learning and Instruction, Nijmegen, Netherlands, August, 1995.
6. Lowe, R. K., Background knowledge and the construction of a situational representation from a diagram, *Euro. J. Psychol. Educ.*, 11, 377–397, 1996.
7. Lowe, R. K., Processing challenges of understanding complex animated pictures, *German J. Educ. Psychol.*, 12, 125–134, 1998.
8. Lowe, R. K., Domain-specific constraints on conceptual change in knowledge acquisition from diagrams, in *New Perspectives on Conceptual change*, Schnotz, W., Vosniadou, S., and Carretero, M., Eds., Amsterdam, Elsevier, 1999.
9. Lowe, R. K., Extracting information from an animation during complex visual learning, *Eur. J. Psychol. Educ.*, 14, 225–244, 1999.

chapter eight

The Role of Remote Sensing Displays in Earth Climate and Planetary Atmospheric Research

Anthony D. Del Genio

Contents

Keywords: *Earth, planets, atmospheres, climate, Venus, Jupiter, Saturn, Titan, clouds, storms, dynamics, winds, El Niño, animation, filtering, sunlight, ultraviolet, infrared, false color, precipitation, microwave, lightning, empirical orthogonal function, Hovmöller diagram*

8.1   Introduction

The communities of scientists who study the Earth's climate and the atmospheres of the other planets barely overlap, but the types of questions they
pose and the resulting implications for the use and interpretation of remote
sensing data sets have much in common. Both seek to determine the characteristic behavior of three-dimensional fluids that also evolve in time. Climate
researchers want to know how and why the general patterns that define our
climate today might be different in the next century. Planetary scientists try
to understand why circulation patterns and clouds on Mars, Venus, or Jupiter
are different from those on Earth. Both disciplines must aggregate large
amounts of data covering long time periods and several altitudes to have a
representative picture of the rapidly changing atmosphere they are studying.
This emphasis separates climate scientists from weather forecasters, who
focus at any one time on a limited number of images. Likewise, it separates
planetary atmosphere researchers from planetary geologists, who rely primarily on single images (or mosaics of images covering the globe) to study
two-dimensional planetary surfaces that are mostly static over the duration
of a spacecraft mission, yet reveal dynamic processes acting over thousands
to millions of years.

Remote sensing displays are usually two-dimensional projections that
capture an atmosphere at an instant in time. How scientists manipulate and
display such data; how they interpret what they see; and how they thereby
understand the physical processes that cause what they see, are the challenges I discuss in this chapter. I begin by discussing differences in how
novices and experts in the field relate displays of data to the real world. This
leads to a discussion of the use and abuse of image enhancement and color in
remote sensing displays. I then show some examples of techniques used by
scientists in climate and planetary research to both convey information and
design research strategies using remote sensing displays.

8.2   Novices vs. experts

The problems beginning students face in interpreting remote sensing
displays have much in common with those they encounter with any mathematical representation of the real world:

1. Novices often cannot translate their own observations of the real world
    into more abstract representations of the larger-scale picture. For exam-
    ple, after a lecture on the forces that determine the flow around low
    and high pressure, and how that relates to the isobars displayed on a
    weather map, students in an introductory climate course at Columbia
    University and Barnard College went outside to measure pressure and
    wind direction. Afterwards, the students were shown a schematic
    weather map with a high-low pressure pair and corresponding isobars,

including arrows indicating the approximate flow. Fewer than half the students could identify where on that map we were minutes earlier when we watched the wind carry a balloon away, noted the sky condition, and confirmed that pressure was rising. This presages the problems that more advanced students have in trying to express physical statements as mathematical equations, or to see the ramifications of an equation or symbolic diagram for the behavior of the physical system it describes.

2. Novices tend to seek out isolated features of any data set they examine, and rarely think in terms of the superposition of several phenomena to explain what they see. For example, the students in the same class were asked to draw a graph of the temperature one would measure on a three-day trip from New York to Florida in winter. Many students drew a simple straight line with an increasing trend. Some added an oscillatory pattern to indicate day-night changes. Only a few recognized that there would also be random day-to-day changes as weather systems passed. Later in the semester, the students were given a data set showing the change in Earth's global surface temperature over the past 100 years. Asked to describe the graph's salient features, most could only say that temperature had risen over the past century and attributed this to rising concentrations of greenhouse gases. Few noticed that from 1940–1965 temperatures had actually cooled slightly, a possible indicator of ocean circulation effects or solar luminosity changes that had been discussed in class. Fewer mentioned the random year-to-year variability superimposed on the pattern.

These general difficulties carry over to the realm of remote sensing displays. Given an image of a planetary atmosphere or a false-color contour map of a climate parameter, the novice—with no background in the physics of the system under study—often simply does not know what to look for and what questions to ask. The situation is something like opening the book, *Where's Waldo?* and trying to find Waldo without having seen what he looks like first. The difference between novice and expert here seems to be that the expert goes in with a mental image of what the remote sensing display might look like, based on his current understanding of the system, and thus can react to the actual display with questions about how it departs from expectations.

As an example, students in the climate system course are asked to interpret Earth Radiation Budget Experiment (ERBE) false-color maps of the geographic distribution of absorbed sunlight (see Figure 8.1). They tend to focus on the decrease of sunlight from equator to pole (indicated by the transition from red/orange in the tropics to blue in the polar regions), which is fundamental but is of little interest to the researcher, who takes that well-understood aspect of the map for granted. The expert instead focuses on less obvious longitudinal variations in absorbed sunlight over a homogeneous

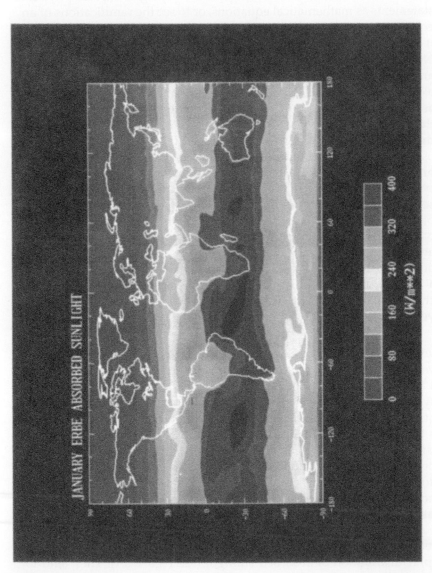

Figure 8.1 False-color contour map of the five-year mean values of solar radiation flux absorbed by the Earth in January (in units of W/m²), derived from satellite measurements made by the Earth Radiation Budget Experiment (ERBE). See color version of this figure in the color section following page 114. (Photo courtesy of NASA.)

surface (e.g., the ocean), which are diagnostic of poorly understood variations in clouds that are of more interest. In Figure 8.1, e.g., the subtle transition south of the equator from the deeper reds in the mid-Pacific and mid-
Atlantic to orange just off the west coasts of South America (20°S, 70°W) and
Africa (15°S, 10°E) reveals the presence of climatically important low-level
stratus cloud decks in the eastern oceans. The expert starts with a mental
model (the intensity of incident sunlight varies with latitude because of
Earth's spherical shape and axial tilt) and a resulting expectation (uniform
solar heating at a given latitude over the ocean because the ocean is approximately equally reflective everywhere), and looks for deviations from the
expectation to learn something. The novice, without a prior mental model,
simply "draws" a mental caricature of the display that emphasizes the major
features and misses the details.

A related bias of the novice is to pay inordinate attention to an obvious
or spectacular feature of a satellite image, at the expense of the more numerous but more amorphous features that are more important indicators of the
climate (the same is apparently true of novice interpretation of weather
maps[7]). Students, for example, enjoy studying pictures of extreme weather
events such as hurricanes. But these storms are rare and affect a relatively
limited area, so their contribution to the seasonal mean temperature and total
rainfall of a region is usually negligible. In the absence of such storms, most
students would guess that skies are clear. But on average, the sky is not much
less cloudy over high pressure centers than over the low pressure centers we
associate with storms. Mainly the type of cloudiness changes, from deep
thick rain clouds in storms to innocuous cirrus or low stratus or fair-weather
cumulus before or after a storm. Storms are present a small fraction of the
time, so the more frequent fair-weather cloudiness may be just as climatically important, but this is rarely anticipated by the novice.

When we image other planets, the playing field becomes more level for
the expert/novice comparison. Our understanding of the other planets is
primitive compared to that of the Earth. Most planets have cloud features
that do not resemble those of the Earth. Figure 8.2 shows Venus, for example,
devoid of the swirling midlatitude storm clouds so well-known to us on
Earth. We understand this as a result of Venus's slow rotation period
(243 days), which eliminates the instability that produces our midlatitude
storms. So we expect not to see such features on Venus. But in the absence of
that process, what other processes prevail on Venus? Can we see evidence of
them in the image? At first glance, the eye is drawn to the planet-sized dark
feature shaped like a sideways letter "Y" that spans the equatorial region.
Analysis of several years of such images by the author has identified this feature as a particular type of wave and documented its characteristics.[3]
Unfortunately, I concluded that this feature is secondary among the processes that maintain the surprisingly strong winds that blow on Venus. The most
important processes occur below the visible clouds, hidden from our view.
We have been fooled into overinterpreting what we see, because it is all we

Figure 8.2 An image of the planet Venus taken through an ultraviolet filter by the Pioneer Venus Orbiter Cloud Photopolarimeter Experiment. The bright regions are clouds composed of a concentrated solution of sulfuric acid in water. The dark regions are locations in which other sulfur compounds have been lifted into view. (Photo courtesy of NASA.)

have to go on! In other words, the other planets can make novices out of experts because their behavior is at least partly unfamiliar to all of us.

The challenge, then, is to manipulate and display remote sensing data in ways that optimize transmission of information, whether in a research or an educational setting. In the next section I describe some common approaches to this problem.

8.3   Image enhancement and color

The image of Venus just discussed does not represent how Venus would look to the human eye. Venus is covered with whitish sulfuric acid clouds; it looks like a featureless tennis ball. However, other sulfur compounds in the clouds absorb ultraviolet (UV) radiation, and when viewed through a UV filter, places where such compounds are lifted up above most of the bright sulfuric acid veil show up as slightly dark regions in a gray-scale image of reflected UV light, which is the Figure 8.2 image. In the "raw" version of this image, even the dark areas are so faint as to be barely detectable by the human eye, both because the contrasts are inherently small and because sunlight falling on a sphere produces larger variations in brightness over the disk, i.e., the image is bright where the Sun is directly overhead, and darkens toward dawn or dusk. The latter effect impedes scientific analysis of the individual features that reveal Venus's weather. Thus, planetary scientists routinely first use a computer algorithm to subtract out global brightness variations due to the different angles at which sunlight falls on different locations. This in turn requires us to know enough about the clouds of Venus to anticipate how well sunlight is reflected as a function of the angle at which it enters and the angle at which we view it.

The next challenge is to enhance the weather features that are really present. This depends on what one wishes to see. In Figure 8.2 we can see both dark regions that span the planet, such as the "Y," and local cloud blobs and streaks reminiscent of things we can see in our own sky. To emphasize one or the other, we filter the image, i.e., we mathematically separate the brightness variations into small and large spatial scales, mathematically boost the strength of the scales we wish to see, and then reconstruct the image. This is the visual equivalent of turning up the bass vs. the treble on one's sound system. In Figure 8.2 a high-pass filtered version of the image (which emphasizes the small features) was added back to the original image (in which the "Y" dominates), to produce a product in which all spatial scales are visible. This makes the image more pleasing for public relations purposes, but it also enhances the scientist's insight—the more irregular nature of small features within the dark arms of the "Y" compared to the more linear nature of the small features in the bright regions to either side contains clues about the processes that form the features and the stability of the underlying atmosphere. This is an example of constructive image manipulation.

Not all such efforts are as successful. Black-and-white imagery is frowned upon by the public relations offices at NASA centers. On a planet such as Venus that does not cooperate by providing much color, one must resort to false colors. A misguided attempt of this sort can be seen on the March 29, 1974 cover of *Science*[12] magazine, which showed a UV image of Venus obtained by the Mariner 10 spacecraft. This image was false-colored blue and white (with the dark regions in Figure 8.2 appearing as blue) to resemble "blue planet" pictures of Earth. The result is visually striking but scientifically misleading (as are many of the planetary images seen by the public[11]): On Earth, clouds (which are white) form in updrafts, while the blue ocean below is visible mostly in places where air sinks and clouds evaporate. On Venus, dark places instead are where the UV absorber is lifted above the bright sulfuric acid, while the bright places are likely to be regions of descending motion. Thus, a terrestrial bias led to a display that obscured the proper scientific interpretation of the image.

Figure 8.3 A false-color composite image of the clouds of Jupiter taken by the Voyager 1 imaging system. The Great Red Spot is visible in the upper right. See color version of this figure in the color section following page 114. (Photo courtesy of NASA.)

Sometimes a planet does contain intrinsic color, though, and false color can be used to create a dramatic and less misleading image. The Voyager 1 image of Jupiter's Great Red Spot and surrounding regions in Figure 8.3 is a good example. This image has a certain basis in truth, because it is a superposition of three monochromatic images sensitive to different colors. But not all colors were included in the Voyager camera filters, so the image is biased. The Jupiter that one views through a telescope is really much more yellow-green and lower in contrast[11]; the Great Red Spot is really a pale pink. Of more concern is how the color scheme influences one's interpretation. Dark regions such as that between the Great Red Spot and regions of swirling white clouds to the west look to the human eye like clearings between the clouds in which we see to great depth, and are thus regions of sinking air. Two decades later, this interpretation is still open to question. Recent Galileo images of lightning on Jupiter suggest that the canonical view of where air is moving up and down on Jupiter may have to be revised.[5]

Aside from images, false color is used to display contour maps of remote sensing retrievals of weather and climate parameters. It is often overlooked that remote sensing retrieval techniques are not perfect—photons emitted or reflected by a planet and received by a detector in space are converted by a computer algorithm to the numerical value of some physical parameter. The algorithm used may be simply empirical, based on observations at one location that are not valid globally. It may assume that other physical parameters that also affect the radiation observed are constant, when in reality they are varying. Or the algorithm may be a physical model of the atmosphere that makes simplifying assumptions. But the result, a color contour map with a title indicating the parameter displayed (e.g., precipitation) immediately attains an air of legitimacy and certainty among scientists who know, but sometimes forget that it is not a direct measurement of raindrops collected in a bucket. The intervals chosen for changes in color sometimes have little relationship to the inherent uncertainty in the algorithm that produced the data set, and users often do not ask how large the errors are. This is a different take on the novice vs. expert issue—professional users of data may be naive about how the data displayed were produced, and hence, erroneous scientific conclusions may sometimes be reached.

The preferred choice of colors depends on the quantity displayed. Sometimes the choice seems obvious based on common associations—e.g., red for warm and blue for cold on a temperature map, or brown for drier and green for wetter on a map of drought severity. When a particular color scheme is not obvious, an effective choice is to color extreme high values red, which draws the eye's attention. Maps of differences (e.g., between a satellite data set and a climate model prediction, or between El Niño years and the mean climate[8]) are commonly used to highlight changes in the real world or errors in a model. A useful color choice in such maps is white for the interval spanning zero, in which changes/differences are too small to be of concern because they are physically unimportant or within the error bar of the data. Figure 8.4 shows such an example. The left side shows a climate model prediction of the coverage of cirrus clouds, with the red areas drawing the eye to the cloudiest places on Earth. The right side shows differences between the model's prediction and the cirrus cloud cover inferred from satellite remote sensing of visible and infrared radiation. It is immediately obvious where the model seriously over- and underestimates cirrus. The spatial pattern of the differences suggests possible causes of the problem to the model developer.

Of more importance than color choice is the parameter interval over which the color changes. Consider precipitation, which varies by an order of magnitude from the tropics to the deserts and polar regions. The novice might choose to display this field using, e.g., 6 colors with equal spacing at precipitation intervals of 2 mm/day, producing a map that resembles a more exaggerated version of the left side of Figure 8.4. For the novice, such a display conveys information, namely that rainfall is highest near the equator and on the western sides of ocean basins. To the expert, though, this is

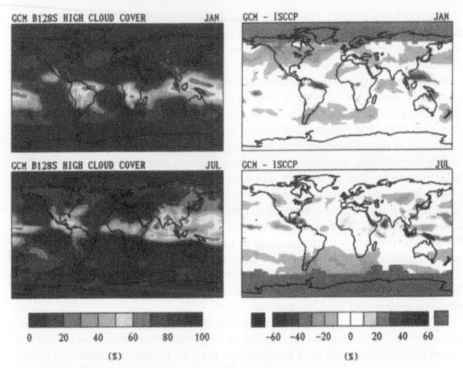

Figure 8.4 Left: Color contour map of monthly mean cirrus cloud coverage (%) simulated by the NASA Goddard Institute for Space Studies global climate model for (upper) January and (lower) July. Right: Differences in cirrus cloud coverage between the simulations at the left and data acquired from visible and infrared satellite imagery by the International Satellite Cloud Climatology Project (ISCCP). The color contour resolution of 10 percent is comparable to the accuracy of the ISCCP satellite retrieval of cloud cover. See color version of this figure in the color section following page 114. (Photos courtesy of NASA.)

well-known and therefore of no research interest. A nonlinear scale that resolves 0.5 mm/day differences in dry regions while sacrificing detail at the high end reveals subtle but interesting variability at middle and high latitudes relevant to drought occurrence and climate changes in ocean currents.

This example points out two other differences between the novice and the expert. The expert is aware of what is already known and selects display characteristics to bring out the unknown, while the novice starts with no such knowledge base and thus makes default choices for a display. Also, novices tend not to appreciate that percent differences are more important than absolute differences, and thus that a 1 mm/day anomaly in a region whose mean rainfall rate is 2 mm/day is more significant than a 2 mm/day anomaly in a region whose mean rainfall rate is 10 mm/day. Similar thinking pervades the general public—100 point daily swings in the Dow Jones Industrial Average were news when the average was near 1,000, but it has taken the media many years to realize that a 100-point swing in today's 10,000-point Dow is cause for neither alarm nor excitement.

With these general concepts as background, we next discuss some of the specific techniques that scientists use to manipulate and display remote sensing data to understand Earth's climate.

8.4   Earth remote sensing for climate research displays

8.4.1   Displays of the atmosphere's variation with time

Satellite imagery is a static display of a dynamic field, and it is the dynamics that best reveals the underlying physical processes. Remote sensing scientists use a variety of techniques to gather and represent dynamic information. A climate expert can deduce a great deal just from the morphology of clouds in a single image. For example, a well-defined comma-shaped cloud pattern is good evidence of the mature stage of a strong midlatitude storm. But patterns in single images are sometimes ambiguous—an amorphous cloud pattern may either be the beginning stage of such a storm or a minor disturbance that never organizes into something stronger. Only animation of a series of images can distinguish the two possibilities.

The shape of a midlatitude storm cloud pattern is immediately interpreted dynamically by the expert, who recognizes the tail of the comma as the cold front, knows that southwesterly flow of warm humid air and northerly flow of cold dry air (if the storm is in the Northern Hemisphere) usually lie to the east and west, respectively, and sees the cloudiest regions as locations of upward motion. The novice may recognize the pattern shape but make no dynamical associations. Understanding can be enhanced for the novice by superimposing other fields on the image, e.g., vectors indicating wind direction and strength and color contours displaying temperature. However, unless a prior mental model of the dynamics exists, the observer has difficulty integrating the individual parts into a comprehensive picture.[7]

Sometimes there is no alternative but to display the time dimension itself. Increasingly, animation is used to track movements of features and to reveal interactions between different geographic regions. Only in a movie can one appreciate the "rivers" of upper troposphere moisture that originate in the tropics and flow all the way to midlatitudes. Figure 8.5, for example, shows a Geostationary Operational Environmental Satellite (GOES) water vapor image. It is obvious to the novice and expert alike that high humidity along the east coast of the U.S. on this day is spatially linked to convection (the bright specks of humidity seen throughout the tropics) occurring near 10°N, 120°W, and that a similar relationship exists between convection west of Hawaii and the Pacific Northwest U.S. The expert has a mental model that transforms this static display into a dynamic interpretation: updrafts in tropical thunderstorms loft moisture to high altitude, and the prevailing winds near the tropopause in the tropics move this humid air poleward, ultimately affecting the sky condition and weather in the U.S. The novice, with no

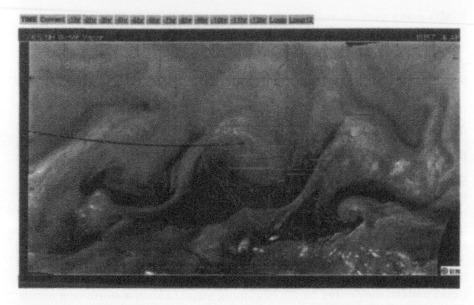

Figure 8.5 Northern Hemisphere GOES water vapor channel gray-scale image for April 4, 2000. Brighter pixels indicate regions of enhanced upper troposphere humidity and high-level cloudiness. (Photo courtesy of NOAA.)

mental model, cannot tell whether the tropics is affecting the midlatitudes or vice versa, or whether the pattern just forms as a single entity at all locations at the same time. By animating the images, though, the novice can watch variations with time in the tropical convection and see how their effects move along the "river" to higher latitudes. The cause-effect link is established via the animation.

Another important aspect of time variation is characterizing propagating wave features. A common way to do this is to construct a Hovmöller diagram: A latitudinally thin (5–10°) strip covering a broad range of longitudes is extracted from a satellite image. A similar strip from the next day's image is placed directly above, and the process is repeated for perhaps a month or more. The result is a composite image in which many two-dimensional arrays of longitude vs. latitude have been converted into a single display of longitude vs. time. In a Hovmöller diagram, a propagating wave shows up as lines of clouds tilted with respect to the horizontal, with the sense and angle of tilt indicating the direction and phase speed of propagation. Persistent stationary features are solid vertical lines, while nonpropagating oscillations are the image equivalent of a dashed vertical line, with the length of the dashes indicating the period of oscillation. False-color Hovmöller displays of tropical Pacific monthly sea surface temperature over several years have become a common means of portraying the onset and decay of El Niño.[8]

Figure 8.6 shows Hovmöller diagrams of GOES visible, water vapor, and "window" (outside the wavelengths of strong water vapor absorption) infrared imagery for a region in Oklahoma over the month of June 1999.

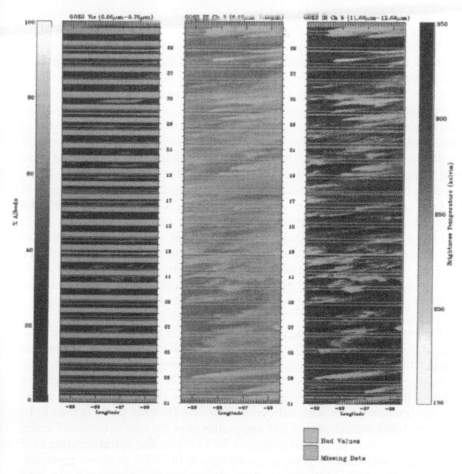

Figure 8.6 Hovmöller diagrams constructed from visible (left), water vapor channel (center), and window infrared (right) GOES-8 hourly imagery of northern Oklahoma for June 1999. The ordinate indicates time (in days of the month), increasing from bottom to top. The abscissa is west longitude in degrees. Bright areas in the visible images represent reflective clouds at any altitude. Bright areas in the window infrared indicate mid- and high-level cloudiness usually associated with synoptic storms. (Figure courtesy of U.S. Department of Energy.)

Storm cloud patterns (the bright features in the middle and right images) tilt from lower left to upper right, indicating that the storms propagate from west to east with time. The degree of tilt tells us how fast the storms move. For example, the storm that originated near 98°W on June 25 had moved to 95.5°W (a distance of about 225 km) by the end of the day, giving a propagation speed of about 2.6 m/sec. Another advantage of the Hovmöller diagram is the ease with which the observer can mentally assimilate missing data. Horizontal lines in the image are times at which the satellite did not acquire or transmit useful data, yet even the novice should be able to guess what the missing data would have looked like by mentally connecting the pattern below the horizontal line to the pattern above.

As mentioned earlier, real atmospheres are a superposition of processes occurring on different temporal and spatial scales. Separation of the different contributions to what we see can be difficult for novices and experts alike, especially when a subtle long-term climate trend must be detected in a parameter that fluctuates more strongly on shorter time scales. Mathematical techniques such as empirical orthogonal function (EOF) analysis separate space-time data sets into a few characteristic modes of variation.[6] The EOF displays the spatial pattern; it is accompanied by a function of time, the principal component (PC). The decomposition is mathematical and is not guaranteed to provide physically meaningful results, but the combined display of the EOF and the PC can often be interpreted as a physical process by the expert. For example, an analysis of monthly sea surface temperature (SST) anomalies has a first EOF showing anomalies of opposite sign north and south of the equator, with an accompanying PC that is sinusoidal with a period of one year. To novice and expert alike, this is obviously capturing the seasonal cycle. The second EOF may show large anomalies in the tropical east Pacific and a PC that oscillates somewhat irregularly with a time scale of a few years; this is El Niño.

One research value of such a decomposition is that if the dominant features of the EOF and PC suggest a particular physical process to the person viewing the display, unanticipated spatial relationships can be discovered. For example, Figure 8.7 shows the first PC and EOF of the twentieth-century record of precipitation for rain gauge stations over all land areas of the globe, after subtraction of the seasonal cycle.[1] The first PC time series is seen to be well-correlated with observed SST anomalies over the east equatorial Pacific, which are known to be caused primarily by El Niño. The corresponding EOF shows some well-known geographic effects of El Niño: negative precipitation anomalies (drought) over eastern Australia, the Amazon Basin, and equatorial Africa, and wet anomalies over the western half of the U.S. But the EOF also suggests more subtle "teleconnections" to places thousands of miles away that were not previously known to be affected by El Niño, e.g., wetter than normal conditions in Europe and western Asia. The second PC (not shown) is an upward trend over the century that might be an effect of anthropogenic global warming but which is undetectable in a simple animation of the data due to the large El Niño signal. The corresponding EOF indicates that midlatitudes have become wetter and the tropics a bit drier over the past century.

8.4.2   The use of displays in computer algorithm development

As noted above, short-term climate changes such as El Niño produce large weather perturbations in certain parts of the world that are clearly noticeable to people (e.g., the flooding in usually dry California in 1997–1998). Long-term anthropogenic global warming due to building concentrations of greenhouse

[previous] [next]

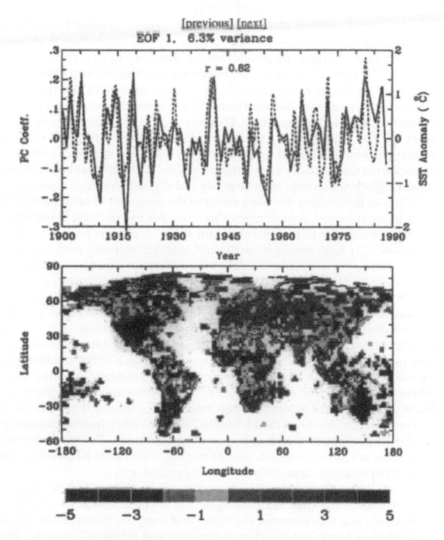

Figure 8.7 Top: The first PC of the record of observed monthly precipitation variations over land for the Twentieth Century (solid line), and the time series of SST anomalies in the equatorial east Pacific, an indicator of El Niño (dashed line). Bottom: The corresponding first EOF of the Twentieth Century land precipitation record, with blue indicating wetter than normal conditions at times when the PC coefficient is positive, and orange/red indicating drier conditions at these times. See color version of this figure in the color section following page 114. (From Dai, A., et al., *J. Climate*, 10, 2943–2962, 1997. Photos courtesy of NASA.)

gases is more gradual and smaller in magnitude. Thus, it is detectable only as a subtle change in the frequency of occurrence of unusual weather, e.g., more or fewer droughts or strong storms over decades. These changes may be barely noticeable, but collectively they have the potential to impact society via the availability of water, the growth of crops, the spread of diseases, erosion of shorelines, and summer electricity demand. Remote sensing scientists use satellite data to understand how the climate responds to changes in temperature, but such changes are much smaller than day-to-day fluctuations in weather. The human eye-brain combination cannot sense such changes reliably, since (1) it notices the obvious, spectacular aspects of an image at the expense of the more mundane but numerous features that weigh more heavily in determining the climate change, (2) many images spanning seasons or even years must be analyzed to get a statistically significant result, and (3) visual displays of 8-bit data, which resolve 256 brightness levels, cannot easily communicate net shifts of only a few brightness levels that represent the collective sum of slight brightenings in some pixels and slight darkenings in others.

Climate researchers therefore resort to the computer to tally statistics for them in an unbiased, representative fashion. But the scientist needs to program the computer to look for the right thing. A current project involving New York City high school students and teachers working with NASA scientists seeks, for example, to determine whether clouds in midlatitude storms are systematically different in either visible brightness, cloud top height, or coverage under warmer vs. colder conditions, and in years when the temperature difference between the tropics and poles is larger vs. smaller. To do this we require a program that recognizes and tracks storms as they grow and decay; this is done objectively using ancillary data on surface pressure patterns to locate storm centers. How big an area of the satellite image should we include in our definition of a storm, though? In other words, where does a storm begin and end? For some storms, with vigorous cold fronts and clear skies behind, the rear boundary of the storm is obvious. For others in which low-level cloud "debris" remains after frontal passage and gradually dissipates, the choice is more problematic. Pattern recognition techniques are not yet sophisticated enough to encompass all possible storm cloud morphologies, especially the less organized ones.

Thus, the student observers determine a plausible storm definition by visually examining a number of images, and we incorporate their subjective impressions into the computer algorithm that compiles the statistics. We then must address Mark Twain's "lies, damn lies, and statistics" warning about being skeptical of what we cannot see. We run the computer algorithm for a month of images and use displays to see whether it detects anything our eyes tell us is not really a storm or misses things we would identify as storms. As a final check, we can test the sensitivity of any conclusions to the assumptions we have made by rerunning the program with an altered storm definition. In this way, the human and the computer work hand-in-hand to do what neither can do alone.

8.4.3 Displaying vertical structure in the atmosphere

Another challenge for Earth remote sensing is the vertical dimension. Images project a 3-D world into two dimensions, and the scientist must know what altitude is being observed, because understanding sometimes depends on knowing how things going on at one level in the atmosphere are influenced by things happening at a lower level or at the surface. Atmospheres usually work from the bottom up—the warm dense lower atmosphere is the "dog" wagging the "tail" that is the cold, tenuous upper atmosphere. For example, an increase in cirrus clouds near the tropopause observed in isolation cannot be interpreted, but that observation combined with the knowledge that temperature or humidity near the Earth's surface had increased at about the same time might enable the scientist to explain the change in clouds, since the expert knows that warm moist air near the ground destabilizes the atmospheric column, and that thunderstorms that originate near the ground and transport moisture to high altitudes are the atmosphere's response to this.

The problem, though, is that satellites view a planet top down, and we cannot always see through the complete atmosphere. Climate scientists deal with this difficulty in a number of ways:

1. By simultaneously observing at two wavelengths, one a "window" of weak absorption in which the atmosphere is transparent and we see to the surface, the other a wavelength of strong absorption by atmospheric gases in which we "see" only part of the way down, we can sense both top and bottom.
2. By looking up from the ground with surface-based remote sensing instruments, we see lower levels better locally but not globally.
3. Clouds are at least partly opaque to the short and moderate wavelengths of most planetary radiation, so active remote sensors such as radars, which emit their own long-wavelength radiation that penetrates through clouds, now fly on spacecraft.
4. The atmosphere changes faster than the Earth's surface beneath it, so we can observe the surface by waiting for the clouds to clear.

Figure 8.8 shows an example of the latter technique, a single frame of an animation of three months of operational weather satellite data.[10] The analysis uses visible and window-infrared images to distinguish clouds from the underlying surface. The visible channel analysis makes use of our knowledge that clouds are brighter than most surfaces, and the infrared analysis uses the knowledge that cloud tops are usually colder than the surface because temperature decreases upward in Earth's troposphere. Figure 8.8 uses four color bars, one each for clouds, ice/snow-cover, continents, and open oceans, with different hues for each type and different levels of saturation distinguishing higher vs. lower temperature. The simultaneous polar projections allow us to compare clouds in the two hemispheres. When the display is animated, even beginning students are able to detect temporal and spatial relationships between surface and atmosphere, e.g., the increase in high thick tropical clouds in the midafternoon when the temperature of the land surface is warmest, and the association of persistent high clouds in the equatorial west Pacific with the warm sea surface temperatures there.

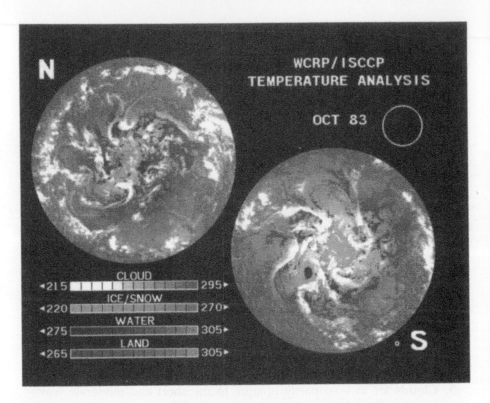

Figure 8.8 Northern and Southern Hemisphere polar projection false-color temperature maps for October 1, 1983, derived by the International Satellite Cloud Climatology Project from operational satellite infrared imagery. Separate color bars differentiate temperatures at cloud tops, ice/snow-covered surface regions, oceans, and continents. Temperatures are expressed in units of kelvin, which are identical to degrees Celsius but shifted upward in value by 273.15. For example, the freezing point of water is 32°F = 0°C = 273.15 K. See color version of this figure in the color section following page 114. (Photo courtesy of NASA.)

This works as long as one can distinguish cloud from surface. In the polar regions this is difficult, because snow and ice are just as bright as clouds in the visible channel analysis and the atmosphere can be warmer than the surface, which can confuse the interpretation of infrared images. The apparent absence of clouds near the North and South Poles in Figure 8.8 is partly a failure to detect them. Such regional errors in remote sensing data sets wreak havoc among climate scientists who are remote sensing novices. At one extreme, the naive user accepts Figure 8.8 as fact and worries needlessly that his climate model produces "too much" polar cloudiness. At the other extreme the skeptic who knows that the error bars in the polar regions are large, dismisses good data in other parts of the world and refuses to use the data set at all. In my experience, both types exist in the supposedly objective, meticulous scientific community.

A recent trend is to use multispectral microwave emission to separate cloud from snow/ice effects in the polar regions, since higher microwave frequencies are more sensitive to clouds and lower frequencies to sea ice.[1] Unfortunately, the separation is not complete, and ambiguity remains. Thus, at any instant a bright region in an image may be a cloud, an ice-covered ocean location, or ice hidden beneath a cloud. Animation allows both novice and expert to use the different morphologies of cloud systems and sea ice, and the different time scales of variation (days for clouds, weeks for sea ice) to separate the two. The observer can see a spiral cloud shape over the dark ocean disappear as it passes over ice and then reappear over the ocean downstream and link the two as the same entity. The observer can separate the primarily north-south seasonal growth and decay of sea ice from the primarily west-east movement of cloud systems. Whether such interpretation capabilities can be translated to the computer to enable the processing of years of such data remains to be seen.

Challenging as it is to understand Earth remote sensing data, we at least have the advantage of everyday experience and routine surface weather observations to guide our development of effective display strategies. When we remotely sense another planet, though, the same rules may not apply, and our approach therefore is somewhat different.

8.5   Remote sensing of planetary atmospheres

In principle, remote sensing of other planets is no different from remote sensing of Planet Earth, but in practice this is not the case. The volume of data on all the other planets combined is a small fraction of that for the Earth, although the advent of long-term planetary orbiters has finally begun to create a data volume issue in planetary research. In any event, our conceptual understanding of other planetary atmospheres still greatly lags that of our own atmosphere. Consequently, even the expert is something of a novice, attempting to make sense of cloud patterns that bear little resemblance to those we see on Earth (Figures 8.2, 8.3). The expert draws upon terrestrial experience to interpret these cloud features. For example, the Voyager imaging team routinely referred to isolated small white clouds (such as that below and to the left of the Great Red Spot of Jupiter in Figure 8.3) as "convective clouds," i.e., scientific jargon for thunderstorms, because of their resemblance to such features in Earth imagery. But this association implies the presence of a specific type of instability, and in truth there was no independent corroborating evidence to assure us that convection was indeed the process producing the clouds. Theoretically, we expect convection to exist sporadically on Jupiter, but to this day we cannot demonstrate why those clouds appear different from the surrounding larger-scale clouds tinged with pink, brown, or blue/gray. Depending on the final outcome of this story, the expert's experience may turn out to have been a boon or an obstacle to true understanding.

The other major difference between Earth and other planetary atmospheres is that most of the other planets are completely cloud covered (Venus, Jupiter, Saturn, Titan, Uranus, and Neptune) and we therefore either cannot see the surface, or no solid surface exists. This has two implications. First, since atmospheres work from the bottom up, what we see with remote sensing on other planets is only the tail of the dog, and it is hard to know what the rest of the dog looks like. Second, since atmospheres are dynamic entities, we have no fixed reference for mapping, and thus there is no such thing as a map of the world for planetary atmospheres. Figure 8.9 shows an attempt to create a rectangular world cloud map of Venus by digitally combining Pioneer Venus images spaced to correspond to the mean rotation rate of the "Y" feature.[2] The result is partly a success, partly a failure (note the discontinuities at image boundaries), because from one day to the next individual clouds grow and decay, and because the rotation speeds of the atmosphere and its waves are different at different latitudes. This is less of a problem on Jupiter, where the rotation rate of the planet far exceeds any fluctuations due to winds.

As on Earth, we use multispectral imaging to sense different altitudes of other planetary atmospheres, but with greater ambiguity. UV filters show sunlight scattered from small haze particles at high altitudes in the stratosphere, while near-infrared filters probe beneath the high hazes to sense sunlight reflected from clouds deep in the troposphere. Longer wavelength thermal infrared radiation senses the planet's own emission, which increases with temperature and therefore depth below the highest cloud tops. Maps of such thermal features side-by-side with images of reflected sunlight tell the expert whether a specific cloud feature is higher or lower in the atmosphere, or perhaps not a cloud at all. We can observe a planet with a filter that admits radiation at a wavelength at which a specific gas is known to absorb (e.g., methane band imaging of the Jovian planets). The higher the cloud top, the less overlying gas there is to absorb, and therefore the brighter the feature in the image. Finally, we can image the nightside of a planet in visible filters, looking for lightning flashes that mark the locations of thunderstorms at great depths that might otherwise be hidden from our view by the overlying cloud layers. Figure 8.10 shows such an example from the Galileo mission to Jupiter. Although this image is a view of the nightside, one can see both the lightning flashes from deep levels and the clouds at upper levels, because the latter are weakly illuminated by moonlight from Jupiter's closest satellite Io.

In all of these cases, interpretation is almost impossible for the novice. It depends on having not just a mental model of the weather of the atmosphere, but also a mental model of how specific types of electromagnetic radiation interact with a specific type of atmosphere. The expert must know the source of the radiation (reflected sunlight vs. the planet's emitted heat), the composition of the atmosphere and whether the gases present absorb or not at the wavelength being observed, and whether the atmosphere contains small haze particles (which reflect short wavelengths well but long wavelengths

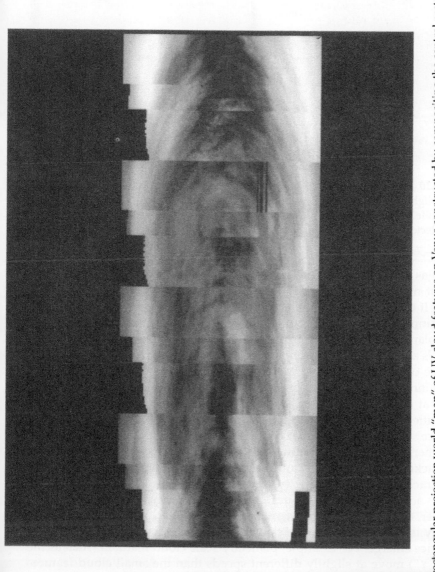

Figure 8.9 A rectangular projection world "map" of UV cloud features on Venus constructed by compositing the central sectors of 12 consecutive Pioneer Venus images acquired over a 4-day period, the nominal rotation period of planetary-scale cloud features. Discontinuities visible at image boundaries are caused by evolution of cloud features over time intervals of a few hours and by departures of the atmosphere's rotation period from 4 days at some latitudes. Solid black areas represent missing data. (Photo courtesy of NASA.)

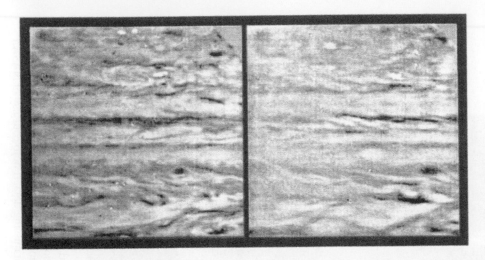

Figure 8.10 Galileo Orbiter visible images of the nightside of Jupiter. Bright specks indicate lightning flashes from water clouds located at depth below the visible cloud deck, while the background shows clouds at higher altitudes illuminated by moonlight reflected by Jupiter's innermost satellite Io. (Photo courtesy of NASA.)

poorly) as opposed to large cloud droplets (which reflect all wavelengths well but may be hidden below the reflective hazes in a short-wavelength image). If there are multiple haze/cloud layers of different particle size and composition (as is the case in most planetary atmospheres) and a heterogeneous planetary surface, the interpretation can be ambiguous even for the expert. Is a near-infrared feature in a Hubble Space Telescope image of Titan evidence of surface topography or ice, a tropospheric methane cloud, or a local thinning of the overlying stratospheric haze? Only by comparing images at different wavelengths and tracking motions over time can such ambiguities possibly be resolved.

Since we do not routinely launch weather balloons into other planets' atmospheres, most of our knowledge of these planets' circulations comes from tracking the motions of cloud features. The novice can do a fairly good job of tracking cloud motions by observing the same cloud shape in two images acquired several hours apart but displayed simultaneously. However, once the zeroth-order information has been gathered and higher accuracy is needed to detect subtle variations in the flow, the limitations of the novice emerge. For example, planetary-scale cloud features (such as the Venus "Y") move at slightly different speeds than the small cloud features in Figure 8.2 because the large features are propagating waves, and the up-down motions that produce wave crests and troughs look to the eye like horizontal motions of the air but are not (imagine, e.g., spreading ripples from a rock thrown onto a pond). It is easy to train the novice to focus only on small features more indicative of the true wind speed, and to avoid alternating dark-bright series of linear features that are obviously small-scale waves.

It is much harder, though, to train the human eye to detect both well-defined cloud objects and disorganized fields of brightness variation. Thus, even the expert detects only some of the possible cloud features that might provide information, given a sparse sample of the wind field. Even worse, since the human is drawn to certain types of features and develops an expectation of how far and in what direction features should move, the resulting wind field may be biased. Finally, from recent multiyear planetary orbital missions, thousands of images have been obtained, and the time it would take a human to process all images from a single mission becomes prohibitive.

We therefore use automated digital tracking algorithms, based on cross-correlations of image brightness fields for limited areas of a pair of images, to try and objectively map wind speeds in planetary atmospheres.[9] This maximizes the information from each image and allows large volumes of data to be processed, giving the statistics needed to answer some current research questions. As with the Earth storm-tracking program, though, the human and the computer must work together to optimize the algorithm. For example, we use visual impressions of cloud feature sizes that provide the most reliable wind estimates to specify the size of the array of pixels that the algorithm tries to cross-correlate. We define a minimum acceptable correlation coefficient by visually inspecting the kinds of feature motions the algorithm derives under different conditions (ideally we would like perfect correlations, but real clouds change shape with time). Most important, after the fact we can look at a frequency histogram of wind speeds derived by the algorithm. This will appear as a well-behaved Gaussian distribution of speeds, plus secondary distributions of outliers that are clearly not part of the main population of vectors. By visually displaying the cloud features that the computer tracked to obtain each outlier, we can throw out the spurious vectors (which may be due to periodic features that fool the algorithm, large-scale brightness gradients not removed in our image enhancement phase, etc.) and retain the "real" outliers for in-depth analysis. This iterative procedure allows us to refine the algorithm so that fewer outliers appear in future versions.

Unlike terrestrial images, where the expert can visualize the dynamics from the static display of a familiar feature, no such baseline of knowledge exists for less familiar planetary cloud features. Thus, movies are becoming an important tool for the planetary fluid dynamicist. Movies of rotating vortices on Jupiter and Neptune allowed Voyager scientists to watch individual vortices merge or pass by without interacting, and to detect individual vortices wiggling as they rotated. This in turn provided information about the otherwise unobserved vertical structures of these atmospheres.

Thus far, I have discussed remote sensing display as an after-the-fact exercise: a spacecraft instrument observes a planet, the data are processed and displayed, and the scientist manipulates and observes the display to understand what the planet *was* doing at the time of the observation. But (albeit in a limited way) we can also use displays to look into the future. This becomes important when scientists plan specific observations they are going to take during a planetary mission. We next discuss the use of displays in planning planetary observations.

8.6   The future: remote sensing displays as planning tools

Unlike Earth-orbiting satellites, which cover the globe and have regular, repeating orbits, planetary missions are either one-time flybys of one or two satellites or orbiter missions in which each orbit has a different shape and orientation to meet multiple scientific objectives (e.g., nearly circular vs. highly elliptic, closest approach to the planet on the dayside vs. the nightside, etc.) Instructions to point the spacecraft in a specific direction, image through a specific filter, set an exposure time, and shutter the camera at a certain moment must be relayed to the spacecraft far in advance of the time the image is taken (because of human limitations in planning and execution and the finite travel time of radio waves to a distant planet). The Voyager imaging team would not have acquired the image of the Great Red Spot in Figure 8.3 if they had not had some idea in advance when and where the Spot was going to come into view.

Such observation planning can of course be done by examining graphs of a spacecraft's latitude, longitude, distance from the planet, and time of day as a function of time during the mission. What we would really like, though, is to be able to visualize what the planet is going to look like from the vantage point of the spacecraft at any future moment, so we know when the most useful imaging opportunities arise and what type of observation is warranted. Projects such as the Cassini-Huygens mission to the Saturn system, already launched for arrival at Saturn in 2004, are using computer software that allows that to be done.

Figure 8.11 is a schematic example of what Saturn will look like to the Cassini Orbiter about a day before it goes into orbit. We can visualize what latitude and longitude are in direct view, where the day-night boundary is, how good a view of Saturn's rings we have at that time, and whether any of Saturn's moons are visible. The superimposed square representing the camera's field of view tells us whether a single image frame will cover the planet or whether we need a mosaic of many images to see everything. Once Cassini gets close enough to do an initial imaging survey of Saturn and its moons, the schematic diagram can be replaced by a projection from a data base of previous images, allowing us to use remote sensing displays to *predict* what Saturn and its moons will look like to Cassini at any time. No one is an expert on the future—since atmospheres evolve in time, these simulated images will only be educated guesses. But they will allow us to optimize the science return by planning the right type of image at the right time.

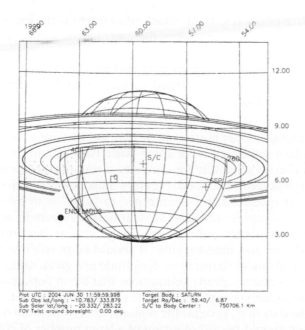

Figure 8.11 A schematic view of the appearance of Saturn as it will be seen by the Cassini Orbiter spacecraft the day before it goes into Saturn orbit on July 1, 2004, computed using the Cassini Sequence Planner (CASPER) algorithm developed by the project for planning mission observations. The superimposed squares are the fields of view of the Cassini Imaging Subsystem Wide and Narrow Angle Cameras. Dotted areas on the left represent the nightside of the planet. "SSP" indicates the point on Saturn directly beneath the Sun, and "S/C" the point directly beneath the spacecraft. According to CASPER, Saturn's moon Enceladus will also be in view just to the lower left of Saturn at that time. (Figure courtesy of NASA.)

8.7   Conclusion

Consider three people looking at a yellow layer cake with chocolate icing: one has never seen a cake before, another has eaten cakes but never made one or seen a recipe, and the third has baking experience. Only the third would know most of the ingredients used to make the cake. Furthermore, there are limits to experiential learning: placed in a fully stocked kitchen, neither of the first two people would be likely to stumble upon the recipe in any reasonable amount of time.

The second person starts out with some advantages over the first: previous experience that although only chocolate icing is visible, there is probably cake and a layer of icing or fruit inside, and that usually the cake is either yellow or chocolate. The first person can advance to the expertise level of the second simply by cutting into the cake, looking at the inside, and tasting it.

Both are then in a position to think about what might make the cake yellow, perhaps leading to an inference about the use of eggs, and so on, although they will never reach the expert level on their own.

The novice in remote sensing display and analysis is in much the same situation. What lessons can be learned to make remote sensing display a more useful learning tool?

1. A prior mental model must exist. It may not be wise to have students use displays until they have some basic background in the subject. There is also no substitute for curiosity, a trait that seems to diminish from childhood to adulthood. Novices must be trained first and foremost to ask questions and encouraged to "play" with data displays.

2. Flexibility in display is crucial. Most atmospheric remote sensing data are two-dimensional (latitude vs. longitude, or horizontal-vertical cross-sections) and time-varying. It should be possible to look at the data from all angles (latitude vs. longitude at a given time, latitude vs. time at a specific longitude, animations that blend both spatial dimensions with time) via menu choices. It should be possible to select subsets of the data (e.g., geographic regions) to view in more detail. Color bar design should permit selection of a large number of colors from a palette, flexible choices of dynamic range, and variable data range definitions for different colors. Each of these features can be found in existing commercially available graphics packages; rarely are all found in the same package.

3. The display software should permit a variety of mathematical manipulations of the data: Anomalies with respect to a user-defined baseline, frequency histograms, lag correlations, spectral analysis, filtering with user-defined bandpass, EOF and/or related orthogonal function analysis, and mathematical function capability, i.e., the ability to calculate and display a function of two or more existing display data sets.

4. Novices must be trained not only how to use all the "bells and whistles," but also why they might want to use each one. For example, a novice who notices the big midlatitude comma cloud patterns but tends to miss the small cloud blobs indicating thunderstorms must be trained not only how to use the filtering function, but why he or she might want to notice both the big things and the small things in an image. Analogies to other fields might help, e.g., the importance of both bass and treble to the overall impact of music.

5. In meteorology and climate, the whole is greater than the sum of the parts. Remote sensing displays should permit the user to superimpose multiple fields on the same display. Satellite image gray-scale displays with superimposed color maps highlighting precipitation, contour maps of pressure and temperature, and wind vectors can be a useful way to allow the student to think about physical relationships, especially if the display can be animated. Simultaneous display of

fields at different altitudes, such as that in Figure 0.0, can be used to help students see how one part of the atmosphere does or does not communicate with another.

6. Novices must be trained to describe what they see in more detail than that to which they are accustomed. An exercise replicating the experience of someone describing a criminal to a police sketch artist might be useful. Two novices, one viewing a display and the other not having access to it, work together. The first describes the display to the second, whose job it is to draw the display only from the description offered by the first.

These points highlight the need especially for training documentation written from the standpoint of the novice user, rather than from the standpoint of the expert. A common flaw of software manuals is that they are so intent on demonstrating all the capabilities of the software, they overwhelm the novice who wishes to get started doing a few basic tasks and has no idea why the advanced capabilities even exist. Meeting the users at their level of expertise is and will continue to be the most effective strategy for widening the novice-to-expert bottleneck.

References

1. Dai, A., Fung, I. Y., and Del Genio, A. D., Surface observed global land precipitation variations during 1900–1988, *J. Climate*, 10, 2943–2962, 1997.
2. Del Genio, A. D. and Rossow, W. B., Temporal variability of UV cloud features in the Venus stratosphere, *Icarus*, 51, 391–415, 1982.
3. Del Genio, A. D. and Rossow, W. B., Planetary-scale waves and the cyclic nature of cloud top dynamics on Venus, *J. Atmos. Sci.*, 47, 293–318, 1990.
4. Gloersen, P., Nordberg, W., Schmugge, T. J., Wilheit, T. T., and Campbell, W. J., Microwave signatures of first-year and multiyear sea ice, *J. Geophys. Res.*, 78, 3564–3572, 1973.
5. Ingersoll, A. P., Gierasch, P. J., Banfield, D., Vasavada, A. R., and the Galileo Imaging Team, Moist convection as an energy source for the large-scale motions in Jupiter's atmosphere, *Nature*, 403, 630–632, 2000.
6. Lorenz, E. N., Empirical Orthogonal Functions and Statistical Weather Prediction, Sci. Rep. 1, Statistical Forecasting Project, Department of Meteorology, MIT (NTIS AD 110268), 49 pp, 1956.
7. Lowe, R. K., Components of expertise in the perception and interpretation of meteorological charts, this volume, Chapter 7.
8. McPhaden, M. J., Genesis and evolution of the 1997–1998 El Niño, *Science*, 283, 950–954, 1999.
9. Rossow, W. B., Del Genio, A. D., and Eichler, T. P., Cloud tracked winds from Pioneer Venus OCPP images, *J. Atmos. Sci.*, 47, 2053–2084, 1990.
10. Rossow, W. B. and Schiffer, R. A., ISCCP cloud data products, *Bull. Am. Meteor. Soc.*, 72, 1–20, 1991.
11. Young, A. T., What color is the solar system? *Sky and Telescope*, 69, 399–403, 1985.
12. *Science*, 183, 4131, March 1974.

chapter nine

The Skilled Interpretation of Weather Satellite Images: Learning to See Patterns and Not Just Cues

H. Michael Mogil

Contents

Keywords: *weather satellites, image interpretation, perceptual learning, atmospheric dynamics, radar, weather maps*

9.1 Introduction

The purpose of this chapter is to describe how an expert learned to perceive patterns (i.e., organized and discernible arrangements) in the weather satellite images used in forecasting, and now commonly seen on televised weather broadcasts. This skill—some would call it an art—is only now coming to be taught more widely in college-level course work on meteorology. A great many forecasters—old-schoolers who began in the days of hand chart analysis and witnessed the advent of weather satellite imagery—have spent decades interpreting images. They have developed an extensive new vocabulary, rich in terms that make sense describing patterns as seen from the vista of space but that do not fit well (or at all) with the traditional ground-based descriptors. From space you see patterns called "popcorn," "comma clouds," "leading edge gradients," "enhanced-V's," and "plumes," each of which suggests specific causal dynamics.

To explain the interpretation skills of the expert, I have covered them in this chapter through a format familiar to meteorology—the case study. Throughout, weather satellite images (in many formats—some familiar, some not), radar displays, weather maps, and other visual information will be used as illustrations. On most images, there will be many more patterns present than can be addressed in the text. As a result, some images may be referred to several times for different reasons. Information about each image, including Web addresses, as appropriate, is included.

9.2 A life story

When I was asked to write about pattern recognition for meteorological applications, I had to ponder how I ever came to do it well. Some would say that I am justified in regarding myself as a very good pattern recognizer, having spent 10 years teaching image interpretation at the Training Branch of the National Environmental Satellite Data and Information Service, an arm of the National Oceanic and Atmospheric Administration (NOAA). I was of the generation that was not formally instructed in the process, although that is what I do now with students of all age groups—from school children through adults. The easy answer to the question of how I became good at it was that I began studying clouds at a very early age, and kept on doing it for some 45 years.

From my family's 14th-story Manhattan apartment I used to watch the clouds. I was especially intrigued by clouds that lined up in "rows" or "streets." I watched snow showers march down the Hudson River. I recall being fascinated by how the clouds hid the sun and moon, and at other times, how the sun or moon could be seen through the clouds. I started counting the seconds for each type of event by day (sun) and night (moon). I discovered that the moon was visible through the clouds more often than the sun. I also noticed that the sun was more easily hidden by thin cirrus clouds than the moon was.

When we moved to the borough of Queens, I discovered that tides provided patterning experiences. Water came up from the nearby bay and occasionally flooded the streets. I remember being fascinated with how the water moved into and out of our neighborhood. I would note the high water marks and eagerly await the next event to see if the level rose even higher.

I understood none of these patterns at the time, but I consciously knew that I had become a watcher. A watcher is someone who looks for patterns and can see them within a larger frame of reference. This can often be accomplished due to contrast when one is able to distinguish color variations, shape variations, and/or movement variations. This was step one in becoming skilled at pattern recognition—noticing differences.

Step two developed over the years. I became a counter. A counter is a person who is always counting things or creating patterns or designs with numbers. I would count the numbers on license plates and add them. I would make a game out of the number of cars we passed vs. the number that passed us. I counted the exits until we reached South of the Border's "Pedro" at the North Carolina-South Carolina border on Interstate 95. (Billboards were strategically placed about 1 mile apart for 100 miles.)

Steps three through five, which will be described throughout the rest of this chapter, involve the linking of pattern recognition with principled understanding, and using that understanding for some purpose (usually analysis and/or forecasting).

- Step three is linking patterns to some process (i.e., physical understanding).
- Step four involves linking the pattern to some future event.
- Step five is bringing the understanding and prediction together.

Thus, if I know why a pattern is like it is, then I can use pattern recognition and go beyond simple observation or noticing of isolated cues.

9.3   Steps three to five: Linking patterns, principles, and prediction

9.3.1   The development of understanding

In high school, I took the New York State Regents' diploma curriculum. This program was for students planning to go to college and involved lots of math and science. In science we studied many concepts including the periodic table of the elements, planetary orbits, and rock formations. All of these were filled with patterning. Also in my math courses, almost everything keyed on patterning (but no one never really stated it that way). We worked number sequences, geometric proofs, and algebraic relationships and formulas. I was literally in heaven (and never had a clue).

Although I am avid cloud and weather watcher (see http://www.weatherworks.com/cool_clouds.html), I was always fascinated by other patterns in nature. This led me into photography and videography, where I can now capture my images of patterns for later study and enjoyment. In photography, I noticed that I was starting to look for the artistic aspects of scenes, not just the cloud types that were present. This artistic facet often involves recognizing and showcasing some type of pattern. It might have been the rolling hills, how haze in mountain areas increased with optical depth, or even how a row of parked aircraft at a terminal building presented a pattern. It also often involves taking photographs of mountain, river, and urbanization patterns from as high as 39,000 feet as I fly to various cities across the U.S. and the world. Figure 9.1 shows the pattern of streets and houses in an urbanized area from an aerial perspective. Figure 9.2 shows the patterning created by wave action interacting with human constructed structures in New York City. The pattern is especially clear because there is little vegetation to block the view or to protect the ground from erosion.

However, it is weather patterns that have driven me since the fourth grade. I recognized that a certain cloud sequence foretold a certain type of weather event. I knew that when the wind blew from a certain direction, a corresponding (and seasonally appropriate) temperature change followed. And during a winter storm along the mid-Atlantic coast, I knew that a wind from the northeast was more likely to mean snow than a wind from the southeast. I remember drawing weather maps at a young age, showing wave cyclone evolution. One of these appears in Figure 9.3. The low pressure center

Figure 9.1   An aerial photograph of an urban residential area. Not only are the houses patterned, but the meandering character of the natural, tree-lined river valley is quite evident.

Figure 9.2 An aerial photograph of a high-density urban center (foreground) and barrier island (upper right). There is active sand/silt transport here (from background toward foreground) as shown by collection of sediment behind the closest jetty. Notice the scalloped pattern on the water side of the sand deposits (and associated wave action on the water surface).

Figure 9.3 Here is a weather forecast I map made as a seventh grader. Note that a series of low pressure systems lies along the east coast and snow is forecast for New York City (my hometown) and parts of the Deep South. The low over Georgia would be the next snow-maker for New York. The symbols are those that typically appear on weather maps.

was always to the south of where I lived, the winds were always blowing from the northeast, and the temperatures were always cold enough for snow.

My interest arose some 6 years before the first weather satellite was launched and some 30 years before I became interested in weather satellite imagery. It is satellite imagery that can make it especially easy—today—for people to start forecasting even at a young age. The waviness of the jet stream, the circular banding of hurricanes, and the shape of a middle-latitude low pressure system with its "legs" (warm and cold fronts), all present and easy to recognize patterns.

At Florida State University (where I earned both undergraduate and graduate degrees in meteorology) I learned a great many more weather patterns, and how the patterns related to the underlying causal dynamics—thunderstorm structure, mesoscale meteorology, tornado characteristics, hurricane evolution, climatology and singularities, and much more. In 1971, I began my formal career at NOAA (I had worked as a trainee while at college during summer months in the late 1960s). It was then that perhaps the most notable pattern event in my life occurred. One evening while watching the evening television weather report, the local weatherman described a line of showers and thunderstorms on radar off to the northwest of Washington, D.C. The weatherman noted that heavy rain was likely in that area. At 11:00 P.M., the weatherman voiced concern that the line of thunderstorms had not moved in five hours and that flooding was probably occurring. He obviously did not fully understand atmospheric processes. The atmosphere was too stable to support the formation of thunderstorms. All that he knew was that he saw a pattern, recognized what he believed the pattern to be, and reported his observation (plus his incorrect interpretation). Most unfortunately, the weatherman did not know about radar "ground clutter." (A glance ahead to Figure 9.16 on page 259 will give the reader some idea of the clutter that appears in radar images.) Furthermore, the weatherman did not understand how local geographical patterns can cause and enhance clutter. He was not seeing thunderstorms at all, but rather the radar reflection off the eastern range of the Appalachian Mountains! Topography is illustrated in Figure 9.4. In this Geostationary Operational Environmental Satellite (GOES) image we have a clear view of the terrain of much of the eastern U.S. One can see the topography of the Appalachian Mountains revealed in the snow-cover pattern.

This event was significant to me because it showed me that a pattern could be caused by different things. The shape shown on the radar image that evening could have been thunderstorms, but it could also have been false echoes or ground clutter. Without the understanding behind pattern recognition, prediction or even simple interpretations can be seriously flawed.

Over the next 30 years, I further built my pattern recognition skills by working at various National Weather Service (NWS) facilities across the country. Following in the footsteps of many who preceded me, I made a concerted effort at understanding the physical processes behind what I could see in weather maps, data from balloon-borne sensors (radiosondes), and

Figure 9.4   As shown in this multispectral satellite image, an intense winter storm (with an eye-like center) spins off the New England Coast on January 21, 2000 Strong northwesterly winds (blowing cold air over relatively warmer waters) are contributing to "lake effect" snow bands and cloud streets off the coast (including longer cloud bands at the exits of larger bays where over-water trajectories are longer). Due to differences between forested and unforested ground, snow cover variations highlight the Appalachian ridge-valley pattern from Pennsylvania to Virginia. There are also some mountain wave clouds present in Virginia due to the wind flow perpendicular to the ridge axes. (GOES Image courtesy of NOAA.)

radar patterns. My work at the National Severe Storms Forecast Center (NSSFC), now known as the Storm Prediction Center (SPC), led to many insights. The myriad patterns created by wind currents at different levels in the atmosphere, moisture variations, and associated pressure, temperature, and dew point changes showcased how the atmosphere could prime itself for a severe weather outbreak.[9,10,32,37] The depiction of how weather parameters *change* can be as important as the raw numbers, since changes often pinpoint where significant thunderstorm development and/or tornadoes are most likely to occur.[17,30]

In all my years of forecasting since working at NSSFC, I always searched for and tracked small and large scale pressure change centers on weather maps.[31] I did this because I recognized the pattern and its association with severe weather; but I also knew that surface pressure change provided an integrated measure of all the pressure variations going on above ground level; this process cannot be measured directly level by level in the atmosphere.

Thus, I came to add physical understanding to the pattern recognition-prediction couplet. Doswell,[9,10] Lemon and Doswell,[26] and Moller et al.[32] have applied similar approaches to forecasting severe mesoscale weather events. Burgess and Lemon,[5] Wilson and Fujita,[47] Forbes,[16] and Petit[39] are among those who have applied pattern recognition techniques to understanding and forecasting radar-based severe weather signatures.

In 1981 I moved to San Francisco. My job was to forecast for a large part of the west coast. After noticing just how little weather data was available for the eastern Pacific Ocean, my comment to the lead forecaster my first day on the job was, "How do you forecast anything out here? There's no data!" His reply was, "We use satellite data." From that moment on, I began to examine clouds from the viewpoint of space on a daily basis. Lacking other data sets to prove or disprove my assessments, I began to see myriad patterns including storm swirls, weather fronts, different cloud types, and snow coverage.

The jet stream (a band of high speed winds at altitudes generally above 20,000 feet) is often quite evident in weather satellite images. It can appear as a meandering band of bright clouds in all three types of imagery—visible, infrared, and water vapor. In multispectral imagery (where different bandwidths are superimposed on the same image), cirrus often appear as a thin purplish shade. Jetstream bands in multispectral imagery are illustrated in Figure 9.5.

Figure 9.5 Large comma cloud in the central Pacific Ocean shows the presence of another ocean storm. The thin band cutting across the comma at nearly a right angle (on this February 25, 2000 multispectral image) indicates cirrus associated with a jet stream. In addition, the snow-covered mountains in the western United States have a much different pattern than the clouds in the region. The snow-covered Sierra Nevada Mountains of eastern California help to highlight the adjacent Sacramento-San Joaquin Valley. (GOES Image courtesy of NOAA.)

The subtropical jet stream is the easiest to recognize. Moving at 35,000 feet or more around 30° latitude, this relatively low amplitude wave often has large sheets of cirrostratus clouds on its equatorward side. The polar jet, typically at much lower altitude, but higher latitude and much greater amplitude, can extend from 30 to 60° latitude depending upon the season and weather pattern. The polar jet stream is often associated with stronger weather fronts and low pressure or storm systems. However, the polar jet is often more discontinuous and cuts across the sharp cloud edges of middle-latitude storms and frontal systems at varying angles. In Figure 9.5, the polar jet is cutting almost directly across the frontal band that lies to the south of the low pressure system.

9.3.2 Patterns at larger and smaller scales

While large-scale patterns on satellite images often "jump out at you," smaller scale features require more scrutiny. For example, in Figures 9.6 and 9.7 notice the effects of coastal geography on fields of low-lying fog and stratus clouds near the California coast (Figure 9.5 also shows the mountain valley pattern). Tule fog, the name given to fog that fills most or all of California's Central Valley after a winter rain, is another fog feature that is relatively easy

Figure 9.6 This visible image shows how mountains and valleys constrain the inland movement of coastal fog and stratus in central California. Also vegetation differences make California's Central Valley easy to locate. (GOES Image courtesy of NOAA.)

Figure 9.7 This visible image shows how coastal fog and stratus tend to hug the west Coast throughout the day. This patterning is significant in understanding microclimates of the region. As in Figure 9.6, vegetation differences make California's Central Valley easy to locate. (GOES Image courtesy of NOAA.)

to see. It literally fills the central valleys of California (seen as gray shades in Figure 9.7). The mountains that surround the rain-cooled air help to frame the fog, creating an image that looks like a giant bathtub filled with soap bubbles. Animated imagery sequences often show how the fog sloshes in the valley, driven largely by differential solar heating on nearby hillsides.

Fog was not the only weather pattern I discovered while working in San Francisco. As the persistent northwest surface winds interact with the coast and nearby islands, circulations or spins (similar to those of tornadoes and large scale low pressure systems) are created. A striking example of this is in Figure 9.8. There is an outstanding animation of this phenomenon (created as winds flow past Guadeloupe Island off the Baja California coast) at the University of Wisconsin Web site (http://cimss.ssec.wisc.edu/tropic/temp/eddy/eddy.html). Generation of eddies by other phenomena is discussed by Chen (see Web site http://www.eng.umd.edu/~chenjh/wakes/wakes.html).

The effect of the western mountains on weather amazed me. The Sierra Nevada Mountains provided me with insights into mountain induced cirrus and cumulus cloud formation, thunderstorm evolution, and snow cover patterning. (See Figure 9.5 for an example of snow coverage over the entire

Figure 9.8   As northwest winds blow across and around Guadeloupe Island (off the Baja California Coast), the wind field is disrupted. Due to the persistence of the winds, both in speed and direction, island eddies often form and move downwind from the island A string of these eddies (called von Karman vortices) can be seen in the stratocumulus cloud layer. (GOES Image courtesy of the University of Wisconsin—http://cimss.ssec.wisc.edu/goes/misc/von_karman.gif.)

western U.S. Differences in color—purplish vs. whitish hues—reveal clouds vs. snow cover.)

Meteorologists (both forecasters and researchers) have discovered an array of additional patterns in satellite imagery. Ellrod and Nelson,[14] Maddox et al.,[28] Purdom,[40] and Scofield et al.[42] have led efforts at applying pattern recognition of satellite cloud signatures to severe weather and/or heavy convective rainfall events. Ellrod has used satellite imagery to detect fog at night[13] and also assess clear air turbulence.[12] Dvorak[11] and Smigielski and Mogil[43] have developed decision-tree approaches which allow meteorologists to look at satellite imagery almost exclusively to obtain estimates of the central pressure inside tropical and middle latitude oceanic cyclones, respectively. Figure 9.9 contains two multispectral images of Hurricane Alberto in the summer of 2000. The top figure shows Alberto as it was "spinning up" and the bottom figure shows the subsequent organization of the storm and a well-defined eye. Alberto would have been classified as a strong storm using the Dvorak Technique and was measured as a strong storm by hurricane hunter aircraft.

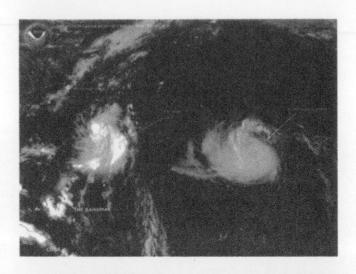

Figure 9.9 Hurricane Alberto undergoes changes in its cloud pattern from the afternoon of August 10, 2000 to August 11, 2000. In this multispectral image pair, notice how the circulation is more rounded and an "eye" has appeared by the August 11 image. According to NOAA, the sustained winds in Alberto had reached hurricane force by the time of the August 11 image. (GOES Image courtesy of NOAA.)

Pattern recognition also plays a role when one takes an even-larger scale perspective. Leonard Snellman, head of the NWS Western Region Scientific Services Division in the 1970s and 1980s, demonstrated relationships between the location of high altitude long wave troughs (low pressure centers) and ridges (high pressure centers). He used the word "teleconnections" to describe how weather patterns in one place can be related to patterns in other places.[44] A teleconnection is a "recurring and persistent, large-scale pattern of pressure and circulation anomalies that spans vast geographical areas"[46] (see also [1,34]).

Gray uses a similar approach to produce his annual forecast of Atlantic Ocean hurricane frequency and storm strength.[22,23] He relies on the strength of El Niño, the presence and strength of westerly winds at high altitudes in the tropics, and African rainfall among his key predictors.

Recently, patterns such as El Niño and La Niña have gained international attention. These patterns are revealed in displays of the type shown in Figure 9.10. The patterns involve variances from average sea surface temperatures in the tropical eastern Pacific Ocean and are part of a larger-scale teleconnections pattern known as the El Niño Southern Oscillation (ENSO).

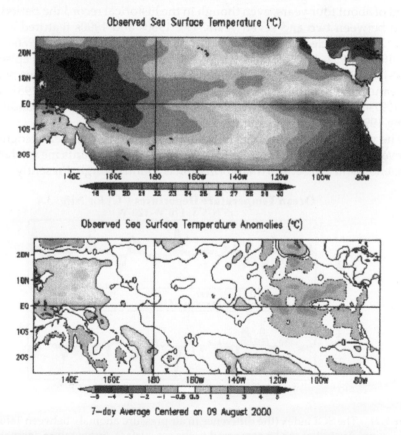

Figure 9.10   Using satellites, ships, and data buoys, NOAA scientists create maps showing sea surface temperatures and departures from average in order to monitor the onset and demise of events such as El Niño and La Niña. See color version of this figure in the color section following page 114. (Maps courtesy of NOAA's Climate Prediction Center—
http://www.cpc.ncep.noaa.gov/products/analysis_monitoring/lanina/.)

One way to measure the pattern is by examining images of sea surface temperatures in the tropical eastern Pacific Ocean which are created from satellite imagery, ship reports, and data buoys. The most current analysis of sea surface temperatures can be found at http://www.cpc.ncep.noaa.gov/products/analysis_monitoring/lanina/.

The Southern Oscillation Index (SOI) is another measure of the El Niño and La Niña pattern.[35,36] Here, the large-scale fluctuations in air pressure occurring between the tropical western and eastern Pacific (i.e., the state of the Southern Oscillation) are examined. Traditionally, this index has been calculated based on the differences in air pressure anomaly between Tahiti and Darwin, Australia. The inverse relationship between the SOI and sea surface temperatures anomalies in the eastern Pacific shown by the time series in Figure 9.11 is striking. Notice too that the cycle of the ENSO has an average period of about four years, even though in the historical record the period has varied between two and seven years. The 1980s and 1990s featured a very active ENSO cycle, with five El Niño episodes (1982–1983, 1986–1987, 1991–1993, 1994–1995, and 1997–1998) and three La Niña episodes (1984–1985, 1988–1989, 1995–1996) occurring during the period. This period also featured two of the strongest El Niño episodes of the century (1982–1983 and 1997–1998), as well as two consecutive periods of El Niño conditions during 1991–1995 without an intervening cold episode.

The wide-reaching impacts of these ENSO patterns are well-recognized and even predictable to a large extent. The thought that haunts me is whether the science which describes their formation is sound enough. Presently, scien-

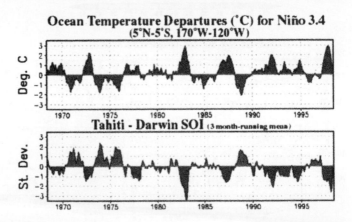

Figure 9.11 The SOI index (the difference in air pressure anomaly between Tahiti and Darwin, Australia) can be compared to the sea surface temperature anomalies (departures from average) found in the tropical eastern Pacific Ocean. The inverse relationship between the SOI and sea surface temperature anomalies in this time series is dramatic. (Graphs courtesy of NOAA's Climate Prediction Center— http://www.cpc.ncep.noaa.gov/products/analysis_monitoring/ensocycle/soi.html.)

tists note the SOI pressure pattern and its associated link to a weakening of the easterly winds in the southeastern North Pacific Ocean. This, in turn, leads to a decrease in upwelling (rising of cold bottom ocean water due to wind stress on the ocean's surface). However, at this time, no one seems to know exactly what causes these pattern changes to occur. Without completing the entire picture (the understanding to support the pattern recognition), the forecasting of these climatological scale oscillations is still in its infancy.

Finally, there are long-term climatic patterns. While satellite imagery (and other forms of remote and *in situ* sensing) may begin to help us understand these, the data record is incomplete, at best. Clearly, with global warming in the news almost daily, there are many valid reasons to document and understand and long- and short-term climatic trends. Some of these include the effects of climatic change on agriculture, water resources, energy use, the potential rise in sea level, insect populations, and spread of disease.[15]

9.3.3 Repeating patterns

During my years working at the NWS, I also learned another aspect of how pattern recognition (on scales shorter than climatic or El Niño) applies to forecasting. It seems that once a certain pattern becomes established, it often repeats itself over time. Even if the pattern weakens or changes, it often quickly re-establishes itself. This was evident during the drought in the eastern U.S. during the summer of 1999 and the cool, wet pattern in the Great Lakes-New England regions during the summer of 2000. There are also some classic semipermanent weather patterns that are often very evident in satellite imagery:

- *The east coast's "Bermuda High,"* a high pressure system which is located near Bermuda during the summer months. With its broad clockwise wind circulation, this weather feature brings warm, humid air (and scattered afternoon thunderstorms) to large parts of the eastern U.S. This is illustrated in Figure 9.12.
- *"Lake effect" snow bands* usually occur throughout the late fall and winter months (and sometimes into spring) when northwest winds blow persistently across the warmer waters of the Great Lakes. As the cold air flows over the warmer waters, it picks up heat and moisture, destabilizing the atmosphere and allowing convection to occur where it normally would not. Due to their narrow nature, the bands often produce large snowfall gradients—excessive snowfall on one part of town and clear skies a few miles away. Figure 9.4 shows these bands extending from the Great Lakes all the way to the Delaware and Chesapeake Bays in the wake of a large winter storm.
- *The "four corners high"* is a semipermanent wintertime high pressure system found near the intersection of Colorado-New Mexico–Arizona-Utah. This high brings light winds and cold temperatures to much of

Figure 9.12 This visible image shows a large, mainly cloud-free area off the U.S. East Coast. Suppression of cloud development over warm ocean waters is one key to the presence of a large high pressure system. Some small cloud lines extend in a curved arc from north of Puerto Rico northwestward toward a few small thunderstorms and then recurve toward the northeast. These cloud lines often reflect the low-level wind pattern. This counter-clockwise curve to the clouds is another clue to the presence of a high pressure area. Because this high is located near Bermuda, it is referred to as the "Bermuda High." (GOES Image courtesy of NOAA.)

the intermountain west. If it shifts to the west slightly, it can alter the normal pressure pattern along the southern California coast and create Santa Ana winds—hot, dry downslope winds that occasionally blow into the Los Angeles basin and nearby locales. Any coastal fog that may be around is quickly swept out to sea by these winds. A similar pattern can occur when a high pressure system builds into the northern and central Rockies and causes onshore winds in California to weaken or shift to an easterly component.[6]

- *The normal pressure pattern along the U.S. west coast* (San Francisco-San Diego) has higher pressure offshore. Likewise, temperatures are much colder offshore, especially in summer. This combination of factors results in an almost constant sea breeze, especially along the central California coast, and most noticeably in the San Francisco Bay Area. As cooler ocean air moves inland toward the hot interior region of

California's Central Valley, it has only one way to go geographically—
through the Golden Gate Bridge area, past Alcatraz and Angel Islands,
northward through San Pablo Bay, and then eastward through Suisan
Bay and the Carquinez Strait. This creates a perpetual "wind tunnel"
in the area where onshore winds of 20 to 30 mph are common. Not surprisingly, comments such as "the coldest winter day I ever experienced was a summer day in San Francisco" have been widely ascribed
to the weather in the City by the Bay. Null[38] notes that Mark Twain
apparently never said these words; nonetheless, the value of this
urban legend is inescapable. Ask the hapless tourists who are caught
in shorts and tee shirts as the fog rolls in through the Golden Gate
Bridge. Figure 9.6 shows how the coast fog and stratus field has
moved ashore overnight to fill nearly all the coastal valleys of the central California coast.

- *The "dry line" from west Texas northward to western Nebraska* is a semipermanent boundary between dry, desert-like air to the west and
warm, humid Gulf of Mexico air to the east. The dry line often migrates
to the east when a large-scale storm system develops over Colorado
and moves into the Great Plains and is occasionally accompanied by
blowing dust. The dry line is often readily detected in surface observations, but when cumulus and cumulonimbus (thunderstorm) clouds
develop along the boundary and/or wind picks up dust to the west of
the dry line, it becomes observable in satellite imagery. This is illustrated in Figure 9.13. Both boundary clouds and dust to the west of the
dry line can be seen in Figure 9.13, across north Texas and southern
Oklahoma where the dust cloud is actually hiding land features. To the
east of the dust plume (and to its far northwest), contrasts between different types of land features (including forests and rivers) are evident.
As the storm moves away, the dry line usually returns to its usual position in west Texas. Many significant tornado outbreaks in the central
U.S. are linked to the dry line.[33]

9.3.4 Dynamic patterning

As the above examples suggest, the patterns in weather can be discussed in
terms of the configurations of cues and cue relationships in a particular data
set (i.e., a GOES image), but they can also be regarded as dynamic and evolving due to the underlying cause-effect relations, which end up leaving their
traces in the static images (or dynamic image loops).

Sometimes a weather pattern will establish itself and a series of storms
may bring excessive rain to one part of the nation, while another part
remains dry. Then the pattern "flips" and the storm track shifts to another
place. The winter of 1995–1996, for example, exhibited such a persistent pattern, with storm after storm bringing the northeast record-breaking snows.
The winter of 1996–1997 was almost the reverse, with record snows falling

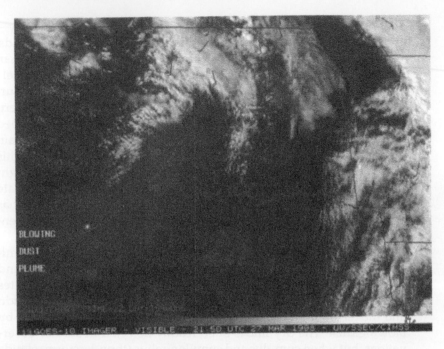

Figure 9.13   A satellite image that reveals the "dry line" in two features—boundary clouds and a dust plume to the west of the dry line (shown in a gray shade subtly lighter than the land). BD signifies blowing dust. Wind flags showing direction and speed are those typically used on weather maps. (GOES Image courtesy of the University of Wisconsin—http://cimss.ssec.wisc.edu/goes/misc/980327_2150_vis.GIF.)

over the northern plains states. The establishment of a pattern could easily be linked to the presence of a snow cover. Once established, the snow on the ground often affects the larger-scale air temperature pattern such that storm tracks move along the snow-no snow cover boundary. Ensuing precipitation events over snow-covered areas tend to be more often of the frozen variety. The boundary becomes further enhanced due to the effects of radiational cooling and reflection of sunlight from different surfaces. This unwritten rule works very well east of the Rocky Mountains. In short, snow often begets more snow!

Dryness (and a record number of forest fires) was the rule over the western U.S. during the summer of 2000. The cause-effect relationships have not been well-established (and are likely very interrelated). For some reason, dry areas tend to remain dry. The 2000 drought could be related to lowered evapo-transpiration rates as well as an associated large-scale high pressure or upper air ridge weather pattern due to decreased cloudiness. Conversely, rainy areas (with higher evapo-transpiration rates and a large scale low pressure system or upper level trough) tend to continue to receive rain.

Daily national high temperatures across the U S are most frequently observed in the desert southwest, Texas, and Florida. This pattern is driven by latitude, sun angle, and amount of cloud coverage. The chilliest spots are in northern states and/or in mountain areas of the west where latitude and altitude factors prevail.

Yet, even persistent patterns can and do change. Meteorologists sometimes refer to this as "flip-flopping." Periods of heavy rainfall may be followed by periods of dry or even drought conditions, only to be followed by periods of heavy rains.

Each year, the classic hurricane and tornado seasons occur during expected time periods. And *within* these trends one can easily find subpatterns involving the concentration of storminess in certain areas, the movement of storms, and the number of storms. For example, hurricane frequency was high along the U.S. east coast in the 1950s. It was not until the 1990s that the east coast frequency peaked again. Fujita[20] noted a periodic, clockwise migration of the tornado frequency centroid across the central U.S.

In addition to the generally repetitive daily weather cycle pattern (cold in the morning and warmer in the afternoon), periods of warm air for several days are often followed by periods of cold air for several days before the warmer air returns. Seasonally, the colder months are followed by warmer ones and then that pattern repeats itself. These ground-based weather patterns are linked closely to similar changes in the upper level wind and pressure patterns.

Have you ever heard the expression, "It always rains in Seattle"? Well, the pattern of prevailing storm tracks and Seattle's special geographical flavor make Seattle a rather cloudy and damp place. Although it rains often, Seattle does not receive a large amount of rain each year, and summertime in Seattle is often not marked by precipitation. Southern California's sun-filled beaches are generally sunny, but only after the nighttime and morning coastal low cloudiness "burns off" or evaporates due to solar heating.

All these instances of dynamic patterning show that the patterns perceived in data and imagery (of any type) are related in a direct way to the underlying causal dynamics. The achievement of expertise at interpreting data and/or imagery means that the person no longer perceives only the information shown. The expert interpreter *sees* the data or the image, and can tell you things about it (e.g., there is a coffee stain in the left corner). *But what the expert perceives is the underlying causal dynamics.* It is because of the expert's understanding of the underlying causal dynamics that the expert can perceive patterns that the novice cannot. Fronts do not appear on satellite images, but the expert can tell you where the fronts are. The jet stream leaves its footprint on both weather charts and satellite imagery. High and low pressure systems, upper-air disturbances, the list goes on and on—these are things that can be *perceived* in the images, but cannot be *seen* in the images.

Let me illustrate.

9.4   Skywatching

Of all the weather possibilities, clouds (from the ground up) first hooked me on patterning. Clouds offer an incredible array of patterns even within the basic set of cloud types. Looking up from the ground, cumulus clouds are puffy, often with white tops and darker bottoms; stratus clouds appear flat; cirrus clouds are wispy; and altocumulus and stratocumulus often have alternating dark and light bands or cloud bands interspersed with clear areas (see   http://www.weatherworks.com/cool_clouds.html).   Although   each cloud type may be different, each one is formed by an associated weather pattern and its appearance is linked closely to physical processes.

Classic cloud patterning involves winter storms (east of the Rockies) and thunderstorms. High-flying cirrus clouds often herald the arrival of a winter storm. The cloud sequence—cirrus-cirrostratus-altocumulus-fractostratus—followed by snow or rain is what is typically observed. As is true in the interpretation of cloud patterns from a space viewpoint, the patterns seen from the ground hinge on the underlying dynamics—they are keyed to a gradual uplifting of moving air, followed by falling precipitation that moistens air below cloud level. As the air between cloud and ground becomes saturated, fractostratus clouds form; this signals that falling precipitation is almost ready to reach the ground.

Look at an approaching thunderstorm (in most parts of the U.S.), and it often involves a description such as "dark west." This is expected since towering thunderstorm clouds are blocking the late afternoon sun (most thunderstorms occur during the time of maximum solar heating of the ground) and the cloud we see is really shadowed (most sunlight has been reflected back toward the sun). No wonder that with five to eight miles of cloud between a ground observer and the sun, a thunderstorm cloud really appears dark!

Cumulus clouds, which generally form in late morning and dissipate around sunset, are the result of a repeating daily pattern associated with solar heating and radiational cooling of the Earth's surface. Land-sea breezes and mountain-valley breezes are driven by this same cold-warm-cold daily temperature cycle and differential heating or cooling related to land-water temperature differences or terrain variations.

Contrails (condensation trails or cirrus-type clouds formed by high-flying jet aircraft) mark the highways in the sky that jet planes use. That is why so many of the trails parallel each other and you can see planes follow planes across the sky. If the contrails last for a long time, chances are the air at flight level was already moist; if the contrail disappears almost as fast as it forms, the air aloft is likely dry.

I have also noticed that some cloud types had patterns within them. Altocumulus usually have alternating bands of clouds and clear spaces. Stratocumulus are similar, but with larger individual cloud elements. Sometimes there are two patterns that seem to crisscross in these layered cumulus-type clouds. At the time I first noticed these subtle patterns, I did not fully appreciate the interactions taking place in these wave pattern clouds. Now that I have taken trips to the beach, seen a tidal bore in Alaska, and watched raindrops splashing in puddles, this patterning seems almost too obvious for me not to have not recognized earlier. Basically, these events all involve transverse wave patterns. Either air or water rises in one place, and sinks in another. The ripple marks left behind in sand or soil by moving water or wind show the presence of the same type of wave pattern. Ripple marks found in wind-blown snow are not much different.

9.5 Patterns in weather analysis

Since I have been largely focusing on satellite image interpretation, I should point out that the understanding of weather involves looking at many different data types (including—but not limited to—clouds from the ground up, radar maps, surface and upper air weather maps, and data from balloon-borne sensors). All of these data types are rich with patterns and one can achieve expertise at interpreting them. An example would be the "meteogram," which depicts the weather for a specific location as a time series. The meteogram shown in Figure 9.14 (from the U.S. Weather Web site— http://www.uswx.com/us/wx/) provides an easy-to-see example of patterns and pattern relationships among weather variables for a 10-day period for Rapid City, SD. (By visiting the U.S. Weather Web site, one can find similar meteograms for cities across the U.S. for 2-, 10-, 30- and 60-day periods.

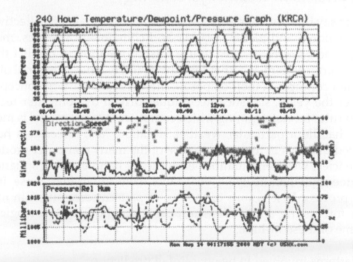

Figure 9.14 A meteogram for 10 days in August 2000 for Rapid City, SD. Notice the daily patterns for temperature, dew point and relative humidity. (Graphs courtesy of the U.S. Weather Web site—USWX at http://www.uswx.com/us/wx/.)

To find the meteograms, click on any city, once you get to the state map page you are interested in. The two day meteogram will initially appear at the bottom of the page; you can toggle among the other three choices.)

Patterns abound in weather charts. There are isotherm bands, warm and cold fronts, and the ongoing progression of highs and lows. One can see jet stream meanders. One can see squall lines go through a formation-decay process that repeats itself over and over again. One can see the preferred locations for highs and lows to form, tracks for them to take, and places for them to die.

Storm chasing provides another venue in which pattern perception plays a major role. Before storm chasing began formally in 1970, meteorologists noted recurring patterns in photographs of tornadic thunderstorms.[21] As a result, the basic structure of tornado-producing storms was specified. This became the basis for the ensuing storm chase programs operated by NOAA, universities, and other organizations. Photography, videography, and *in situ* and remote sensing data were examined to determine patterns and revise our models of storm structure. Photographic evidence provided by storm chasers supported hypotheses developed concerning the dynamics of multivortex tornadoes (smaller tornadoes rotating around the main tornado).[8,18] Most recently, Doppler radar evidence confirmed the existence of this phenomenon.[4] Richardson[41] was correct when he suggested that "big whirls have little whirls which feed on their velocity; little whirls have smaller whirls and so on to viscosity."

9.6   Patterns in weather forecasting

It is safe to say that weather *is* patterns! From individual and collective clouds to local, national and global weather and climatological scales, meteorologists examine patterns and try to use this information to predict the future state of the atmosphere. Weather forecasters today have an arsenal of pattern-recognition concepts at their disposal. These include pattern concepts developed over the years, statistical techniques driven by computer technology, and even rules for determining which computer forecast model is most likely going to handle a particular weather situation. Yes, forecasters have even recognized patterns in the performance of the many computer models (biases, tendencies, weather situations each model handles well, situations each model does not handle well, etc.), and have integrated these into their forecast process. Discussions of the use of pattern recognition in numerous weather forecasting applications appear throughout meteorological literature. Some of these include:

- Patterns involved in heavy rainfall prediction[28]
- Conditions needed for major east coast cyclogenesis[45]
- The relationship between winter lightning in the southeastern U.S. and heavy frozen precipitation[24]

Most of the forecasting techniques used by NWS forecasters today are based not only on patterning, but also sound scientific principles that support the pattern.

The same types of pattern recognition have forged breakthroughs in how forecasters interpret radar (both conventional and Doppler) and weather satellite imagery to create forecasts and warnings. Techniques key on the shape, movement, intensity, temperature, temperature gradient, and other measurable characteristics in either satellite or radar data. For example, a v-shape signature atop a thunderstorm in satellite imagery often indicates the presence of a strong updraft (and possible overshooting cloud tops) that is blocking the horizontal wind flow.[29] As the wind is forced around the updraft, it creates a v-shaped pattern downwind. This is easily seen in the cloud tops on enhanced infrared satellite imagery (hence its name, "enhanced-V") and may also be evident in visible imagery. Figure 9.15 (top) is a color enhanced infrared image at a 4 km resolution. It shows the temperature pattern associated with an enhanced-V cloud-top signature. The strongly rising air inside the thunderstorm causes environmental winds to split apart and move around the storm. A similar effect happens at the top of the storm. Notice the location match of the "V" with the overshooting cloud top in the corresponding, higher 1 km resolution visible image in the bottom figure. You can also see this type of feature as water flows down a curb and passes over or by an obstacle (see Figure 9.8).

The circulation associated with a tornado can sometimes be seen on conventional radars as a "hook echo." This shape results as rain is curled around the circulation of the tornado's parent mesocyclone. Where rain is not present, the radar detects nothing. The contrast between coiling rain and rain-free areas yields the hook shape in conventional radar reflectivity images. This is illustrated in Figure 9.16.

Here, the green yellow and red colors show increasing reflectivities (which mean heavier rain and/or larger hail are reflecting the radar signals). NEXt generation RADar (NEXRAD) is the new NWS Doppler radar system. While this system can detect rainfall, it also has the added capability of measuring the motion of raindrops (hailstones, other airborne particles) toward or away from the radar site (the Doppler effect). This means that air that is moving quickly toward the radar at one place and moving quickly away from the radar next to it shows two sides of a circulation pattern. Figure 9.16 (bottom) shows a Doppler velocity profile (red = winds moving away from the radar; green = winds moving toward the radar; white = very strong winds moving toward the radar). Depending upon the strength of this "gate-to-gate shear," the phenomenon can be classed as a mesocyclone or the more dangerous tornado vortex signature. These radar images in Figure 9.16 were obtained just before a large F5 tornado struck Moore, OK on May 3, 1999. A similar hook-shaped pattern, although at a much larger scale, is often observed in satellite images. Clouds (and associated precipitation) wrap around a low pressure center in a comma-shape pattern, shown in Figure 9.17 (see also Figure 9.4).

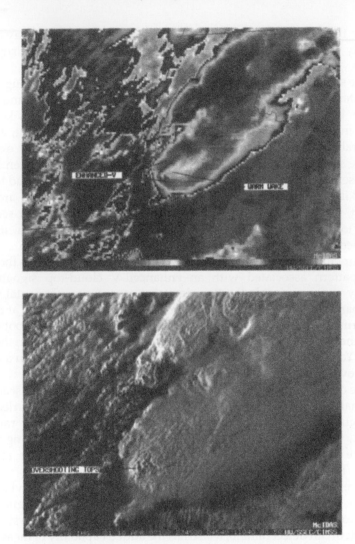

Figure 9.15   Top: A color-enhanced infrared image showing the temperature pattern associated with an enhanced-v cloud-top signature. Bottom: The corresponding visible image. See color version of this image in color section following page 114. (GOES images courtesy of the University of Wisconsin—http://cimss.ssec.wisc.edu/goes/misc/warm_wake.html.)

A cloud pattern that typifies a high pressure system is the meso-scale convective complex (MCC). The meso-scale of weather is for phenomena that are at a scale small in areal extent and which last for periods of only a few hours to a day. An MCC is a large cluster of thunderstorms that persists for a long time. Most commonly observed in the central U.S. during the summer months, MCCs also move off the west Africa coast and can develop into Atlantic hurricanes. Many MCCs produce strong outflow wind patterns

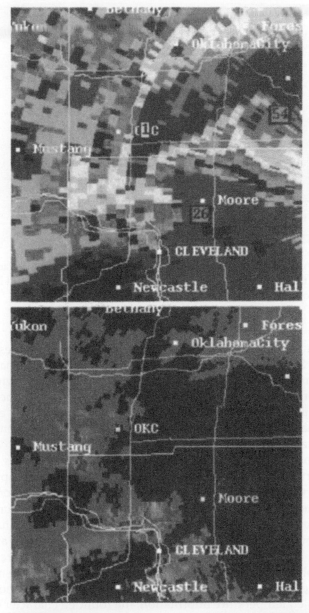

Figure 9.16   NEXRAD base refectivity and velocity images for a major tornado event on May 3, 1999. Base reflectivity shows the classic hook-shaped image associated with a tornado just west-southwest of Moore, OK. Velocity data show a corresponding gate-to-gate (or pixel-to-pixel) shear of velocity inward toward the radar (green) and outward from the radar (red). This wind shear couplet shows two parts of a corresponding complete circulation pattern. See color version of this figure in the color section following page 114. (Image courtesy of NOAA's National Severe Storms Laboratory—http://www.nssl.noaa.gov/~tsmith/may3/0017-8panel.gif.)

Figure 9.17 Another example of a large comma cloud in the central Pacific Ocean on February 16, 2000. Compare to Figure 9.5. (GOES Image courtesy of NOAA— http://www.osei.noaa.gov/.)

known as microbursts or downbursts. Some produce tornadoes and excessive rainfall. Some give rise to straight-line outflowing winds that in satellite and radar imagery appear as easily recognized patterns known as leading edge gradients or LEGs (in satellite images) and bow echoes (in radar images). Fujita,[19] Johns and Hirt,[25] Maddox,[27] and Bently et al.[2] have described many of the patterns showing MCCs that are evident in surface weather, radar, and satellite data.

MCCs form because thunderstorms transfer large amounts of heat and moisture vertically through the atmosphere. Heat helps to evaporate water from the Earth, oceans, and vegetation. During the condensation process in the clouds, heat is released. As heat builds in these long-lived thunderstorms, it helps to create an upper level high pressure system over the thunderstorm. Often the cloud top pattern associated with an MCC is rounder and contains sharp cloud top temperature gradients. This enhanced infrared image in Figure 9.18 shows many of these features. Figure 9.19 shows a smaller MCC over the Ohio valley in unenhanced infrared imagery. Even without the presence of detailed temperature information, the rounded character of this large thunderstorm system tags it as an MCC.

Figure 9.19 shows the satellite imagery near the onset of an MCC event. Meteograms for that event showing data from Huntington, WV, and Richmond, VA in Figure 9.20 show how the temperature, wind, and pressure changed as the strong wind passed those locations. The storm report map compiled by the NWS's Storm Prediction Center, Figure 9.21, shows the fan-shaped collective of high winds and dense agents resulting from the thunderstorm cluster as it grew and expanded southeastward in an arc-shaped

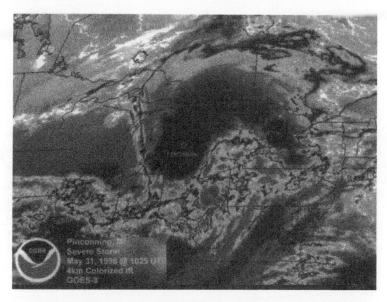

Figure 9.18   A large mesoscale convective complex (MCC) over Michigan on
May 31, 1998. In this enhanced infrared image, the coldest and highest cloud tops
(and the clouds likely producing the heaviest rainfall) are indicated by purple. Reds
also show heavy rainfall. The rounded pattern of this weather feature makes it easy
to identify. See color version of this image in color section following page 114.
(GOES Image courtesy of NOAA's National Climatic Data Center—
http://www.ncdc.noaa.gov/pub/data/images/storm-pincon-19980531-g8ir.gif.)

Figure 9.19   A much smaller, but still rounded, MCC over Illinois and Indiana on
August 9, 2000. This MCC grew throughout the day and spread severe weather to
the U.S. east coast. (GOES Image courtesy of NOAA.)

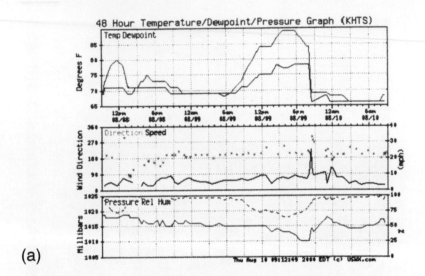

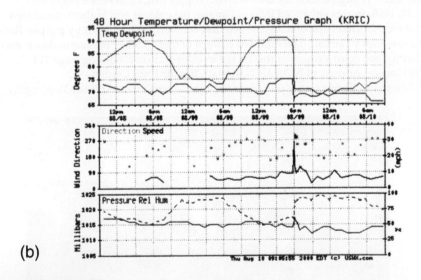

Figure 9.20 Meteograms for 2 days in August 2000 for Huntington, WV, and
Richmond, VA. Both locations were impacted by the MCC shown in Figure 9.19.
Notice the similar pattern involving a large decrease in temperature and dew point
with a rise in pressure and a peak in wind speed. These are the signatures associated
with the arrival of a strong thunderstorm and an accompanying small scale high
pressure system. (Graphs courtesy of the U.S. Weather Web site—USWX at
http://www.uswx.com/us/wx.)

Figure 9.21 NOAA's Storm Prediction Center keeps track of severe weather reports each day. This map summary clearly shows the diverging storm report damage pattern associated with the growing MCC on August 9, 2000. Most reports with this MCC were of strong winds and/or wind damage.

pattern (northern boundary, Indiana to Maryland; southern boundary, Indiana to the western Carolinas).

The book, *An Introduction to Satellite Image Interpretation*[7] provides further background information about basic satellite imagery interpretation and pattern recognition. Similarly, radar interpretation concepts can be found online at the National Severe Storm Laboratory's Operations Training Branch Web page (at http://www.osf.noaa.gov/otb/otb.htm).

9.7 Learning to perceive patterns can be easy

In the natural and man-made world around us, patterns abound. We recognize car types by their characteristics or styling patterns. We assign names to certain housing styles based on their individual characteristics, features, or cues. Identify a bird or a flower, and chances are you will use the patterns associated with it (e.g., wing shape, colors, beak length, and size). Look at the bands in snow drifts or sand dunes, the shapes and designs in icicles, and planted or unplanted fields (especially if snow is present) for still more patterns. Sedimentary rocks afford outstanding examples of patterning, whether they are flat, tilted, or folded. Stir your coffee gently and add some milk to create your own hurricane-like swirls. Stock market investors know about patterns. Simply listen to a market news report and you will hear the reporter talk about "double bottoms," "resistance levels," and more. We live in a world filled with man-made mathematical-based patterns, including bar codes, Web addresses, zip codes, interstate highway numbering, and house numbering.

Our ability to recognize (and understand) the myriad patterns around us helps us survive in our day-to-day world. Yet, we are often not formally taught how to do this. In the case of weather satellite image interpretation, now that we know what some of the patterns are, learning to perceive them can be easy.

Several years ago, my wife and I developed a set of cloud picture cards that we use to teach basic cloud identification to elementary school students. The card set contains three each of cumulus, stratus, and cirrus cloud pictures. Students are instructed to sort and classify the cards according to the three basic cloud families. Not knowing a thing about clouds, or even the names of the clouds, students are able to quickly group the clouds via pattern recognition and provide a list of descriptors that can be used to identify the clouds.

We next replicated the cloud-card concept, and achieved similar results using newspaper weather maps and weather satellite images. Students from elementary through college level (and even some TV meteorologists), were asked to group a set of 12 satellite images (four of each type—infrared, water vapor, and visible, over a 4-day period) by imagery type and cloud features/patterns. Then they were challenged to order the images chronologically, looking for clues in any of the image types to help them determine ordering for all images. The set was chosen to intentionally show a repeating pattern in which day one and day four were remarkably similar. In contrast with the younger participants, many of the college-age students had trouble with this activity at first, because they were not pattern-oriented. (Were they so focused on finding the forest that they could not find the trees, or had pattern recognition been "educated out of them"? We fear that the latter possibility is the truer.) Once they were shown patterning concepts, however, they were better able to perform the activity on another set of images.

Recently, I taught a class of 18 first graders about storms. I keyed on "swirls" as my theme and we examined Hurricane Floyd from a satellite perspective. The students initially patterned the image as representing the globe (because it had all the colors the globe has on it and it was round). This is another great example of how youngsters can develop patterning skills. Then they investigated swirls in a bowl and a pie plate and discovered how swirls form, change, and create smaller swirls inside them. At the end of the hour, students were given take-home copies of weather satellite images in which they were able to pick out storm swirl patterns. They were now ready to explain satellite imagery via pattern recognition to their parents.

In my case (and for others who practice meteorology), there is little doubt that pattern recognition and understanding has played a role in making us better at what we do. It has guided us through the scientific process and helped us uncover relationships we might never have seen otherwise. It also enabled us to take the recognition phase and move into understanding and prediction, thereby advancing the state of knowledge of the science and using it toward a common good. And as Berra once said "you can observe a lot by watching."[3]

Figure 9.22 presents three (unenhanced) satellite images (one visible, one infrared and one water vapor image) from the University of Wisconsin Web page (http://www.ssec.wisc.edu/data/eastsnap.html) showing the Western Hemisphere in the late morning of August 14, 2000. Even if one does not know the meteorological or physical forces that may be creating a particular pattern, it is interesting to see how many patterns can be uncovered. The Reader is invited look at these individually and collectively for patterns, without first looking at Table 9.1, which presents some interpretations.

There are many Web sites that provide real-time satellite imagery in various formats. A list of some of them appears in Table 9.2.

Figure 9.22   This set of images (visible, infrared, and water vapor) shows cloud and weather conditions across the U.S. in the late morning (eastern time) on August 14, 2000. This is a visible light image. (GOES Image courtesy of the University of Wisconsin.)

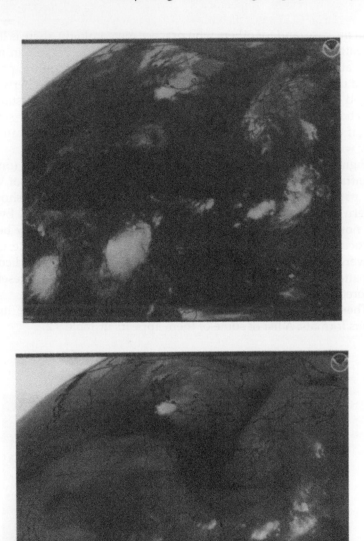

Figure 9.22 (*Continued*.) Top: an infrared image. Bottom: a water vapor image. For an interpretation, see Table 9.1.

Table 9.1 Features Seen in Three Images in Figure 9.22.

Visible light image on page 265
Clouds appear whitish because they reflect solar energy.

- Swirl along middle Atlantic coast. Is this a "Nor'easter?"
- Band of speckled clouds from Texas coast eastward to just west of Florida having a distinct "edge" at its northern side. Why? Why is the band inland over Texas but over water in the Gulf Coast?
- Two large clusters of clouds on either side of Mexican coast. Are these tropical storms?
- Some cloud streaks near Hudson Bay, Canada.
- Land is light gray and water in Gulf of Mexico is darker gray. Why?
- Dark areas sprinkled throughout southwestern U.S. What are they?
- White Sands, NM can be seen.

Infrared image on page 266 (top)
Clouds appear whitish because they are radiating infrared energy, but the color code is counterintuitive: cold = white, warm = dark.

- The swirl along middle Atlantic coast now has a "hole" in the center.
- Band of small rounded clouds from Louisiana coast eastward to central Florida; clouds are larger over Florida.
- The two large clusters of clouds on either side of Mexican coast now have brighter spots embedded in their central regions. What might this indicate?
- Why do the cloud streaks near Hudson Bay, Canada look different in the visible image?
- Hudson Bay itself is lighter colored than land nearby. Why?
- The cloud-free areas in the western U.S. are darker colored than areas in the east. Why?
- From Minnesota eastward to New England (and in corresponding regions of Canada), there are definite variations in the gray shades of the clouds. Why?
- Outer space looks white. Why?

Water vapor image on page 266 (bottom)
The sensor picks up radiated infrared energy that is partially to totally masked by atmospheric water vapor. Clouds appear *very* whitish; areas of water vapor appear milky white; drier regions appear as dark gray—this is related to temperature in the same way as in infrared images (cold = white; warm = dark).

- The swirl along middle Atlantic coast shows circulation well into eastern Canada and southward as far as the Carolinas. The swirl is linked to a larger-scale wave pattern (a "long-wave trough") that extends all the way from central California to northern Nebraska to western Tennessee to the South Carolina-Georgia coast. The thin band of clouds lying along the northern edge of the lighter gray region over the Rockies is a manifestation of the jet stream.
- Note the sharp cloud edge from eastern Canada to western Pennsylvania. What might be the cause of this?
- The two large clusters of clouds on either side of Mexican coast have many bright spots in them. Might these be storm cells embedded in a tropical storm?
- The cloud streaks near Hudson Bay, Canada now appear as rippling layers. Might these be manifestations of the jet streams in those areas?
- What are the large areas of light gray and large areas of dark gray? Might they be high altitude moisture and dry air aloft (respectively)?

Table 9.2   URLs of Web Sites Showing Weather Satellite Images.

Site URL	Notes
HOWTHEWEATHERWORKS http://www.weatherworks.com/links/ satellite_links.html	Current weather Archived images
HOWTHEWEATHERWORKS "Cloud" page http://www.weatherworks.com/cool_clouds.html	Cloud interpretation guidance
Colorado State University http://www.cira.colostate.edu/Special/CurrWx/ currwx.htm	Current weather
Colorado State University, Cooperative Institute for Research in the Atmosphere http://www.cira.colostate.edu/ramm/visit/istpds/ awips/page1.asp http://www.cira.colostate.edu/ramm/advimgry/ enhance0.htm	GOES imagery and how it is processed
NOAA—National Center for Environmental Prediction http://www.cpc.ncep.noaa.gov/products/ analysis_monitoring/lanina/	Current and archived ocean data
NOAA—National Environmental Satellite Data and Information Service http://goeshp.wwb.noaa.gov/	Current weather
NOAA—National Environmental Satellite Data and Information Service http://orbit-net.nesdis.noaa.gov/arad/fpdt/5_enhan/ enhance.html	GOES imagery and how it is processed
NOAA—Operational Significant Event Imagery http://www.osei.noaa.gov/	Archived images
NOAA—National Climatic Data Center Historically Significant Events Imagery Files http://www.ncdc.noaa.gov/ol/satellite/olimages.html	Archived images
University of Wisconsin http://www.ssec.wisc.edu/data/eastsnap.html	Current weather
University of Wisconsin http://cimss.ssec.wisc.edu/goes/ http://cimss.ssec.wisc.edu/tropic/temp/eddy/eddy.html http://cimss.ssec.wisc.edu/goes/misc/ interesting_images.html	Archived images
Goddard Space Flight Center http://goes1.gsfc.nasa.gov/	GOES imagery and how it is processed

(continued)

Table 9.2 (Continued)

Site URL	Notes
Jeng-Horng Chen's Fluid Dynamics Web Page http://www.eng.umd.edu/~chenjh/wakes/ wakes.html	Understanding fluid dynamics of the atmosphere
National Severe Storm Laboratory's Operations Training Branch http://www.osf.noaa.gov	Training in many aspects of meteorology and forecasting
U.S. Weather http://www.uswx.com/us/wx/	One of many sites that provide weather observations and forecast information

References

1. Barnston, A. G. and Livezey, R. E., Classification, seasonality and persistence of low-frequency atmospheric circulation patterns, *Mon. Weather Rev.*, 115, 1083–1126, 1987.
2. Bentley, M. L., Mote, T. L., and Byrd, S. F., North Central Great Plains Derecho Producing Mesoscale Convective Systems (DMCSs): A forecasting primer, U.S. Dept. of Commerce, National Oceanic and Atmospheric Administration, National Weather Service Technical Note CR 08, Scientific Services Division, Central Region, Kansas City, MO, 1999.
3. Berra, Y., http://www.yogi-berra.com/yogiisms.html, 2000.
4. Bluestein, H. B., *Tornado Alley—Monster Storms of the Great Plains*, Oxford University Press, Oxford, 1999.
5. Burgess, D. W. and Lemon, L. R., Severe thunderstorm detection by radar, in *Radar in Meteorology*, Atlas, D., Ed., American Meteorological Society, Boston, 619–647, 1990.
6. Canepa, R. and Miller, M., A record heatwave along the central California coast: October 7–8, 1996, NWS Western Regional Technical Attachment 97–29, 1997, http://www.wrh.noaa.gov/wrhq/97TAs/TA9729/TA97-29.html
7. Conway, E. D., *An Introduction to Satellite Image Interpretation*, Johns Hopkins University Press, Baltimore, 1997.
8. Davies-Jones, R., Tornado dynamics, in *Thunderstorm Morphology and Dynamics*, 2nd ed., Kesler, E., Ed., University of Oklahoma Press, Norman, OK, 1986.
9. Doswell, C. A., III, The operational meteorology of convective weather, Volume I: operational mesoanalysis, NOAA Technical Memorandum NWS NSSFC-5, National Oceanic and Atmospheric Administration, U.S. Department of Commerce, Silver Spring, MD, 1982.

10. Doswell, C. A., III, The operational meteorology of convective weather, Volume I: storm scale analysis, NOAA Technical Memorandum NWS NSSFC-5, National Oceanic and Atmospheric Administration, U.S. Department of Commerce, Silver Spring, MD, 1985.

11. Dvorak, V. F., Tropical cyclone intensity analysis using satellite data, NOAA Technical Report NESDIS 11, NESDIS, Camp Springs, MD, 1984.

12. Ellrod, G. P., A decision tree approach to clear air turbulence analysis using satellite and upper air data, NOAA Technical Memorandum NESDIS 23, NESDIS, Camp Springs, MD, 1989.

13. Ellrod, G. P., Detection and analysis of fog at night using GOES multispectral imagery, NOAA Technical Report NESDIS 75, NESDIS, Camp Springs, MD, 1994.

14. Ellrod, G. P. and Nelson, J. P., Experimental microburst image products derived from GOES sounder data, in *Proc. 16ᵗʰ Conf. Weather Anal. Forecasting*, American Meteorological Society, Boston, 43–45, 1998.

15. Epstein, P. R., Is global warming harmful to health? *Sci. Am.*, 50–57, (August, 2000).

16. Forbes, G. S., On the reliability of hook echoes as tornado indicators, *Mon. Weather Rev.*, 109, 1457–66, 1981.

17. Fujita, T. T., Analytical mesometeorology: a review, *Meteorol. Monogr.*, 5, no. 27, 77–125, 1963.

18. Fujita, T. T., Proposed mechanisms of suction spots accompanied by tornadoes, in *Preprints of the 7ᵗʰ Conference on Severe Local Storms*, American Meteorological Society, Satellite and Mesometeorology Project, Report, Department of Geophysical Sciences, University of Chicago, 203–213, 1971.

19. Fujita, T. T., Manual of downburst identification for Project NIMROD, Satellite and Mesometeorology Project Report, Department of Geophysical Sciences, University of Chicago, 1978.

20. Fujita, T. T., U.S. Tornadoes, part 1, 70 year statistics, report, Satellite and Mesometeorology Project Report, Department of Geophysical Sciences, University of Chicago, 1987.

21. Golden J. H. and Purcell, D., Photogrammetric velocities of the Great Bend, Kansas tornado of 30 August 1974: accelerations and asymmetries, *Mon. Weather Rev.*, 105, 485–492, 1977.

22. Gray, W. M., Landsea, C. W., Mielke, P. W., Jr., and Berry, K. J., Early August updated forecast of atlantic basin seasonal hurricane activity and landfall probabilities for 2000, Report, Department of Atmospheric Science, Colorado State University, Fort Collins, CO, 2000.

23. http://typhoon.atmos.colostate.edu/forecasts/2000/august2000/

24. Hunter, S. M., Steven, M., Underwood, S. J., Holle, R. L., and Mote, T. L., Winter lightning in the southeast U.S. and its relation to heavy precipitation, in *Proc. 19ᵗʰ Conf. Severe Local Storms*, American Meteorological Society, Boston, 23–37, 1998. http://www.srh.noaa.gov/mrx/research/Lgtg/slspaper.htm

25. Johns, R. H. and Hirt, W. D., Derechos: widespread convectively induced windstorms, *Weather and Forecasting*, 2, 32–49, 1987.

26. Lemon, L. R. and Doswell, C. A., III, Mesocyclone and severe thunderstorm structure: a revised model, in *Preprints of the 11ᵗʰ Conference on Severe Local Storms*, American Meteorological Society, Boston, 1979.

27. Maddox, R. A., Mesoscale convective complexes, *Mon. Weather Rev.*, 111, 1475–1493, 1980.

28. Maddox, R. A., Chappell, C. F., and Hoxit, L. R., Synoptic and mesoscale aspects of flash flood events, *Bull. Am. Meteorol. Soc.*, 60, 115–123, 1979.
29. McCann, D. W., The Enhanced-V, a satellite observable severe storm signature, NOAA Technical Memorandum NWS NSSFC-4, U.S. Department of Commerce, National Oceanic and Atmospheric Administration, Silver Spring, MD, 1981.
30. Magor, B. W., Mesoanalysis: some operational analysis techniques utilized in tornado forecasting, *Bull. Am. Meteorol. Soc.*, 40, 499–511, 1959.
31. Mogil, H. M., Pressure change—its use in forecasting the Atlanta tornado of March 24, 1975, in *Preprints of the 9th Conference on Severe Local Storms*, American Meteorological Society, Boston, 25–32, 1975.
32. Moller, A. R., Doswell, C. A., III., and Pryzbylinksi, R., High-precipitation supercells: a perceptual model and documentation, in *Preprints of the 16th Conference on Severe Local Storms*, American Meteorological Society, Boston, 52–57, 1990.
33. National Oceanic and Atmospheric Administration, NOAA Natural Disaster Survey Report—Wichita/Andover, KS Tornado of April 26, 1991, National Weather Service, U.S. Department of Commerce, Silver Spring, MD, 1991.
34. National Oceanic and Atmospheric Administration, www.cpc.ncep.noaa.gov/data/teledoc/teleintro.html, National Oceanic and Atmospheric Administration, Washington, D.C., 2000.
35. National Oceanic and Atmospheric Administration, www.cpc.ncep.noaa.gov/products/analysis_monitoring/ensocycle/soi.html, National Oceanic and Atmospheric Administration, Washington, D.C., 2000.
36. National Oceanic and Atmospheric Administration, www.cpc.ncep.noaa.gov/products/analysis_monitoring/ensocycle/enso_cycle.html, National Oceanic and Atmospheric Administration, Washington, D.C., 2000.
37. National Oceanic and Atmospheric Administration, www.outlook.noaa.gov/tornadoes/torn50.htm, National Oceanic and Atmospheric Administration, Washington, D.C., 2000.
38. Null, J., Personal communication, 2000.
39. Petit, P. E., Doppler Radar detection capabilities at Montgomery, Alabama, 1982–1988, *Natl. Weather Dig.*, 15, 23–28, 1990.
40. Purdom, J. F. W., Convective scale weather analysis and forecasting, in Rao, P. K., Ed., *Weather Satellites: Systems, Data, and Environmental Applications*, American Meteorological Society, Boston, 285–304, 1990.
41. Richardson. L. F., http://robby.caltech.edu/~mason/quotes.html#onscience, 2000.
42. Scofield, R., Vicente, G., and Rabin, B., The use of water vapor (6.7 micron), precipitable water, and relative humidity for detecting environments that lead to heavy precipitation and flash floods, in *Proc. 16th Conf. on Weather Analysis and Forecasting*, American Meteorological Society, Boston, 37–39, 1998.
43. Smigielski, F. J. and Mogil, H. M., A systematic satellite approach for estimating central pressures of mid-latitude oceanic storms, NOAA Technical Report NESDIS 63, NESDIS, Camp Springs, MD, 1992.
44. Snellman, L., Personal communication, 1981.
45. Uccellini, L.W. and Kocin, P. J., The interaction of jet stream circulations during heavy snow events along the east coast of the United States, *Weather and Forecasting*, 2, 289–308, 1987.

46. Wallace, J. M. and Gutzler, D. S., Teleconnections in the geopotential height field during the Northern Hemisphere winter, *Mon. Weather Rev.*, 109, 784–812, 1981.

47. Wilson, J. W. and Fujita, T. T., Vertical cross section through a rotating thunderstorm by Doppler Radar, in *Preprints from the 11th Conf. on Severe Local Storms*, American Meteorological Society, Boston, 447–452, 1979.

Images from GOES Gallery in this chapter were produced by Scott Bachmeier, Cooperative Institute for Meteorological Satellite Studies, Space Science and Engineering Center, University of Wisconsin–Madison.

Author Index

Author Index

A

Abidi, M. 179
Abler, R. F. 51
Aguilar, M. 145, 148, 147, 157, 163, 164, 170, 171, 174, 175, 180, 181, 182
Alexopoulos, J. S. 88, 96, 111
Allen, L. 20, 54, 117, 136, 143,181
Allen, S. W. 26, 52, 28, 29
Altrock, C. 72, 77, 79
Anderson, J. D. 143, 178
Anderson, J. R. 28, 37, 43, 45, 50, 51, 54
Anderson, R. B. 19, 20, 51
Antonio, J. C. 118, 130, 132, 135, 136
Arbib, M. A. 53
Argialas, D. xi, xiii, 5, 9, 59, 61, 63, 71, 73, 74, 76, 77, 78, 79, 80
Arndt, D. R. 20, 49
Artis, D. A. 15, 45, 31, 32
Aston, B. 28, 45
Atwood, W. W. 74, 75, 80
Austin, A. A. 26, 45
Ayala, B. 140, 178

B

Baer, G. 94, 107, 112
Baker, V. R. 60, 80
Baldwin, R. B. 91, 93, 96, 97, 98, 100, 108, 111
Balzer, W. K. 37, 45
Banfield, D. 214, 233
Barham, P. 140, 178
Barnston, A. G. 247, 269
Baruch, T. 20, 54, 117, 136, 143, 181
Bates, R. L. 73, 80
Bathurst, D. 10, 19, 47
Bathurst, R. 10, 19, 47
Bauer, M. I. 19, 45

Beatty, J. C. 10, 20, 26, 34, 54
Bechtoldt, H. P. 143, 178
Beck, J. 140, 178
Becker, A. H. 28, 54
Beishon, R. J. 20, 47
Bennett, K. B. 20, 45
Bentley, M. L. 260, 269
Berkeley, W. E. 118, 135
Berra, Y. 265, 269
Berry, D. C. 33, 45
Berry, K. J. 247, 270
Berson, E. L. 140, 178
Bertin, J. 9, 19, 45
Biederman, I. 43, 45, 146, 178
Bindschadler, D. L. 94, 107, 112
Binkley, M. 50, 55
Bizot, E. 28, 29, 50
Blair, R. W. 60, 80
Bluestein, H. B. 256, 269
Booth, W. 17, 45
Boyce, J. M. 89, 96, 113
Brabb, E. E. 87, 108, 112
Bransford, J. D. 43, 45
Braun, M. 145, 147, 148, 155, 163, 175, 182
Breed, C. S. 86, 91, 111
Breen, T. J. 28, 47
Britton, B. K. 50, 55
Broadbent, D. E. 28, 33, 45, 49
Brodley, C. E. 84, 85, 87, 110, 111
Brooks, L. R. 26, 28, 29, 45, 52
Brooks, M. J. 93, 112
Bruner, J. S. 26, 28, 45
Bucha, C. T. 118, 136
Bullemer, P. 28, 52
Burgess, D. W. 242, 269
Burgstaller, J. 93, 111
Burke, B. E. 144, 145, 147, 148, 150, 155, 170, 171, 182
Burke, K. 89, 113

Subject Index

Subject Index

Printed and bound by CPI Group (UK) Ltd, Croydon, CR0 4YY

23/10/2024

01778227-0015